Stay in the Room

INDIGORIVER
PUBLISHING

Stay *in the* Room

How a Gay Son and a Mormon Father Found Themselves and Each Other

Jeff McLean & Michael McLean

WITH BRAD M. REEDY, PH.D.

Stay in the Room: How a Gay Son and a Mormon Father Found Themselves and Each Other

LCCN: 2025928188
ISBN: 978-1-969935-05-3 (paperback) 978-1-969935-06-0 (ebook)

Editors: Megan Carver, Jennifer Casey
Cover and Interior Design: Emma Elzinga
Cover Art: Justin Wheatley

Printed in the United States of America

First Edition

3 West Garden Street, Ste. 718
Pensacola, FL 32502
www.indigoriverpublishing.com

Ordering Information:

Quantity sales: Special discounts are available on quantity purchases by corporations, associations, and others. For details, contact the publisher at the address above.

Orders by US trade bookstores and wholesalers: Please contact the publisher at the address above.

For Simone, who saw me.
J.M

INTRODUCTION

Jeff

The book you're about to read has been seven years in the making. When I started writing it, I was still processing the trauma of growing up as a closeted gay Mormon[1] in small-town Utah in the 1980s and 1990s.

Some days, I would find myself trembling or bawling at my computer as I tried to write. An invisible force was reading over my shoulder, telling me I was wrong and bad for trying to be authentic and tell the truth. How dare the son of Michael McLean, prominent Mormon director and musician, not only step outside of the mold but also tell the whole world about it?

---

1 The Church of Jesus Christ of Latter-day Saints has asked that it no longer be referred to as the Mormon Church or the LDS Church and that its members no longer be called Mormons. But since the term *Mormon* is familiar to a wide audience and is the term I am most comfortable with in reflecting on my experience, we have chosen to use this moniker throughout. The Church itself uses *Mormon* in some contexts it deems valid, so we're actually following their lead in this.

But as I revised and revisited difficult passage after difficult passage, I found that I was healing. Repetition is a balm for trauma. In fact, as I found words for my experiences and expressed myself, my trauma was set free. What was left was simply the memory of difficult situations I had worked through. The sting and terror were gone.

It wasn't just repetition that healed me. As I wrote my story, Brad M. Reedy, Ph.D., an extraordinary therapist, responded with insights and commentary that blew my mind with their accuracy and expansiveness. My editor, Laura Summerhays, validated my voice and experiences. And Dad did me the honor of making himself vulnerable alongside me.

I know some of the people reading this book don't have their dads or other supporters to hold them compassionately as they confront the scary parts of their stories. But Brad, Dad, and I are here for you.

You're going to get interrupted a lot while you're reading this book. My story is the framework, but Dad pipes in now and then, reflecting on how he learned to fully accept me. Brad pops up between our chapters, making expert observations about our experiences, answering questions you and other readers might have, and offering lists of reflection questions.

When some people read earlier drafts of the book, I received pushback on our approach. Some of my queer friends said, "I don't want to hear from your Mormon dad! He's the oppressor!" Some of my Mormon friends felt betrayed by how I talked about my former religion. A few readers said they just wanted a good story with no interference from a therapist.

But all of the book's parts make it more human and more essential. The "oppressor" gets to have his say because he's my dad and I love him—and because his experience can help other religious parents with queer children. Brad's commentary is indispensable. You can't read all of my story and not get a little time off! Just as I sometimes had to put my emotionally exhausted self to bed after writing for just an hour or two, you get the chance to rest and reflect when Brad's sections come along.

Writing set me free, and I hope that you can find the same freedom as you read the story and then take time to write out answers to Brad's reflection questions. Use them as a blueprint for processing your own issues, and discuss them with your therapists, sponsors, or other confidantes.

Let's heal together.

PART 1

Unlovable

1

BRAD

Reconciliation

If you speak to somebody at the level of the mind, you will speak to their mind. If you speak from your heart, you will speak to their heart. But if you speak through your life and your life is the story, then you will change lives.

– Deepak Chopra

This book speaks to all of the above—mind, heart, and life. It is the true story of Jeff McLean, the son of religious-music icon Michael McLean, Mormonism's answer to Billy Joel. It is about the gulf that was exposed between Jeff and his family when he came out as gay. And while it takes place in Utah and within the context of The Church of Jesus Christ of Latter-day Saints—also known as the Mormon Church or the LDS Church—it is not necessarily a Mormon story. It is a human story. It is a story about a father and son as they find their way back to each other from across a seemingly insurmountable chasm.

I am Brad M. Reedy, Ph.D., a marriage and family therapist, and a few years ago, I met Jeff through a therapy retreat I run with my wife.

As a former Mormon, I was familiar with Michael's prominence in Mormon circles, and I was curious how Jeff's coming out had affected their relationship. I asked, "How are you with your father?"

Jeff explained that he and his dad were close but that it had taken fifteen years and an incredible effort to get to where they were. Jeff had left the church, spent some time in active drug addiction, and married and divorced his first husband during this time. Michael confronted his own crisis of faith. What did God[2] want him to do, he wondered? What did it look like to love his child while staying connected to a faith that rejected that child?

I had witnessed similar stories in my therapy practice, and they did not always turn out with parent and child in a relationship that I would describe as "close." I pressed Jeff for more detail.

Jeff said, "Dad would tell you that my coming out was the best thing that ever happened to his faith. It challenged him to look deeper into his relationship with God and the church. My dad is more than supportive. He actually celebrates who I am. And I love myself, and I know my value no matter what anyone else thinks."

I must admit that I was a bit skeptical about the rosy picture Jeff painted of his relationship with his father. I have seen children carry the weight of their parents' pathology, suppressing their

---

2 Throughout this book, we attribute male pronouns to the word *God*. This reflects the religious tradition of the authors, but as you read, you'll see that all three of us have different definitions of God. So does each reader. You may be very comfortable with the word *God*, or it may be a word fraught with pain and disillusionment. We invite you to substitute in any other name that works for you—fate, the universe, the divine self, etc.

own needs in an effort to preserve some place in their family.

So I went to see Michael. As I asked questions and listened, Michael expressed gratitude for his son, celebrated his son, and even gave his son credit for his own deeper connection to his faith. He shared, "If I were to write a book about my son and our journey, the title would be *How Crystal Meth and Having a Gay Son Helped Me Find God*."

Michael and Jeff's relationship had clearly evolved beyond resignation to agree to disagree. Jeff told me that despite the pain of growing up gay in a conservative culture and community, he would not change it if he could. Michael arrived at a similar conclusion after having traversed his own desert of fear and prejudice. Michael eventually found the heaven available to all of us when we learn to love and embrace our children as they are. Jeff and Michael each shed parts of themselves and fought to find hope and connection.

Now convinced that this father and son had found true reconciliation, I poked at Jeff a little: "I imagine your story could be very healing to many Mormon LGBTQ+ youth and their families," I said. "What are you doing to help?"

This book is his reply. He enlisted his father in the project and asked me to provide commentary on their stories. The book alternates between Jeff's and Michael's narratives, and I offer insights and pose questions throughout.

The title of the book, *Stay in the Room,* comes from a part of Michael's story when he received inspiration during a particularly contentious moment with Jeff. He realized that in order to save the relationship, his son, and himself, he would need to listen to difficult things. He would need to stay in the room.

When I shared the title with a friend, they asked me, "Is it okay to leave the room too?"

"Of course!" I said. "We stay when we can and leave when we must."

Healthy relationships are difficult and often painful, but healthy relationships do not require us to sacrifice important aspects of ourselves in order to belong. So if you are being abused or mistreated, if you are being asked to give up who you are, this is your doctor's note granting permission to leave the room.

However, if we can stay in the room when someone is telling us how we hurt them, we learn to expand. We learn to see ourselves in others, whether we are children or parents, gay or straight, conservative or liberal.

2

JEFF

Before I Knew Anything Else

Before the terror came wonder. Before the terror came the Cinderella dress.

I discovered it among my sister's things when I was three—a glory in pink tulle and satin. The first thing I remember is the texture of the tulle, rough in my hands. And then I remember pink. And the smell. And how much I loved the way the dress made me feel. I wore it every single day for years, complemented, of course, by divine white patent-leather Mary Janes and a white straw bonnet bedecked with a pink bow.

My love for that dress was the purest expression possible—no contrivance. I just liked the way it felt, and I liked how it moved when I twirled.

My dad recalls the time when he asked me why I wore the dress. Little Jeff looked at him and said, "Dad, look at you." I pointed at him in his just-after-work clothes, furrowing my brow in disapproval. "Now look at *me*." I spun around and said, "I look fabulous."

Kudos to my parents for letting me wear a dress every day. But everything changed when I was five. That's when we moved from Salt Lake City to the nearby mountain town of Heber City, Utah, to combine households with my strict, conservative paternal grandparents. That is when I found out the dress was—and I was—wildly inappropriate.

I remember going to the supermarket in the dress and everyone staring at me, some even rolling their eyes. I never wore the pink dream in public again.

At home, it was all hushed tones and weird looks. I heard the conversations through the wall: "What are we going to do about that boy and that dress?"

No one thought to talk to me about it, but I felt the disapproval and anxiety. It became crystal clear to me at five years old that wearing what I wanted to wear was wrong. More than that, I knew there was something fundamentally wrong with *me*. I was petrified and genuinely fearful of being abandoned or losing my life because of who I was.

As I look back, I know that everybody did the best they could. I've come to understand new levels of healing and acceptance, but I carry a sadness in accepting the damage that can't be undone. I hope that by telling my story, I can validate and give voice to feelings—both mine and yours—that are often hidden in shame. I believe that the more we talk about our feelings and experiences, the more we heal. Naming something takes away its power. It's when we keep things under wraps that they turn on us.

One evening at Brad's house, Dad asked me a pointed question: "So, Jeff, what are you doing to help Mormon LGBTQ+ youth?"

His query struck a chord so powerful that it became the catalyst for this book. I hope I can help prevent others from feeling the invisibility and despair that had colored my whole life as a gay kid growing up Mormon in 1980s and 1990s Utah.

Before I dive into my story, I want to make a few points clear, just in case you don't keep reading. These are the book's absolute can't-miss ideas:

First, anyone who suggests that being gay is a choice hasn't had to give up everything to be gay. Believe me, if I could have picked the easier road, I would have. I had a perfect life set up for me as heir to Mormon music icon Michael McLean. But being gay messed it all up. So, no, I did *not* choose this.

Second (in case the first point made you doubt it), I love being gay. Being authentic to yourself is a wildly fun and amazing ride. When I came out, I didn't want to waste any more time lying. And I didn't want to be angry and gay. I wanted to be gay and gay.

Third, I could not have come out at any time before I did. If I'd come out before I left home, my parents would have tried to "fix" me. I weep for anyone who has gone through conversion therapy and am grateful I was able to avoid that persecution and torture.

Fourth, coming out didn't immediately change my beliefs about myself. It was just the first step.

Fifth, parents, please don't lie to your children. Lies can be told on purpose or by accident. For example, here are some inadvertent lies my parents told me: "You aren't gay" and "You can't be gay unless you've been molested (or unless you had a domineering mother or an absent father)." Maybe you have believed lies like these and passed them on. Own the limits of your understanding and tell your kids you're sorry. An apology from a parent goes a long way.

Sixth, it is abusive to rob people of the chance to feel that there is a God who can love them.

Seventh and most important: stay alive, kids (and former kids). I completely get the drive to escape. But the incredible thing about staying alive is that things do change. I know it feels hopeless sometimes. But then moments come that show you how truly valuable you are. Moments when you look in the mirror and feel proud of the person looking back at you. My journey has not been easy (suffering is just part of the deal), but it has absolutely been worth it.

Here is the truth: Telling my story has taken me through shades of panic. I've felt the pressure of creating something important that might bless lives and change people. But honestly, there's nothing special, unique, or fabulous about my story. It's just me figuring out who I am. Figuring out who we are is the journey we all take. Writing this book has become part of my journey. It helped me reclaim my childhood and my life.

Here is another truth: This book is a love story. No, it's not about my romantic conquests (though you'll see a few of those). It's not that kind of love story. It's a self-love story, an accepting-myself-and-others-as-they-are love story.

My self-love, you will soon see, was hard won. But I want you to know, as you read about my darkest times, that the light is coming. "It gets better," as they say. I actually struggle with that particular encouraging phrase because sometimes life gets worse before it becomes *different*. Becoming different is your own fight. Becoming different comes from healing. And carving through the darkness and sitting in the pain is the only way to heal.

For years, I clung to the religion I was raised in, but those beliefs did not serve me. I eventually freed myself, but I went a little too far in the other direction. I rejected God, and life became harder. I banished love, kindness, and understanding from my soul. God eventually broke through my defenses and revealed a path that those who raised me would have thought impossible. I encourage you to challenge your beliefs—about God, yourself, your world. Reject any perception that you and your sexuality are the problem. You are, in fact, a gift from God, sent to those around you so they can learn to love better and grow closer to God. If certain beliefs don't serve you, it is okay—rather, it is vital—to lovingly let go of your culture, your church, your family's expectations and find a better path. *Your* path. God is bigger than you think and doesn't want you to stumble down paths that other people chose for you. You will find God wherever your explorations take you because God is in everything.

✣

When I first came out, a lot of people asked me when I first knew I was gay. The answer is a little surprising.

After a church mission, when I was in my early twenties, I went on a journey into alternative healing. I went to several energy healers and therapists, and every single one of them asked me two questions: "What happened to you in the womb?" and "Were you supposed to be a twin?" No joke. Six different practitioners asked me the same questions, and none of them had any knowledge of the others.

I had definitely never been a twin, but since all of these people kept asking about it, I decided to find a therapist who could uncover the origin of this line of questioning. A few trusted friends highly recommended a hypnotherapist in my area who believed in past-life regression. I approached the session the way I approach most things—like they're a crock of shit and at the same time deeply cool.

When I was under hypnosis, the therapist took me back in time. We landed in a place that was warm and safe. She asked, "Where are you?"

"I'm in the womb," I replied without missing a beat.

"Why are you smiling so much?"

"Because I'm discovering everything I'm going to be. I'm going to be tall and dark-haired. I'm going to be a singer."

Then I began to tremble and whimper.

"What's wrong?" the therapist asked. "Why are you so sad?"

I could barely speak. "Oh no. I'm going to be gay. In fact, I am gay. And my mom isn't going to like it."

At this moment, I felt a loss—a splintering—and woke up.

So the answer to that question of when I knew I was gay is indeed surprising: I knew in the womb. I knew before I knew anything else.

Why had my prenatal self been so sad about being gay? Because I knew I was being born into a family that could answer every question I could ask—except the ones that mattered most. Amid that profound prebirth grief, another embryo started to develop alongside me: a shadow twin who would live inside me. This dumb, dismal monster knew just three words, three words I would spend nearly forty years running away from:

You are unlovable.

3

BRAD

The Call to Adventure

Famed mythology expert Joseph Campbell says that the call to adventure is the moment we feel a pull to leave the comfort of our ordinary lives and seek treasure. Initially, the call may be an invitation to rescue others, but if we accept the call, the journey reveals who we are, unveiling aspects of ourselves that we've denied in order to fit into our families and cultures.

In the previous chapter, you witnessed Jeff's call to aid Mormon LGBTQ+ youth by writing this book. As you observe how Jeff unveils his true self over the course of this book, think about what might be calling to you. Something may be sparked through the questions and answers I offer here.

Questions for Brad

Young Jeff takes on the anxiety of the adults around him. Why do children do this?

One understanding is that children's unconscious thinking goes something like this: *If I am causing these adults distress, they might abandon me, so I had better do all I can to help get rid of their distress. My survival is at stake.* Jeff's early childhood serves as a powerful illustration of how children unconsciously sense others' anxiety and similarly charged feelings. Not only do they sense the feelings, but children tend to believe that they themselves—not the people having the emotions—are in the wrong.

Jeff points out that everybody "did the best they could." Is that enough?

This is a tricky one. First, it is usually true that parents in challenging situations are doing their best. Second, it is also true that their best is often not good enough. In therapy, we learn that some seemingly incompatible ideas can actually be true at the same time. Replacing either/or with both/and is a sign of emotional and spiritual growth and complexity: I am doing the best I can, AND I can do better. Dialectical ideas like this may be particularly challenging for those raised in religions that reduce ambiguities by positing things in terms of opposites: right/wrong, us/them, and good/evil.

It is interesting to me that Jeff has carried into adulthood the idea that his caretakers did their best, but this is not uncommon. It is likely that such beliefs arise out of a desire to take care of the parents' egos. Imagine a parent who is overwhelmed by a child's feelings or needs. The parent may not admit their own lack of capacity but instead communicate to the child that the child is too big or too much. The child learns that their parent is fragile, and lurking beneath is a deeper inference: *I cannot get mad or fault my parent because I know they can't handle it, and they might abandon me.* So the anger and blame are shunted to the side, and "they did their best" takes their place.

Even after reaching adulthood, a child raised in such an environment may be reluctant to express—or incapable of expressing—any rage toward not only their parent but also toward nearly anyone. Thus, the parent pleaser has become a people pleaser. This repressive pleasing pattern leads to mental, physical, and spiritual illnesses like depression and addiction.

Jeff implores readers to stay alive. What if that feels too difficult to me or someone I love?

First of all, no matter your sexuality or gender identity, you are not disqualified from a happy life worth living.

I have personal experience with suicidal ideation, and I would like to share the insight that brought me through the darkness. I cannot emphasize enough that anyone experiencing suicidal ideation or making suicidal plans needs immediate help from a licensed medical or mental health professional. The method that helped me may not help you, and I also did not do this work alone. I was under the care of a skilled therapist.

More than a decade ago, I was struggling with my own demons and fantasizing about ending my life. I told myself I would never do it, but the pain and the bleak future I envisioned were overwhelming.

I shared my thoughts with my therapist, and she said something so profound it shifted my life forever: "The suicidal impulses have merit; however, the mistake most suicidal people make is thinking that they have to kill the whole self. In reality, they just have to kill part of themselves to be freed from their prisons of despair. They need to discover which part is causing the despair and kill only that part. Then they can be free." And often, the part that we need to kill is the part that cares what others think about us.

The dark clouds parted at that moment. I realized she was right. I didn't immediately figure out which part of me was causing me the most pain, but over time, I realized that it was the part that cared what others thought. Preoccupation with others' opinions is a common villain for suicidal individuals. For many queer people, this is certainly the case. If they stay alive, they can find freedom from the ideas and expectations that others have imprinted on them.

Analytical psychologist Robert A. Johnson, who takes a similar approach to my therapist, suggests what comes next after eliminating the most damaging parts of us: "The urge toward suicide signals an edge of a new level of consciousness. If you can kill . . . the old way of adaptation . . . and not injure yourself, a new energy-filled era will begin."[3] I think of this energy-filled era as the beginning of a lifelong love affair with yourself. As self-love grows, your relationships with others take on a new form. I have seen this transformation so often. Those who have suffered—those who have been left out, rejected, or forgotten—become capable of reaching others who suffer. Jeff was able to write this book and reach out to those who suffer exactly because he stayed alive and abandoned what didn't work for him.

Jeff felt unlovable almost from the start. Why is loving so difficult between queer people and conservative religious people?

I believe we are dealing with different conceptions of love. Those from conservative religious cultures like Mormonism do not consider their lack of acceptance to be a lack of love—"Love the

3 Robert A. Johnson, *She: Understanding Feminine Psychology* (New York: HarperCollins, 1976).

sinner, hate the sin," they profess. And those in the LGBTQ+ community don't experience their identity or orientation as a choice (let alone a sin) but rather as something central, something core, to who they are. If you can't accept that part of them, you can't love them. It's a seemingly insurmountable divide.

To any religious parent struggling with this divide, I'll tell you what I told an Orthodox Jewish father who approached me. He said, "I love what you teach, but I am struggling because I hear something so contrary from my rabbi."

I said, "I am not a rabbi. I'm a therapist, and my answer is practical. The consequences of rejecting your child are too dire, so I choose the side of acceptance."

I was not trying to convince this father—nor am I trying to convince you—to take my position. I am simply sharing how, within one's religious context, one might arrive at simply loving members of the LGBTQ+ community.

My close friend shared with me a simple story illustrating these ideas. She and her wife moved into a new house and found themselves neighbors to the son of an Apostle (a high official in the Mormon Church). When the Apostle's daughter-in-law asked the Apostle how she should respond to the lesbians living across the street, he replied, "Just love them." It was that simple. Just love them. No need to stand in judgment. Just love.

You can reserve judgment without leaving behind your religion. Clearly, that son of the Mormon Apostle did not leave his religion behind. But if you have lived a life abiding by strict religious tenets, you may need to strengthen your capacity to think independently.

Reflection Questions

1. Have you taken on others' anxieties, or have you seen this behavior in your children or other loved ones?
2. Do you feel resistant to expressing anger, hurt, or other difficult feedback toward your parents or others? Could this resistance be tied to a belief that you need to protect them, so they won't reject you?
3. How does it make you feel that you or others have done their best, but it wasn't good enough?
4. How does it make you feel when others excuse hurtful behavior by stating that they did it "with the best of intentions"?
5. Have you experienced suicidal ideation? What type of help have you sought? How do you feel about my suggestion to reframe these impulses as teachers that show you which parts of yourself—or beliefs about yourself—to let go of?
6. Have you ever used the phrase "Love the sinner, hate the sin" or heard it used by someone you love? Has your opinion about this phrase changed? How?

4
MICHAEL
Something Perfect

In the summer of 2017, Jeff and I were invited to perform together at the first-ever LOVELOUD concert organized by Dan Reynolds, lead singer of Imagine Dragons. The purpose of the show, which featured other well-known music artists, was to support the LGBTQ+ community and build bridges across cultural divides. Held in Orem, Utah—a town that is 93 percent Mormon[4]—the concert sought to encourage the conservative religious community to open their hearts and minds to those who have felt marginalized and shamed within the religious culture.

Jeff and I sang "Safe Harbors," a song I had written years before Jeff came out. When I wrote it, I had no idea how prophetic it would become for the two of us fifteen years later:

There are refugees among us, that are not from foreign shores
And the battles they've been waging are from very private wars

---

4 "Religion in Orem, Utah," Bestplaces, accessed October 24, 2022, bestplaces.net/religion/city/utah/orem.

And there are no correspondents documenting all their grief
But these refugees among us all are yearning for relief
There are refugees among us, they don't carry flags or signs
They are standing right beside us in the market checkout lines
And the war that they've been fighting, it will not be televised
But the story of their need for love is written in their eyes

This is a call to arms to reach out and to hold
The evacuees from the dark
This is a call to arms to lead anguished souls
To safe harbors of the heart

The significance of Jeff and me singing together on that stage for twenty thousand people cannot be overstated. Having sold millions of albums to members of the church during my career, I have become a celebrity among the Mormon faithful, and here I was, singing with my gay son who'd left that very organization when he came out. The juxtaposition of our relationships with the church was on full display.

Since our performance, Jeff and I have been asked over and over again, "How did *THAT* happen?" What they meant was, "How have the two of you reconciled the vast gulf between the Iconic Mormon Dad and the Prodigal Gay Son?"

The short answer is that it's just like all things human: it's messy, it's imperfect, it's a work in progress. I assure you that coming to a place of healing and acceptance has been an experience of deep humility.

⁂

A few weeks after he was born, I took Jeffrey Thomas McLean into my arms on a Sunday morning in church. I stood in a circle of good, God-fearing men—disciples of Jesus and my brothers in the gospel—and introduced Jeff into the church community. I gave him a blessing, a prayer that faithful Mormon fathers say over the newest members of their families.

In these blessings, we don't ever say, "My son, I bless you that you won't be gay. I'm not sure anything would be harder on me or you. And please don't leave the church and become a drug addict. Your mother and I will try not to make joy seem impossible. We don't want you to kill yourself, no matter what."

No, we don't say those things. We try not to even think those things. We pray for the good things, the happily-ever-after-things—the perfect things. But in recent years, I have come to wonder if this journey I've been on with my son *is* something perfect.

Since Jeff came out, so many people have asked me, "How could you not have known that your son is gay? Were you in denial? Were you embarrassed?"

I was in denial.

When Jeff was three and always wearing his sister's pink Cinderella dress, he had also started noticing things like his grandmother's nail polish matching her scarf, so I trusted him to be my fashion consultant. Before I headed to work each morning, Jeff would help me pick out my tie. I thought he might grow up to be a talented designer or artist. Whatever was going on, he couldn't be gay because, based on the church's propaganda, being gay was a choice. How could a three-year-old possibly make that choice? I never allowed these gay-related thoughts to enter my conscious mind. Everything I'd been taught, everything I believed, told me my son's sexuality would put our eternal family in jeopardy. The math was simple: God wouldn't send me a challenge I couldn't bear. Therefore, my child could not be gay.

When I shared memories of Jeff's early childhood with Brad, he said that Jeff had told him I'd let him wear the Cinderella dress for quite some time. I can't remember how long it went on, but I know I never said anything like, "Get that girly stuff off."

Brad then offered this insight: "It seems you tolerated what your religious culture would not have tolerated. You stood up against what people thought of you and your family. You parented from your heart."

But somewhere along the way, I dropped the ball. Soon after he came out, Jeff told me I had failed him as a father. Nothing had ever been quite as humbling as hearing this from my son. Acknowledging this specific failure was harder than processing all of my professional failures put together—the scripts that never got produced, the albums that bombed, the books that went out of print within a year, the bad reviews in *The New York Times*. None of that held a candle to Jeff's words, which I knew to be true. I'd been taught that success as a husband and father is the only real success in life. A much-loved Mormon leader said something that I memorized as a child: "No other success can compensate for failure in the home."[5]

My soul wept and died a little the day Jeff told me I'd failed him, and he didn't stop there. He said, "Dad, I'm gay, and everything you have ever said about homosexuality was just talking points from the church's playbook. Those points haven't been true for me. You lied, and you did it in the name of God. So where does that leave me, Dad?" His eyes flashed with anger, and in my sorrow and confusion, I could not find the words to respond. He pushed on.

---

5 David O. McKay, 105th Annual General Conference of The Church of Jesus Christ of Latter-day Saints, April 1935.

"I've done everything you expected of me. I went to church every week, I was an Eagle Scout, I served a mission, I fasted, I read my scriptures, and I said my prayers. But none of it changed the fact that I am an abomination! You taught me that being gay was a choice, that no one is 'born that way.' You said God doesn't make mistakes—and yet here I am! Everyone would be better off if I were gone."

As these last words poured out of my son, my every impulse was poised to volley a defense against Jeff's indignation—or at least to storm theatrically out of the room. Jeff was clearly a hedonist under the devil's sway. I didn't need to listen to him anymore! But something stopped me before I could open my mouth or make a move.

It was a feeling more than a voice in my head, but the communication was nonetheless painfully clear:

You must stay in the room. But you can't fight back.

Then what can *I do?* I responded.

Listen, the voice said. *And learn.*

Listening and *learning* were not my focus when I became a father at the tender age of twenty-three. I didn't even know these tasks were in the job description. For me, it wasn't those two Ls but the three Ps of parenting that I was worried about: providing, protecting, and preparing. To paraphrase a famous Mormon children's song, my job was to lead my kids, guide them, walk beside them, help them find the way. Teach them all that they must do to live with God someday.[6]

---

6 Naomi Ward Randall and Mildred Tanner Pettit, "I Am a Child of God," in *Children's Songbook* (Salt Lake City, UT: The Church of Jesus Christ of Latter-day Saints, 2011), 2–3.

It isn't surprising to me that my instinct was to double down on my parental duties and to teach, defend, and justify. But now it was time for Jeff to teach me.

Jeff invited me to imagine that I lived in a gay world and that heterosexual people were considered an abomination to God. He asked me to imagine that I'd been raised in a church that said eternal blessings would come only from marrying someone of the same sex. "Now imagine, Dad," he said, "that you fell in love with Mom."

"Everyone said you'd been deceived by Satan, that you had sinfully chosen Mom. It was a horrible sin—everyone agreed on that—but they said that if you'd leave Mom and seek repentance, you could be forgiven and find true happiness with a worthy male companion. 'Date Pete Jones,' they would say. 'Kiss him, and in time you'll learn to feel the way you felt about Lynne.' Would you leave Mom and say it was because you were following God and keeping His homosexual commandments? Or would you risk an eternity in hell to stay with your wife?"

Pause.

He saw my face, and in that moment, I saw his heart. He said, "Welcome to my world, Dad."

Before I could formulate a response, he mused: "What if your homosexual son decided to live as a faithful, celibate single man his entire life? Then what if he approached the judgment seat and asked God when He would change him from gay to straight? And what if God said, 'You know, Jeff, I can't change your sexual orientation. You've always been gay. It's just who you are.'"

I can't tell you how many sleepless nights I spent reviewing this conversation in my head. I couldn't process it. Jeff's words felt like heresy, and just thinking about them threatened my core beliefs. Yet the better part of me was beginning to get a glimpse into Jeff's real life for the first time in more than twenty years.

5

BRAD

Keeping the Faith

For the parents of LGBTQ+ youth in conservative religious cultures, Campbell's call to adventure comes at the moment when a child ventures beyond where parents can hold both their faith and their child. The journey involves finding and embracing a new faith, one that is expansive and celebrates each person's unique self, one that contributes to a deeper capacity to love. The transition from old ideas to new is like a death. You can grieve the loss of old beliefs. It will likely not be the last time your thinking evolves. The death of ideas may feel difficult to welcome, but it gives way to new contexts, new ideas, new faith, and new companions.

For those who feel that I'm asking them to leave behind a particular religious tradition, I assure you I am not necessarily suggesting this. It is possible to transform *within* a religion rather than transform out of it.

Questions for Brad

Michael seemed to be parenting from the heart when he was so tolerant of the Cinderella dress. What changed?

Early on in fatherhood, Michael had an instinctual resistance to his closed culture. He stepped outside of the circle just enough to be open to something new—a son in a Cinderella dress. That instinct is one he eventually followed to reconcile with Jeff later. But in the interim, Michael spent time not seeing his son and instead prioritizing the family's church and culture.

The draw of church and culture is understandable. Closed cultures, such as conservative faiths, provide a profound sense of belonging. Michael wanted this for both himself and his child. But benefits like belonging and unity come at a cost. When communities are strict, some people are excluded. If a person's identity is at odds with the group, they must leave the group or hide within the group, never to reveal the real self.

Michael learned an important lesson about staying, listening, and learning. How can parents help their children feel heard?

It is as simple as listening without trying to change your children's feelings. The job of parents is certainly not to gaslight their children. Erasing, dismissing, or re-creating a child's truth leaves the most lasting scars. Our children will experience pain no matter what we say or do. A child's pain may be an excruciating burden for a loving parent to bear, but holding our children and their big emotions is the holy calling of parenthood. Novelist Anne Lamott explained, "The most profound thing we have to offer our children is our own healing." So our calling as parents is to become large enough to carry children's feelings without collapsing under the weight of them.

An interesting side effect of listening to children is that they learn to listen to themselves. Children guided in self-listening can also learn to differentiate their inner voice from others' expectations. I'm not sure how Michael came by this powerful inner voice, but it sounds a little like the one that told him to stay in the room.

Reflection Questions

1. Can you find space in your faith tradition that will support your love for those who have left the tradition behind? If you have left your faith, how do you show love to those who remained?
2. Did your parents show support for you sometimes and withdraw it later? Did you ever withdraw support for your children?
3. Did your parents rely on emotional coercion, guilt, shame, fear, and other such tactics? If you're a parent, have you used these methods? Have you seen yourself or your children become more vulnerable to these mechanisms in other relationships?

6

JEFF

The Genie and Pollyanna

I am many things in the world. A gay man, a singer, a teacher, an addict. One of my earliest roles is that of son. And not just any son: a McLean son. Understanding my parents is key to understanding my story.

From my earliest memories, Dad was already a shooting star flying through the sky. Around the time I was born, he produced a short TV film, bagging one of the biggest legends of the silver screen to star as an old man who dreamed of conducting the Mormon Tabernacle Choir. We even have a photo of this Tinseltown icon *holding my infant self.* This is the kind of magic Dad created, and he was just getting started. (I won't steal Dad's thunder and reveal who the movie star was, but if you can't stand the suspense, take a peek at Chapter 14.)

The thing about meteor fathers is that they're gone a lot. Luckily, Mom provided consistency while Dad stepped into the role of grand-gesture guy.

At the center of one of Dad's recurring gestures was a Datsun 240Z, his pride and joy. (You know this car. Google it if you need your memory jogged.) Dad had started writing jingles for companies like RC Willey and Hardee's. Sometimes he'd get paid in cash, but sometimes—say if he wrote a jingle for a car dealership—his payment would come in the form of a badass sports car.

The Z fit only two people, perfect for one-on-one Dad dates. In the days before we moved to Heber, we lived at the top of the super-steep 13th South hill in Salt Lake City. At the bottom sat the pot of gold: the Dairy Queen.

We'd jump into the car, breathing in its leather and gasoline musk, and Dad would sail down the hill. Barely able to see over the dash, I'd throw my hands up like I was on a roller coaster. *Wheee!*

After we practically skidded to a stop at Dairy Queen, it was time for Dilly Bars. We'd sit in the parking lot and talk and laugh and eat our chocolate-coated heaven.

When you live with a genius, you can count on memories like these. But with great genius comes gigantic mood swings, so you also learn quickly that if you challenge the genius, you will lose and lose big. The unspoken rule in our house was that the Michael McLean Show was the only show in town, so you'd better get on board. However, he had some vulnerabilities that I keyed into from a pretty young age. He wanted your attention and applause, whoever you were.

My dad truly loves people and God, and he does the best he can. But in a lot of ways, he completely missed the boat on raising kids, those famous mood swings revealing by turns an overindulgent Z-driving genie or an inaccessible Major Tom.

If Dad was my buddy, Mom was my idol. My mother, Lynne McLean, is hands down my favorite person on Earth. She loves everyone the same. You might think this would make me jealous or resentful, but it doesn't. It's refreshing to experience the way she spreads her love around.

When I was a kid, Mom was generally straitlaced, but she was willing to break certain rules. Runaway Day was the best. She would surprise us by signing us out of school to go skiing or to the movies. She taught me that spontaneity and adventure are exhilarating. I could see that before her life was out, she wanted to try everything. (Within reason. Not heroin. This is Lynne McLean we're talking about here!)

My mom is also a courageous badass. She developed severe chronic PMS after I was born, at a time when women's health issues weren't considered important enough to study. In her work as a nurse, she made it her mission to educate people about PMS, postpartum depression, and other hush-hush women's issues.

My mom is also a doer. Her motto—for herself and for us kids—was, "If you don't feel good, do something to change it!" Stay busy. Organize the drawers. Go on a trip. Do anything that brings you joy and develops your talents.

When she decided she needed some time for herself during the years she was raising the three of us, she took up tap dancing. Among the most adorable displays I've seen in life was Mom at the Christmas talent show performing her number in a black leotard and tights—plus a top hat and cane! My Grandma Eggington had a videotape of the act at her house, and I loved to sneak a view here and there.

Amid grappling with serious gynecological pursuits and "doing" her way out of discomfort, my mom always looked on the sunny side of life. In fact, she just might be Pollyanna. If you haven't read the Eleanor H. Porter novel by that name, you may have at least seen the 1960 screen adaptation starring Haley Mills. Basically, Pollyanna is the most optimistic person on the planet.

Her father taught her to always find something to be glad about in any situation—he called this the "glad game." My mom is a glad-game pro.

Mom chooses to see the best in the world and in every single person. This quality has a magic about it, and it's one of the reasons that people love my mom so much. But this approach to life has a dark side.

Mom doesn't just focus on the happy and glad things of this world. She ignores the bad entirely. I learned early on that if I were less than cheerful and optimistic, she could not fully love me. She may have believed that she loved me unconditionally, but her refusal to accept me as I was, flaws included, taught me that love is conditional. The Unlovable Monster living inside me, the one who had developed along with me in the womb, thrived on this incomplete love, this proof—from my own mother, no less—that it was right about me. If I wanted my mother's love, and I did, I had to hide a fundamental aspect of myself.

Apparently, I did a fantastic job of hiding from her. My gayness became obvious to everyone else on Earth, but for years, Mom ferociously defended the notion that she had no idea. Later, I learned that Mom had actually asked God about my sexuality during my childhood. In her mind, gayness arose from two possible situations: 1) having a domineering mother and 2) being molested. Since neither of these were true of me, she determined that I was just a sensitive soul who would make a great husband someday. And if I were gay—well, God would have some explaining to do. Regardless of whether her ignorance was genuine or born of denial, her inability to really see me was damaging.

Sometimes, as a child, musing on my mother's black-and-white approach, I would ask myself, "Am I a good person if I do bad things? Am I lovable if I allow the negative in?" Once, as an adult, I asked my mom these questions aloud during a very heated conversation about why I didn't want to go to church anymore.

"Can't I be a good person without going to church? I think God is okay with it."

Her reply: "Jeff, don't patronize me. The McLeans are not just GOOD people. We are EXCELLENT people."

If I wasn't excellent according to Lynne's definition, I didn't count as a McLean. Message received, internalized, and fed to my monster twin.

7

BRAD

Stealing the Key

In Robert Bly's *Iron John*, a wild man is caged in the courtyard of a king and queen. On one occasion, the young prince loses his golden ball into the possession of the wild man. The wild man offers a deal to the young prince: the wild man will give up the ball, but the boy must give him the key that unlocks the cage. The queen guards the key, keeping it under her pillow. She will not surrender it, so the boy must steal it.

The key's hiding place—where the mother lays her head to sleep—represents the dreams the mother has for her son, how she thinks his life *should* go.

Like the mother in the story, parents are often unwilling to give up their hopes and dreams for their children. But children must set themselves free from those expectations—steal the key—in order to grow up. That's how *becoming a person* works. Finding out who we are is a personal matter and cannot be dictated. If parents use emotional coercion, threats, guilt, shame, fear, and other such tactics, children become vulnerable to these mechanisms in their other relationships. The antidote is to allow children to develop in such a way that they discover their own truths and their own paths. That is not to say that boundaries shouldn't exist and that parenting must be passive. It's just that we don't try to convince our children that we know their truths.

Question for Brad

I liked reading about Lynne the buddy. Are there benefits to breaking small rules for or with your children?

Yes! Children need to be allowed to break the small rules. It is essential for growth and progress, and, as with most things children learn, they need to see rule-breaking in action.

Laurel Thatcher Ulrich's famous quote, "Well-behaved women seldom make history,"[7] hits the nail on the head and applies to men and women alike. Picasso, Rosa Parks, Galileo, Princess Diana, Harriet Tubman, Einstein, Joan of Arc, Dylan, Malcolm X, Maya Angelou, Moses, Jesus, Joseph Smith—the list of history-making and rule-breaking women and men is lengthy.

Transgressing norms is the context where innovation and invention happen. Beyond the known is the origin of creativity. Astute observers of most religions will recognize that even leaders in the faith break rules in service of larger truths.

---

7 Laurel Thatcher Ulrich, "'Virtuous Women Found': New England Ministerial Literature, 1668–1735," *American Quarterly* 28, no. 1 (Spring 1976): 20.

Reflection Questions

1. Consider the roles Michael and Lynne played in Jeff's young life: idol and buddy. What roles did your parents play? What roles do you play as a parent?
2. Do you need permission from others to express and live your truth?
3. How did you individuate from your parents as you grew up and set out on your own? What was the cost of this individuation?
4. If you are a parent, have you found it difficult to relinquish your expectations for your children and allow them their freedom?

8

JEFF

That Child Is Gay

Sometime near the end of summer 1978, Mike and Lynne McLean resolved a fight through an exchange that inadvertently resulted in yours truly. Oops!

Nothing helps set the tone for your value in the world more than your parents repeatedly telling you and everyone else that you were an accident. Honestly, I think all three of us McLean children were accidents. Meggan was born a mere eleven months after my parents' wedding. I think we can all agree that this pregnancy was definitely not deliberate. I don't know if Scott was planned or not, but he carries the aura of a different sort of accident: my mother was in a serious car accident while pregnant with him.

My parents were practically children themselves when they had us. But hey, it was the seventies—in conservative religious circles, you couldn't have sex before marriage, so you got married young. And marriage was all about having babies. Contraception was a sin.

Based on my relationship with the Cinderella dress, you probably have a pretty good idea of what I was like as a young child. I loved everything that would make anyone sane (and not in deep denial) think, "That child is gay."

When I was three, I asked Santa for a Strawberry Shortcake doll. Christmas morning revealed that Santa had not only come through—he'd surpassed my wildest dreams. I found Strawberry Shortcake herself, but she was not alone. Santa had brought all of her friends as well. Huckleberry Pie, Orange Blossom—everyone! And they had a cozy place to live: a two-story cardboard Strawberry Shortcake dollhouse.

I was a little dumbfounded. Even that young, I had some inkling that Strawberry Shortcake wasn't "for boys," so I'd doubted that Santa would make my strawberry dreams come true. I exclaimed, "I wanted Strawberry Shortcake and got her, which means Santa Claus is real." Good on Santa for not letting me down.

Living in Salt Lake with my immediate family was a delight. Cinderella dresses and puppet shows and pure, unadulterated innocence. Utah Mormons lean toward the conservative, trying to prevent things from changing too quickly. We were just a little behind the times, even when it came to home décor. So my 1980s childhood looked less like *Stranger Things* and more like the 1960s of *The Sandlot*.

Our neighborhood was full of young families. It seemed that every house had kids my age. We would roam the neighborhood, daring each other to walk past the house of the resident crotchety old man, whose dog would surely tear to pieces anyone who took the dare.

I remember an alley full of what we called honeysuckle (actually named common periwinkle or running myrtle)—purple flowers we'd pick off the vine to suck out their sweet stores of nectar.

But this idyllic place had a dark side: the inversion. In this natural phenomenon typically occurring in January and February (and July and August if you're lucky), mysterious meteorological interactions between the Wasatch Range and the Great Salt Lake turn the Salt Lake Valley into a dish with a lid on it. Cold air gets trapped under there, and pollution gets trapped with it.

In 1983, my parents decided that enough smog was more than enough, so we escaped to Heber City on the other side of the Wasatch. Heber is an alpine paradise, but the change for four-year-old Jeff was enormous and traumatic. It wasn't just Mom, Dad, Meggan, Scott, and Jeff anymore. My dad's parents moved to Heber as well, and we went from being a nuclear family to a multigenerational family.

Dad and Grandpa McLean had selected a twenty-acre plot and named it Scotshaven. Grandpa designed a huge Lincoln Log cabin and meticulously built it—inch by inch, log by log, precept upon precept. Construction took three years, and in the meantime, a lot of personality was shoehorned into some very small rental spaces.

My experience of living with Dad's parents was a gift that helped me to see that he came by his parenting style honestly. No way could those two pieces of work—a.k.a. my McLean grandparents—raise anyone responsibly.

Before we delve into life with the McLean grandparents, let me introduce Meggan and Scott, my siblings. Meggan, our fearless leader, was the perfect embodiment of an older sister. I believe she was one of the first people in my family to really see me, though she may not have understood it at the time. When I was born, my parents took her to see me in the hospital. I was in the nursery with all the other babies, wrapped in a blue blanket. The girl babies were swaddled in pink blankets and had pink bows stuck to their heads with Karo syrup. When my parents pointed me out, she said, "No, I want a pink one, not a blue one!" Little did she know that I would very soon be a pink one when I commandeered her Cinderella dress and any other hand-me-downs that met with my approval.

Edgy and independent, Meggan defended Scott and me against bullies. The way she saw it, if anyone picked on one McLean kid, they picked on all of us. This attitude wasn't just for the schoolyard. We had to stick together at home, too. During heated battles among the McLean adults, we kids would crawl under the covers of one of our beds, Meggan assuring us that everything was going to be okay. I knew she would never let anyone hurt me.

Meggan's strength barely revealed any vulnerability, but she had some serious struggles. She suffered from seizures as a kid. And as the firstborn, she had an awful lot of songs written about her. You can see echoes of her difficulties in many Michael McLean hits, most notably "If Only You Believe in Yourself."

I can't remember a time when Meggan wasn't my best friend, but I can't quite say the same about Scott. We were nothing alike. He was deeply emotional, frequently flustered, and germophobic—and therefore an easy target for my teasing. When we fought, we fought hard. But when we got along, I was eager to follow his lead.

Scott was obsessed with his role of big brother, even though we were only sixteen months apart. If we made a movie, he was the director, but he'd let me hold the camera. If we recorded a radio play, he'd take most of the parts but would throw in a few consolation lines for me. Even though I was often willing to go along with these plans, I think I disrupted Scott's older-brother image when I quickly caught up with him physically and then just kept on growing. This couldn't have been easy for him.

Despite our differences and our occasional brawling, though, Scott and I developed a strong bond. We had to if we wanted to survive the horrors of living with Grandma and Grandpa McLean.

My very controlling McLean grandparents believed that my parents were ill-equipped to teach Meggan, Scott, and me anything. Instead, our upbringing should rest upon the older generation's venerable shoulders.

We had lessons for everything. How to follow proper etiquette (I know how to eat with all seventeen forks), how to pray and feel the Spirit, how to make our beds. We felt pressure to do everything perfectly. "I don't know" was never an acceptable answer.

And the notes! Just in case our face-to-face interactions weren't sufficient, Grandma and Grandpa left notes everywhere all the time—little reminders that nothing was ever enough. You know who loved those notes? The small but growing Unlovable Monster inside me.

Grandma and Grandpa were very devout Mormons, and Grandpa was fond of leading after-church discussions that went on for hours. And then again on Wednesdays. This was deep-doctrine time: God has a body. He lives somewhere near a planet called Kolob (yes, God has an address). Jesus is His son, and they both look like Brad Pitt.

Because of my grandparents' influence in the home, my parents stopped being parents and instead joined me and my siblings in the child role. That dynamic turned out to be painfully destructive. My mom did everything in her power to cater to her in-laws, and my dad just wanted to be good enough for his parents—an achievement Grandma McLean made sure to keep just out of reach.

If Grandpa or Grandma McLean told Dad that we kids had done something bad, Dad would yell and scream at us or spank us. It wasn't pretty. Years passed before I felt like my dad cared about me and wasn't just being nice so I would say something positive about him at his funeral.

Dad's parents played him like a fiddle. They threw tantrums and found ways to make their son feel small, and the result was that they got whatever they wanted. I watched and learned. These were my first lessons in getting exactly what I wanted from Dad. I saw that he was apt to take on blame whether it was warranted or not, that he wanted to fix every challenging situation he encountered. As I grew, I got better at using this knowledge to manipulate him and to get his attention.

Looking back, it is clear to me that I was living in a house with four adults who were dealing with untreated or undertreated mental illness. I know Grandma McLean struggled with severe anxiety attacks. Dad has those powerful mood swings, and he and my mom have both used antidepressants since I was a kid. In this kind of household, you get two options:

Things are okay

or

Everything is a high-stakes, red-alert trauma that *must* be fixed—NOW!

As time went on in our combined household, World War III became a weekly occurrence. I seemed to always be in the middle of it. The joy of being the youngest and most vulnerable is that everything is your fault. I was always the prime suspect in The Case of the Open Refrigerator, The Unmade-Bed Conundrum, or The Mystery of the Lost Remote-Control Battery.

When that remote-control battery went missing, Dad and Grandpa raged and raged. Care to witness a classic Grandpa McLean interrogation? I thought you might:

Grandpa. What's this?

Young Jeff. A remote control.

Grandpa. What's wrong with this remote control?

Young Jeff. It doesn't work?

Grandpa. Try again!

Young Jeff. Someone stepped on it?

Grandpa. NO. There are no batteries in the remote control. *(Removes the sliding back panel and slowly shows it for all to witness.)* Now. Whose remote control is this?

Young Jeff. The family's.

Grandpa. No. This is MY remote control. Did you pay for this TV? Did you buy the batteries? No, you did not. It's mine, and someone stole what belongs to me.

Young Jeff. (Stunned silence.)

Grandpa. Who took the batteries? Who stole my property?

I finally decided to confess. I hadn't taken the batteries, but I knew even at seven years old that this shaming stream of questions could last all day. So I lied and said I'd lost the batteries—and I got spanked.

To add to our general domestic bliss, my dad drew on an alter ego named Bruise Maker. When he felt overwhelmed, which was often, he would come into our rooms at night, bash a belt on our headboards in the dark, and say that if we didn't do what we were told, Bruise Maker would come get us.

And Bruise Maker came. I'm sure it was less often than what I recall, but he came nonetheless.

Bruise Maker had been around since I was about three, even before we'd moved to Heber. Dad was too young to handle three kids under four, and he has said that we ruined the prolonged date he was trying to have with our mom. He feels bad about Bruise Maker and apologized profusely, but the consequences of Bruise Maker's existence remained.

Eventually, I started to wet the bed, and I stopped wearing my Cinderella dress altogether. My grandparents made it clear that the dress was unacceptable, and they intentionally tried to make me feel awful for wearing it. Wetting the bed was also unacceptable, and Grandpa McLean took it upon himself to help me quit. He would wake me up every night and take me to the bathroom. Once, when I was six, I had an accident, and Grandpa made me drag my mattress onto the front lawn so that everyone in the neighborhood could see that I'd wet the bed. This was just the beginning of years of twisted, culturally sanctioned abuse. I don't have one positive memory of Grandpa McLean. Not one.

In fairness, I want to clarify that not everything on the McLean front was Bruise Maker and pee-stained mattresses on the front lawn. The flip side to all that ugly was a lot of awesome and exciting things: Incredible Christmases with scavenger hunts. Movie marathons. Breakfast in bed every birthday. Elaborate Easter egg hunts. Visiting Dad on movie sets and enjoying craft services. Summers at the Bear Lake cabin—all raspberry shakes and puzzles and card games.

But then a devastating thing happened in our family that would be a turning point for the rest of my childhood. It was the summer I was seven years old. We were going to meet my mom's large extended family for the annual pancake breakfast next to the town hall. My mom's cousin Kim and her husband, Steve, had just moved back to Utah with their two kids. Steve was young, fit, absolutely gorgeous, and an airline pilot to boot. He was on leave from American Airlines, and the Smiths said he'd landed a new job in Utah. But everything seemed hushed. Nobody could talk about why Steve was on leave, why the Smiths had really come back.

The truth? Steve had HIV. Kim had HIV. Steve had contracted the virus through an affair with a man and passed it to his wife. This was 1986, and AIDS was still a death sentence in this country. My mom's favorite cousin had HIV, and the whole family was terrified.

In the months after the Smiths' news, I heard my parents, these supposedly Christlike people, say the most horrible things: HIV was sent by God to kill all gayness. Gay people are murdering everyone. Gay people deserve to die of AIDS. They're disgusting. We should send them to die on an island. Of course, it wasn't just from my parents that I heard things like this. Homophobia was a mainstream pastime in the 1980s. It was considered completely okay—expected, even—to bully gay people, and if you saw gay people portrayed in the media, they were villains or jokes.

The Unlovable Monster inside me fed on this rhetoric and grew. Even at seven years old, I knew I was gay, and I knew my parents were talking about me. And just like that, I was no longer safe in my own home. So I swallowed my truth, believing that silence would be the key to survival. (Note to parents: if you communicate that being gay is the most awful thing in the world, your kids will hide.)

During this time of frequent torch-and-pitchfork conversations, I turned eight, the typical age of baptism for Mormon children. When I look at the photos of my baptism day, I see a petrified boy, a boy who believed he was filthy but who had to make a covenant to be pure. The brilliant God who'd created the stars, the moon, and the universe somehow had no answers for what was going on inside of me. No one said it aloud in exactly this way, but from various conversations I eavesdropped on, I learned that gay was the one thing God could not handle. By all overheard accounts, he could save pedophiles, prostitutes, and adulterers but not a gay little boy. I was an unnatural mistake and the embodiment of evil. Baptism or no baptism, how could a Savior possibly redeem me?

For years, these ideas from my childhood lived and breathed inside me. Once, as an adult, I had a panic attack after watching an HBO special about AIDS in the eighties. I had to work with my therapist to unpack the trauma of seeing witches burned right in front of me, witches who had my face. One day after one of these therapy sessions, my dad asked how I was. I said, "If you were a gay child, how do you think you would have been affected by the way you talked about Steve Smith?"

The color left his face. He exhaled and shuddered. "Oh man, Jeff, I'm so sorry. That would have been awful."

Here is what is amazing about my dad: he stays in the room, and he always attempts to understand how I feel.

9

BRAD

The Sins of the Parents

Multigenerational transmission is a concept from family systems theory that explains how health, patterns, pathology, and trauma are passed to the next generation. This concept provides a compassionate lens through which to explore the wounding we receive from our families, while it places responsibility on the sufferer to do the work. The related concept of ancestral sin is found in scripture, where you can find many examples of parental sins being visited upon subsequent generations.

Questions for Brad

Thinking about harming my children is unbearable. Is there any way around this?

We and our forebears are human, and our collective imperfection is inescapable. We cannot avoid what I call *denting* our children, and those dents are worthy of exploration. Children—that is, all of us—must grapple with ancestral wounds. The greatest harm is not from our mistakes but from our denial of those mistakes. It is the parents' defenses—the need to be right or good—that cause the most damage to children. Parents must look at their mistakes, own them, and do the work to move through them. Speaking to parents on the topic of their own healing I explain: *You were wounded—more than some and less than others. But you were hurt. And the way you protect that pain hurts others, most pointedly your children. Work on yourself, and discover that your fear, hurt, and anger are yours. Take responsibility for those feelings so your children don't have to carry them. This is the greatest love you can give, and it will multiply. Your children will bring even greater healing to their children. And in this very simple way, your love multiplies throughout eternity.*

Jeff talks about his parents being more like his siblings, with the grandparents taking on the parent role exclusively. Why does this happen? Is it unavoidable in multigenerational households?

Parents often allow their own parents to treat their grandchildren the same way they (the parents) were treated. It is what the parents are used to. Harsh words, dogmatic rigidity, violence, and even sexual abuse can move from grandparent to grandchild if the parents are ill-equipped or unable to confront the grandparents and their history. In families where multiple generations cohabitate, the transmission of abuse can go around the parents and straight into the psyches of the grandchildren.

Jeff's grandparents were afforded unchallenged access to their grandchildren, with Michael and Lynne watching impotently from the sidelines as themes of physical and emotional abuse were reenacted upon the McLean grandchildren. When Michael carried out punishment based on his parents' distorted views of his children, he was taking care of his parents rather than his children. This is not uncommon. I see it in my clients frequently, and I often ask them pointedly, "Are you a better parent to your parents than you are to your children?"

As a parent, I have resorted to "bruise maker" behavior. How can I make up for this?

Stop the behavior now if you haven't, and use positive reinforcement more than punishment. Children who have experienced even occasional corporal punishment, like Jeff, may fixate on these experiences. But because Jeff had a lot of positive experiences from Michael as well, he is able to remember a loving family—one with merry Christmases and fun vacations.

If you feel like your children should "get over" your treatment of them, it's important to know that humans are wired to prioritize negative experiences over positive ones. This principle is called *negative bias.* Imagine our ancestors walking across the African savanna. If they missed a threat—a lion lying in the low grass—the result was death. If they missed something positive, like low-hanging fruit, they merely missed a meal. In the modern world, negative bias has fewer immediate lifesaving uses, but our nervous systems have not caught up. This psychological phenomenon of noticing and remembering negative experiences is called *negative bias.* The function of negative bias is simple. Just like you might hear ten compliments about a presentation at work or school and just one criticism, you're likely to remember the critical remark. Children are more likely to remember fear and pain in their growing-up years unless positive experiences vastly outweigh the bad.

Reflection Questions

1. Consider your parents and grandparents. What "sins" from these generations have made their way into your life? What healthier behaviors would you like to pass down?
2. How does negative bias show up in your life, specifically with your parents or your children?

10

JEFF

S-E-X

There's an old Mormon chestnut: having sex with the wrong person at the wrong time is second only to murder. So there in the Sin Olympics, Murder is standing in the middle with the gold medal. Off to the right, silver medal around its neck, stands Having Wrong Sex. I'm not sure who got the bronze.

For a topic so tied up with Mormon salvation, though, sex seemed to be something that no one actually wanted to talk about directly. For example, when I was thirteen—thirteen!—the bishop (the leader over a local congregation) and the youth group leaders decided that I would give my fellow young men a lesson on the evils of masturbation. It was insane—grown-ass men pawning off their dirty work.

It sure would have been nice to learn about sexual development outside of an environment (i.e., church) that was focused on scaring us to death about all the ways you can do sex wrong and the consequences that follow.

Alas, outside of church, I got one conversation about sex, and it was when I was still presexual. My dad briefly told me, Scott, and my cousins about the birds and the bees while we were doing ceramics at a family retreat in the mountains. I guess Michael McLean felt like the crafts pavilion was the perfect setting to talk about sex—primarily, I assume, because my mom was in a cabin giving The Talk to Meggan at that moment.

The whole concept was confusing. Nothing Dad said was relevant to my experience as a nine-year-old boy. I couldn't figure out the actual physicality of it all. You might assume or hope that Dad repeated this information when I was older and could understand it. But no. When it came to talking about sex with his kids, my dad's credo was *one and done*. When Scott had his first wet dream a couple of years later, he thought he had one of those diseases they teach you about in junior high health class. Our family doctor was the one who explained to him that this experience was completely normal. (Note to parents: If your children are struggling sexually, it may be that they have no vocabulary for it. You have to create one. It might be awkward as all get out. Figure it out anyway. If it's mentionable, it's manageable!)

I went through puberty early—around ten. It was a big deal because of how drastically it changed my voice. I don't think that anyone expected it to happen so quickly, but all of a sudden, I looked more mature than Scott. I mean, I had pubes in sixth grade, which made the introduction of compulsory showers in gym class that year a total nightmare for me. I couldn't think of any way to get out of this requirement, so my only recourse was to not look at anyone and pretend that no one was looking at me. I firmly believe that being forced to bare it all in front of my peers played a special role in weaving body-image issues into my DNA.

Starting at age ten, I would masturbate every single day. Only I didn't know what I was doing and didn't have any language for it (my dad's ceramics sex talk from two years earlier had, of course, been useless, and this was a few years before my famous church-mandated masturbation lesson). I just knew I would get funny sensations if I touched my nethers and that those sensations got even better if I touched my nethers on purpose.

Soon, my masturbation habits became even more involved. We had one of those huge 1980s camcorders, the kind that records onto VHS tapes. We had taken it on our recent European vacation, and my dad had used it to film both our wholesome family time among all the famous sights as well as my mom's behind climbing up various hills and staircases. I found a new use for it once we got home. I would film myself masturbating and then watch the video and masturbate to it again. Voila! Homemade gay porn. I didn't really know what I was doing or why I was doing it, but I knew it was shameful and needed to be hidden. So I would tape over my pornos with videos of myself singing sacred songs. I'd obsessively check to make sure that every last second of my skin flicks was erased forever. I would blush when Scott would ask why I sang so much or when my parents would comment about how much they loved to hear me practicing in my room.

Even after I found out that masturbation was a grave sin, I kept doing it. But after each time, I'd cry and plead on my knees for God's forgiveness. Rinse. Repeat.

I had my first crush in fifth grade. Marc. These first feelings of really liking someone were more vivid than anything else I had ever felt before. When I sat next to Marc, my skin burned. But I had no one to share my experience with and nobody to help me understand what was going on.

If I'd liked a girl, I knew my parents would want to hear all about it. They loved to ask me and Scott which girl we'd marry and why. I couldn't say, "I don't want to marry a girl." So I would think for a while and say, "Amy," and they would ask why. And I would say, "Because she is funny and smart and my good friend." I couldn't share my real answer then, but I can now: "Marc, because he gives me butterflies. I would hang the moon for him."

Having a huge part of yourself go unseen by your parents does weird things to your identity and development. I started to establish a clear understanding that the only way to survive was to be what other people wanted me to be. I remember wondering once if I should tell my mom that I was gay. In response to this internal questioning, I received what I believe to be an answer from God: *Absolutely not!* If I had told her at this stage, my mother would have sent me to conversion therapy for sure. My mom recently confirmed that the person she was back then would have stopped at nothing to "cure" her son. My divinely sanctioned secrecy protected me from that horrific abuse.

Church and home weren't alone in teaching me that gay was the worst thing I could be. In 1980s and 1990s America, it was completely acceptable to belittle feminine men. I heard these messages on TV, in music—antigay sentiment was unavoidable. And nowhere was the idea that I was unlovable more relentlessly beat into me than in middle school. Every day, I was bullied for being gay or acting like a girl, and I came to believe I deserved the abuse and public shaming. Middle school is a time of life I would never revisit (though the Unlovable Monster really thrived there). If you are there now, I can tell you truthfully that it gets better.

I grew nine inches the summer after I turned thirteen, reaching my full adult height of six foot two. After this impressive growth spurt, my Boy Scout leader convinced me to join the football team. I decided to sign up, but I realized after two seconds that football for a gay kid in small-town 1990s America was death. In spite of the toxic atmosphere on the team, though, I stuck with it for a while. I was actually quite good, but the better I got, the more ruthlessly a certain group of guys teased me for being gay. I couldn't just quit, because then I'd have to tell my parents why. I knew they'd just say what they had said in response to an earlier bullying situation: "Well, you're not gay, so who cares what those boys think?"

I reasoned that my only way out of football was to break a bone. I threw myself down some stairs but ended up merely bruising my shins. Undeterred, I continued my reckless pursuit. Soon, a trampoline maneuver resulted in a sprained—nearly broken—neck. I had to wear a brace (and now have chronic neck issues), but, hey, it worked! My football days were done. My problems were not.

Life after football was almost worse. A trio of my former teammates made a pastime of giving me shit for quitting, tossing off classic digs like, "He had to quit so he wouldn't get a boner in the shower." It felt like their sole purpose was to ruin my life, and I was terrified to go to school. I felt lucky that I was big enough to actually hurt someone if I had to. I remember worrying about a much smaller fellow student, Jeremiah, who would brush his Barbies' hair on the school bus. I wanted to shake him and say, "Are you nuts? They are going to crucify you!" Why wasn't he doing everything he could to hide his true self like I was?

Jeremiah was one of the five or so noticeably gay kids in our class of two hundred. All of us were treated like shit, but we kept isolated even though we all recognized each other for who we were. It was intensely lonely. Though the Gay-Straight Alliance was founded in 1988, it did not make its way to Heber in time for me and my peers. (If you are wondering about the fate of Jeremiah, he became a drag queen, but he had a rocky road, struggling with drugs and self-worth along the way.)

During this time, the Unlovable Monster grew into a formidable size, threatening to take my life. The truth is that throwing myself down the stairs wasn't just about getting out of football. I was, for the first time, suicidal. My journal from those years is filled with cries of being in hell and wanting to die. I didn't have anyone to talk to. At home, I pretended that everything was fine, because I knew Mom and Dad couldn't handle the truth. And in fact, I started to think that my dad had possibly caused my gayness.

This part of my story is tricky to talk about. Tricky because my experience conflicts with someone else's. It needs to be told, however, because it shows how damaging false beliefs can be. So here we go.

Tingle fingers. That's what my family calls innocuous, pleasant physical touching. Sitting in church and your mom rubs your back? That's tingle fingers. Grandma rubs your feet while watching TV? Tingle fingers. It was all harmless—until it wasn't.

Tingle fingers meant something different for pubescent Jeff, who was attracted to boys. When my dad rubbed my neck or asked me to rub his, I started to experience something completely different from what he intended.

I struggled to comprehend my new reaction to a long-standing family practice, but I eventually seized upon a twisted logic. It went like this: *I've heard over and over again that homosexuality is caused by molestation. I'm gay, so I must have been molested. I never thought I had been, but it must be tingle fingers! Tingle fingers is molestation. Now I have a clear reason for being gay.*

The first part of my logical conclusion was true: I *had* heard repeatedly, both at home and in church, that homosexuality is caused by molestation or some other significant abuse or trauma. My parents and leaders who believed this were misguided, but so were a lot of people back then, even in the larger non-religious culture. Queer awareness wasn't exactly widespread in the eighties and nineties. The Pride movement didn't have the support it experiences today, and the first study about the genetic component of homosexuality didn't come out until 1993. Serious discussions about queer issues were still whispers in the dark. Within this uninformed context, uninformed logic took root. I came to believe that my dad had sexually wronged me. I could barely utter this belief aloud when I excavated tingle fingers in therapy when I was twenty-four. For over ten years, I'd alternated between telling myself that either 1) I was crazy for thinking Dad was capable of molesting me or 2) I was naïve for thinking Dad had meant tingle fingers in anything but a sexual way. When the therapist didn't scold me but rather allowed me to speak, I sobbed for the entire session.

I eventually confronted Dad about tingle fingers. It was not fun. In fact, it brought our relationship near the point of collapse. We have worked through it now, but the whole drama could have been avoided if Dad and I hadn't both fallen victim to unfounded religious and secular conjecture.

11

BRAD

Invisibility and "The Talk"

Jeff says that it did "weird things" to him when his parents could not see him as he was. This is hardly surprising. To be unseen is almost to cease to exist. As Jessica Benjamin explains in *The Bonds of Love*, "Recognition is that response from the other which makes meaningful the feelings, intentions, and actions of the self."[8] When some part of a child (in Jeff's case, being gay) keeps them from experiencing true recognition, they will often disown, repress, or reject that part in order to survive. The repressed aspect of the self will then manifest in symptoms, self-sabotaging behaviors, and mental illness until the child can own the unseen part, promoting it to its rightful place as part of the self.

---

8 Jessica Benjamin, *The Bonds of Love: Psychoanalysis, Feminism, and the Problem of Domination* (New York: Pantheon Books, 1988), 12.

Questions for Brad

Why is it so hard for some religious parents to talk to their children about sex?

In closed cultures, where sex and other subjects are taboo, parents and their children are left to guess their way through complex and emotionally charged issues. Michael had sincere intentions when he broached the topic with his boys under the crafts pavilion, but he was ill-equipped to deal with sexuality and intimacy, let alone to teach others about these topics. Because his culture shrouds sexuality in shame (though calling it *sacred*), Michael was left on his own to teach anything of worth to his children. In this way, Michael was also like a neglected child, thrust into the driver's seat and asked to navigate the complexities of oncoming traffic. He did the best he could with what he had available. Even those of us who might not be immersed in such a religious culture can relate to this overwhelm.

I've had a misunderstanding similar to Jeff and Michael's "tingle fingers" situation? How do I move on?

Tingle fingers is a perfect example of two stories crossing, and such situations often lead to shame, an all-powerful force that prevents awareness.

Jeff was ashamed that his experience of tingle fingers led to some arousal. Michael was appalled that an innocent game could cause such feelings. Both experiences are real, human, and true.

Jeff needs to be heard. When a child feels wronged and abused, the last thing they need is to hold the parent's shame—that sort of lopsided burden is what brings families and children to the edge of disaster. But Michael also deserves to be heard. The parent deserves the same compassion as the child since, in a very real sense, they are also the child.

Reflection Questions

1. What lies did your family of origin perpetuate, consciously or unconsciously, and how can you both name the truth and hold compassion for those who can't see it?
2. If you have had suicidal ideation or engaged in self-harm, can you recognize what part of yourself you are trying to keep unseen?
3. How did your parents talk to you about sex? How can you improve on their approach?

12

JEFF

A Taste of Salvation

Sometimes a phone call changes everything. One day soon after I quit football—and in the nick of time—my friend Andrew Gross called and asked if I wanted to join a singing group in Salt Lake City called Onstage. The woman who directed the group, Jann, had actually debuted one of my dad's most famous songs, "You're Not Alone." It is not lost on me that the first person to sing "You're Not Alone" for a large audience was, in fact, the first person who created a space where I didn't feel alone. Throughout my life, I have had the good fortune to be helped along by mortal representatives of the divine feminine. Jann was the first of these guides. A gregarious perfectionist, she dedicated her life to inspiring her performing groups to exceed expectations. She drew out the best in her students. I started Onstage scared and unsure. I had become resolute that a foundational part of me had to die, but Jann helped me realize that a part of me truly deserved to live. As she paid careful attention to me, Jann revealed that I was more than a struggling, insecure boy. Giving me some of the first unconditional love I'd ever experienced, she made it clear that I was a valued member of her team. The rest of the group followed suit. No one was concerned about my sexuality. Onstage consumed my teenage life, and it got me out of Heber. I met new people and had new experiences that breathed new life into me.

Jann was also the first unorthodox Mormon I had ever known well. She had been married a few times and lived by her own rules. She was okay with her life. Though I wouldn't break out of the mold for several more years, that early example of someone who was good, kind, and not a strict Mormon paved the way for me.

Though it opened up my world, Onstage was not my first foray into music, not by a long shot. Being my dad's son basically groomed me for a life in music. A couple of early experiences had me sold.

Because Dad was always working, he would find ways to bring us along so that he would see more of us than just our sleeping figures in our beds at night. During the summers when I was nine, ten, and eleven, the Promised Valley Playhouse on Salt Lake City's State Street produced my dad's show, *Celebrating the Light*. Dad brought us along to sell cassettes after each show.

I remember the hour-long drive to the theater, sailing down the winding and beautiful Parley's Canyon and into Salt Lake's downtown with its wide streets and remnants of pioneer-era and turn-of-the-century architecture. The theater exterior was ornate and imposing, the interior bright white and gold foiled. (Unfortunately, the theater was gutted in the mid-nineties. Its ornate façade was saved and now provides a front for offices). We'd watch the show and then wait out in the lobby to traffic our wares. We typically sold a hundred five-dollar cassettes per night. I got to handle the money, and all of that cash seemed like a fortune.

The Young Ambassadors, a traveling song-and-dance troupe from Brigham Young University (BYU), starred in the show. I was obsessed with these brilliant performers. They'd come out to the lobby while we were selling cassettes, and I got to know them pretty well. They seemed so grown up and accomplished to little prepubescent Jeff. I felt that since my dad had written the show, I certainly was part of the gang. I actually became a semi-official member when I was fourteen. For a few summers, I went to the Young Ambassadors' Singing Entertainer Workshop at BYU. We'd stay in the dorms and learn from the Young Ambassadors. Some of the crew I'd hung out with at Promised Valley were actually my teachers at camp!

The other formative experience is far more intimate. Dad would take us to his office sometimes. It was airy and hip—the central decorative choice was a huge poster of Bruce Springsteen. Dad was so light-hearted and dedicated when he was at work. I loved hanging out there, befriending the receptionist and other colleagues who are still family friends to this day.

But across the street at Bonneville Communications is where the real fun happened. This is where Dad recorded his albums. One summer, Mom and Meggan went to Europe with my Grandma Eggington, so Dad, Scott, and I spent a lot of time hanging out in the studio. This was the summer he recorded *One Heart in the Right Place.* Sessions would start at 4 p.m. and go until 10 or 11 at night. Big stuff for a ten-year-old.

Between songs, we would play catch and softball in the alley with the band and the engineers. But it was really all about the music. I return to one encounter over and over when I consider how I came to fall in love with music.

We were all in the main studio. Dad was at the piano, and I sat on the floor, literally at the feet of the divine songstress Felicia

Gibbons as she learned Dad's brand-new song "Which Part Is Mine?" I had fallen asleep many nights to Dad composing this number in the great room at home. A piece of music that had simply been a sound of home became glamorous as Felicia sang it there in the yellow-toned, orange-carpeted, instrument- and microphone-bestrewn studio. This was magic.

Besides these experiences in Dad's orbit, I had my own early adventures with music. While I kept my silence about the unspeakable part of my identity, singing became my escape. I sang myself to sleep at night. I sang to make sense of my feelings. I sang and sang and sang. Heber City had an incredible youth choir program. In the eighties and early nineties, choir director extraordinaire Brad Thompson involved everyone—football players, band geeks, skaters, cowboys—in all of the musicals and choirs.

Not only was I involved in Brad's choir at an early age, but I started taking private voice lessons from his assistant, Karen Patterson, at age eight. I worked with Karen for three years, and she coached me for the sixth-grade talent show, where I sang "Whistle a Happy Tune" from *The King and I.* Probably because my classmates were too young and sheltered, I lived it down despite the song's first line: "Whenever I feel afraid to hold my head erect."

In seventh grade, I started taking lessons from Rebecca Dimmick, a popular operatic voice teacher who lived forty minutes away in Provo. It was through her that I met Andrew, my Onstage lifeline. I studied with Rebecca through ninth grade.

When I was twelve, I performed with my dad for the first time. It was a Sunday at the end of January. In fact, it was Super Bowl Sunday, and my dad still managed to fill a 6,000-seat theater. Three stakes had come together to make the concert happen. (A stake is a collection of Mormon congregations, roughly analogous to a Catholic diocese.) This was the first of many church-related meetings, concerts, and gatherings to be graced by the presence of our father-son act.

I remember pulling up in front of a domed building in Bountiful, Utah, a suburb north of Salt Lake City. The venue seemed massive to me. I knew everybody milling around outside was there to see Dad and me. Nerves started to set in as I looked out the car window. Dad was great. He gave me a little pep talk, the first of many through the years. He told me he was a little nervous too, but he reminded me of what he'd taught me: how we represent ourselves as a family (we are casual but dignified) and how to talk to other people (make the conversation about them).

We got out of the car and were ushered through a special entrance. I went into the bathroom and checked myself in the mirror, a ritual that I repeated with each performance for years. Then Dad and I walked into the theater together, and I could feel the audience murmuring, putting it together that I was the great Michael McLean's son.

I watched him tell his funny and clever stories, letting loose his considerable charisma on the rapt audience. I remember marveling that this commanding presence was my dad. I may not have been able to put it into words at the time, but it became clear to me that this was why he couldn't know the intricacies of my life. He was built for the grand scale. He belonged to the converts of the gospel of Michael McLean. Honestly, I've never lost my awe at his prowess as a performer.

That night, Dad was going to have me sing "You're Not Alone." But first, Scott was going to start out. Scott could do all kinds of impressions, so he would sing it in his best Kermit the Frog voice. It was a little bit that Dad thought up. The idea was that we may believe that we most certainly *are* alone, so anyone saying otherwise will sound silly to us. But, he assured the congregation, the truth is that we are not alone. So then I came in, shaking and nervous, singing Dad's words and tune in my little barely-out-of-puberty voice. People told me it was amazing, and I was hooked. I started singing with Dad whenever I could, sometimes for serious bigwigs in the Mormon Church in settings large and small.

The more I sang with Dad, the more I began to think that my voice was connected to God's spirit, and others seemed to agree. *But how?* I thought. Didn't you have to *earn* God's presence by doing the right things? I would masturbate the night before performing and still have everyone crying in their seats. I was proving the rules wrong. I was both good and evil. Sexuality—especially gay sexuality—couldn't be tolerated, but something about me was still special.

After each concert, Dad and I would talk to (and flatter) audience members, graciously receiving their praise (and selling albums). Essentially, my job was to validate members of a community that was fighting to destroy people like me. I didn't yet have a full intellectual grasp on that fact, despite how I'd heard my family talk about Steve Smith. All I knew was that singing with my dad placed me in situations where people listened to me and I was valued. And, well, we were kind of famous, and that was fun. It was also fun to see my dad at work off the stage. He was so kind, so interested in others. I saw that he really loved and took care of his fans in the same way that they loved and took care of him. He would listen to all of their stories, and as a bystander, I would listen to their stories too. The whole thing made me feel proud and grateful to represent my family.

Any discussion of my musical life with Dad would be incomplete without *The Forgotten Carols*, a Christmas show he wrote that he has been touring for over thirty years. It has been wildly successful, with many families turning it into an annual tradition.

In the late 1980s, Dad had several successful albums out, and his production company and publisher, Deseret Book, asked him for a Christmas album. Dad took that request and ran with it. Taking inspiration from Charles Dickens, who used to do *A Christmas Carol* as a one-man show, Dad didn't simply create an album of all-original music. He wrote an accompanying book and started putting together a stage show.

I was twelve years old when Dad first performed *The Forgotten Carols* in our living room for a small group. After that, Christmas changed forever. Thanksgiving became our big family holiday—the last hurrah before tour.

The show has evolved over the years, boasting a larger cast and reaching audiences all over the western United States and beyond. When I was fifteen or sixteen, I started touring with the show, singing some of the more vocally challenging numbers for male voice while Dad and Felicia Gibbons sang everything else.

✣

Once Onstage came into my world, I started thriving in other areas of my life. I got my Eagle Scout award, started applying to colleges, and zeroed in on career goals (I wanted to be a chiropractor). I had actual friends—most of them girls—and was even voted junior class president. My committee and I threw the most extravagant prom Wasatch High had ever seen.

I was set for a regular life, and then came another life-changing call.

A theater owner in Salt Lake was hosting a master class with the acclaimed voice teacher Seth Riggs. (A master class is basically a lesson in front of an audience. Students receive feedback from a master teacher, and teachers in the audience learn new techniques.)

The theater owner called and asked if Dad would like to buy the final master-class lesson. Dad said, "I'm not much of a singer, but can I take that spot for my son?" The perfect gift for my upcoming sixteenth birthday.

I was no stranger to Seth Riggs's reputation. Seth had taught all the greats. And I mean the great greats—people like Stevie Wonder and Michael Jackson. He was a big name with a big personality and a huge, well-deserved ego. We had some Riggs satellites in Utah, and Jann from Onstage was one, as well as Dean Kalin, my voice teacher after I moved on from Rebecca Dimmick (I'd decided that opera was not my thing). In the first half of high school, I hit my stride as a super-low bass. I couldn't sing higher because of my vocal break. Every voice has a break, where you move from chest voice to head voice, and this break is where your voice is weakest. I had a huge break, which is very difficult to hide, but I worked around it the best I could.

I had to pick a song for the master class. At that time, *The Secret Garden* was a hit musical, so I chose the song "A Bit of Earth." It has a G that my bass voice really struggled to hit, and I wanted some help figuring out how to sing it. I'd been told I couldn't sing tenor notes. But tenors get *all* the good songs and are *always* the leads, so I'd been trying to figure out how to sing "those notes."

When I told Dad my plan, he said, "Jeff, why don't you sing something impressive? This voice teacher is a big deal."

"Dad," I replied, "you are paying an insane amount of money for this guy to teach me something. Why don't we let him impress *me* by teaching me something I don't know?"

Dad let it go after that.

The night of the master class, I was given the second-to-last spot, so I sat in the audience with my family, waiting for my turn through lesson after lesson. It was torture. Seth had a brash, bold style I liked, but it was also very intimidating. He had a booming, beautiful voice, and though I could tell whenever he stood up from the piano that we were about the same height, he seemed so much bigger. He was in his sixties, but he was still in his full physical power. As I watched him, I became more and more nervous—and more and more intrigued. What would this commanding, square-jawed wizard teach me? He was so decisive, so quick to pinpoint problems and identify solutions. And the charisma—it was off the charts. He was like your potbellied grandpa turned master of the universe. I knew one thing: I wanted to make this man happy and prove to him that I was good enough to be there.

Finally, I was up. I walked dizzily onto the stage and began my song. I cracked on that G just like I'd known I would, but overall, I did really well. When I finished the song, it was time for Seth Riggs to show his stuff. We did a series of vocal drills, starting with vowels up and down the scale and then some exercises where he took me from chest voice to head voice. I was amazed at how effortlessly I took to his instruction. After ten minutes, Seth turned to the audience and said, "This kid is a tenor."

I laughed a little inside because, according to every teacher I'd ever had, I was and would forever be a bass. "It's crucial to unlock his abilities so he can sing these amazing notes," said Seth.

In the next ten minutes, I felt like I had been sucked into a vortex where only Seth, the piano, and I existed. We returned to "A Bit of Earth," and he told me to do things that I'd never heard before. He had me lower the corners of my mouth, modulate my vowels in new ways. He led me into a mixed part of my voice I'd never experienced—not head, not chest. I went from cracking on the song's high note to not only hitting the note but also feeling it resonate throughout my body.

And then I was out of the vortex, back in the theater, knowing the note was ringing, ricocheting through the audience as well.

The Great Seth Riggs paused. He turned to the audience again.

"Ladies and gentlemen, this is the best young tenor voice I have ever heard in my thirty-plus years of teaching."

The audience gasped collectively. And because of the magic Seth had unlocked in me, I almost believed him.

"It is critical that he find a teacher who can help him reach his ultimate potential."

After my lesson, I sat next to my family to watch the last student. I could tell that the mood in my family had changed.

After the final singer, Seth had to rush off to the airport, but Dad told me to ask Seth what I should do next.

"Call me," said Seth as he walked to his waiting limo.

This invitation didn't register in my intimidated fifteen-year-old brain, and I had no intention of calling him. He was too big a deal, and I was . . . well, just me. The ride home, however, was all cheering and excitement.

I listened to the cassette recording of my lesson at home that night, enthralled with the genius of Seth's teaching and with my voice sounding so different and beautiful in its upper register. I rewound the tape over and over again to listen to Seth's proclamation: "This is the best young tenor voice I have ever heard in my thirty-plus years of teaching."

As I went to bed that Saturday in March, I slept soundly knowing there was more to me and my talents than I had imagined.

Magic . . .

⌖

Like I said before, sometimes a phone call changes everything.

Sunday morning, I awoke to my parents' yelling, "Jeff, get up here! You have to hear this!"

Seth had left a message on our machine.

"Hello, this is Seth. I've been up all night wondering what to do about Jeff. I've decided that I have to teach him myself. We need to get him to Los Angeles. We can work out cost and everything later. I have a really strong feeling that I just have to teach him! Okay, talk to you soon. Goodbye."

What!? What was happening?! We all just started screaming and dancing around the house.

Then Mom said, "Well, you're still in high school, so there is no way we are just going to send you to LA by yourself. What if we all moved?"

We sat in crackling silence until Dad said, "That sounds like the best adventure ever! We moved a lot when I was kid, and I loved it."

Mom said, "If we are moving to California, I want to live on the beach."

Dad had business in LA two weeks later. While driving up the Pacific Coast Highway, he felt divinely inspired to pull over in front of some condos in Malibu. He rented one on the spot, and we moved in a month later.

⁜

Life in Malibu was nuts and exactly what you would think: spectacular. Mom, Dad, and I happily lived like sardines in a one-bedroom loft by the sea. Scott went to college in Pasadena, so he was just an hour away. Only Meggan missed out on our California adventure. She was on a church mission in Madrid.

Starting that summer, I drove to Seth's studio twice a week for hour-long sessions. When someone like Seth Riggs believes in you, it's astonishing how easily everyone else believes in you too. This was evident when Dad pitched an album called *Father and Son* to his label and they ate it up. We had a project for the summer. The album's concept centers on my having the voice that Dad never did. Dad is a great songwriter, but he isn't really a singer. The idea of my taking over his legacy had a special kind of romance.

My senior year at the ultra-fancy Malibu High School was packed with star-studded extravaganzas. At one fundraiser—a black-tie dinner at music producer David Foster's house—we raised over a million dollars. The hosts? Mel Gibson and Daniel Stern. Jay Leno did an act. Natalie Cole and Olivia Newton-John sang.

It was $500 a plate for the dinner, so my parents sprang for the $1,000, and let me just tell you, it was totally worth it. The night was out of a dream. We parked at Cross Creek, and I sent my parents on a shuttle to the Fosters' property. The high school choir would be performing that night, and I gathered with my fellow singers so we could take a separate shuttle. As we passed through a security gate and along a vast lawn, I felt like Nick Carraway entering Gatsby's world for the first time.

We were in for more delight and wonder. The shuttle dropped us off at the gala venue: an enormous white tent that sat on the lawn near an impressive swimming pool and pool house. I saw that we were at base of a mountain, and on a cliff above us stood a beautiful, gleaming mansion. The Fosters' home. I saw a peculiar trolley-like contraption leading to the graceful structure and wondered aloud what it could be. David Foster's daughter was in the choir, and she heard me. "That's our funicular," she said. A *funicular*? What fanciful place had I found myself in? I felt like I'd been sucked into one of Wes Anderson's films—or I would have if this night hadn't predated his entire career.

The choir performed "The Power of the Dream," an Olympic theme song that David Foster had produced for Céline Dion. I had a solo. The soloists had all worked with David to prerecord our parts. I'd had a hard time with the rhythm in the studio because I was so nervous, but David was so patient and such a cheerleader through my four takes. Maybe it was five. Or six. When I stepped forward to lip-synch my solo, feeling like a rock star in my choir uniform of white shirt and jeans, my eyes swept the audience, picking up such luminaries as Ralph Lauren and Jim Carrey. And then there was Dr. Quinn Medicine Woman herself: Jane Seymour, gorgeous in a red floor-length gown. I imagined she must have looked at my flowing shoulder-length hair and mistaken me for Byron Sully, her sensitive yet rugged *Dr. Quinn* love interest. I locked eyes with her and sang, "It's the moment that you think you can't, you'll discover that you can." I felt light years away from suicidal Heber Jeff.

The coolest thing in the world was introducing my parents to David Foster. He was so kind, and he gushed to them about how good I was and how great it was to meet them. Here was one of the world's biggest music producers, and he was gracious and sweet and made me feel like a million bucks. Honestly, some of the most supportive people I've ever met are the ones who have made it big—they don't have anything to prove.

After a whirlwind year of many other such galas (I could name-drop for days here), I spoke at my high school graduation. With a dulcet voice and silky hair, I also sang 1997's hottest graduation choral number, "Seasons of Love" from *Rent*. I threw my mortarboard in the air, believing a life full of promise awaited me.

How quickly life can change. Not three years before, I'd desperately thrown myself down the stairs. Now things seemed to be going my way—at least on the surface. I had managed to get through my adolescence. Sure, I still thought I was irredeemably evil—that malicious Unlovable Monster, though a little smaller, continued to skulk around my head. But I had seen a few hopeful glimmers in my short life: Strawberry Shortcake from Santa. Andrew's phone call. Jann. Appreciative fans at concerts with Dad. David Foster. Seth. And most importantly, some genuine family affection.

Following graduation and the dream of Malibu life, I focused on proving that both my gayness and the monster didn't exist. I became Jeff the Super Mormon.

13

BRAD

Magical Helpers

As we—parents and children alike—begin to align ourselves with life, we attract those who can and will support us on our journeys. Not everyone will have a Seth Riggs experience, of course, with power and fame waiting in the wings. But when we pursue authenticity in some area of our lives, we often find that helpers appear.

Question for Brad

Jeff got his magical helper in Seth Riggs. What can parents who authentically pursue healing with their children expect?

As we become more authentic, we become less interested in superficial friendships. Old dinner-party conversations don't make sense anymore. We feel an aversion to mundane or status-driven questions like, "What school does your child attend?" Instead, we gravitate to sincerely posed questions: "How are you and your children—really?" As we tell the truth about our lives, we weed out people who cannot handle our reality. Our new friends will see and love us as we are. We've "leveled up," finding others who also operate at a higher frequency and who can relate and share their stories in return. These others may be our magical helpers, and we may be theirs.

Reflection Questions

1. Have you had extraordinary opportunities in your life? Did you take hold of them, or did you let them pass by?
2. What do you truly want in your life? If you are a parent, do you know your children's passions? Have you found ways to support them?

14

MICHAEL

A Storyteller

Now that Jeff has shared with you the experience of his young life, I'm going to tell you a little about how I grew up and eventually became a father who was oblivious to his young son's anguish.

My parents were attentive but tough to please. I learned early that I had to earn their love. My father was raised in the Great Depression, and it showed. He was not the guy who took his son fishing or golfing or skiing. Fixing the washing machine together was his idea of a good time. He was a hard worker, and he taught me some valuable lessons. My relationship with my mom was harder. She was talented and funny, but she was deeply broken.

By the time I was eight years old, I had acquired two main survival skills: perfectionism and people pleasing. I'm a storyteller, so here are a couple of anecdotes that may give you an idea where these traits came from.

Around third grade, I got the nicest pair of school shoes I'd ever had. My mother made me promise not to take the shortcut through the field while wearing them. "Stay on the road!" she commanded. The very first day I wore the shoes, I disobeyed and walked across the field. When my mother saw the tell-tale mud all over the shoes, she was furious. She said I could never make up for what I had done, even when I begged her to let me clean the shoes. No, I was not allowed to clean them. Instead, she put them up on display, dirt and all. Then she fell silent and did not speak to her eight-year-old son for weeks.

This is how I learned that you can never make up for your mistakes—so you'd better try your damnedest not to make any.

Now for people pleasing. When I was seven, my mother forced me to take piano lessons, and the inevitable recital came up. I performed selections from John W. Schaum's green book. When I finished my song, the audience momentarily remained silent. And then . . . APPLAUSE! They were clapping for *me*. My soul drank in the sound, and I coined this poem:

When I leave mortality, its pains and fears,
And enter into holier spheres,
Angelic choirs needn't sing, dear God.
Just let me hear them all applaud.

This is how love worked for me for a long time: I would do everything I could to please and entertain you, and in return, you'd clap for me. And if you weren't clapping, I was obviously doing something wrong. I'd try harder.

When I was seventeen, I received a patriarchal blessing, a sacred rite of passage for Mormons. The blessing gives inspiration and direction for your life. The man who blessed me was deeply articulate, even poetic. He said I had a mission to perform. He didn't tell me what it was, but he said that I must prioritize discovering my mission and then do whatever it took to fulfill it.

Worldwide consequences for good would follow, he said.

A divine call was just what my perfectionism and people pleasing needed in order to blossom. The blessing empowered me to do things I might have been too intimidated to try, but I also felt a heavy responsibility to help everyone everywhere. I prayerfully considered every decision in my life, large and small, evaluating which alternative lined up closely with my life's mission.

I met and married Lynne, and by the time I hit the age of twenty-three and a half, we had Meggan. When she was born, I looked at that little face and said to her, "I'll work four jobs to keep you fed and safe. I will be the best father I can possibly be."

Soon, Lynne was pregnant with Scott, and she went on a road trip with her sister. I received the phone call we all dread. Lynne's car had been identified in a seventeen-car pile-up. No word on whether she'd survived.

I entered the hospital fearing the worst, but Lynne and the baby were alive. Lynne had suffered terrible facial injuries, though. When I went into her room, I recognized her only by her clothes. My expectations for everything changed.

I dropped out of school so I could take on more of the labor at home. Lynne took a long time to get back to herself, and we didn't feel quite settled when, only a few months after Scott was born, Lynne became pregnant with Jeff. We would have three kids under four years old. I began thinking, "How do I pay the light bill, build a career, take care of everyone, and nurture my wife? And what about my patriarchal blessing?" It was too much.

When my business partner lost a huge chunk of my money (life can really pile it on sometimes), my lofty ideas of being the best father went out the window. Survival became the goal. I didn't cheat on Lynne, and we weren't starving. Good enough, right? Fatherhood would have to take a back seat because it was time to make good on my patriarchal blessing. I had to find my mission and carry it out!

I'd been steadily working my way up the ladder at the church since Meggan was a baby. I'd started with a part-time job producing radio and television shows featuring the Mormon Tabernacle Choir. I gave it all I had to give and then some. By January 1980, when Jeff was nine months old, I found myself in front of the most intimidating audience I'd ever tried to please: the global leaders of the church. I had thirty-five minutes to pitch a television special featuring the choir and a legendary movie star. I must have aced it, because they gave this twenty-seven-year-old kid approval to produce the TV special "Mr. Krueger's Christmas." I was too young to know that you can't pull off something like hiring the immortal Jimmy Stewart to play the lead in your religious TV special.

So I pulled it off.

This win kicked off twenty years of nonstop obsession with fulfilling my mission. With success after success, I believed that God must be using me as a vessel. I had plenty of proof—albums, famous public service announcements, concerts, movies, stage plays, and a Bronze Lion from the Cannes Film Festival. I had no doubt that my patriarchal blessing had come true. I was a force of good in the world. God could trust me. And I trusted Him.

The irony is that my award-winning public service commercials were all about making family a priority: "Give them your time! Thoughts from The Church of Jesus Christ of Latter-day Saints (the Mormons)." All the while, I was sort of an absentee father. Sure, I tried my best to make up for lost time with trips to the studio and rides in the Z. And I'm happy to say I never put my kids' muddy shoes on display. But I still missed out on being there for Jeff in the ways he needed me to be. While working to fulfill my destiny, I was ignorant of my son's reality.

15

BRAD

A Heroic Admission

When Michael says he was ignorant of Jeff's reality, he is making a heroic admission. The truth is that most parents are ignorant of their children's reality, and to admit this is to heroically admit something true. We've been told that we need to be good parents, so we deny our badness. This denial affects our children because they are consciously and unconsciously asked to take up the banner for us. They have to be supposedly "good" so that they reflect *our* supposed goodness. This can create a loop of denial.

Questions for Brad

How do we break out of the loop of denial?

Someone has to come along and *want* to know about their real and authentic self instead of some polished and "acceptable" version of a self that was sold to them by their parents—and to their parents by their parents, on down the generations. That's why I call Michael's admission heroic. It has the potential to change the course of future generations in the family.

If Michael's parents had showered him with praise more, would he have been a better father to Jeff?

It is difficult to know for sure what the consequences would have been if Michael's parents had been effusive in their support of Michael. What he needed more than anything was what all children need: to be consistently *seen* by someone they value. That is where esteem comes from. It doesn't arise from success or praise. One of the greatest errors we make is conflating praise with love. Praise is valuable, but it is not a substitute for attunement and connection. We don't want our children to develop a sense that only their good parts are worthy of love and compassion—we want them to know that all of them is worthy.

If a child receives *less* praise than needed, they will either act out or learn to not need attention (this is called *splitting*, or disowning part of the self). Acting out or splitting makes the lack of praise more tolerable for the child, for if they retained a conscious need for positive attention, life would be too painful. This child will likely become an adult who has difficulty accepting compliments because they've had to split off the parts of themselves that want attention and praise. Compliments remind them of a need they've repressed, triggering shame and pain.

Reflection Questions

1. Did your parents give you a lot of praise or withhold praise? As a parent, how do you praise your children? How can you prioritize *seeing* your children consistently?
2. Do you feel that only your smart, successful, beautiful parts are loved? When someone admires you, do you say to yourself, "Yeah, but if they knew the real me, they wouldn't love me"?
3. Does your family have a loop of denial? What heroic admission could you make to help break it?

PART 2

Super Mormon

16

JEFF

Father and Son

After high school, most kids I knew left the nest to begin their new "independent" lives at college. I'd been accepted to Pepperdine and could have gone there for a year before going on a church mission, but Dad presented a compelling alternative: "We did an album together. Now we need to go sell it." So instead of individuating by going to college or taking a break to "find myself," I continued working in the family business like I had since I was twelve. It felt so natural, but the *Father and Son* tour also took things to a new level. Now everything in my life was about my family and singing for Dad's predominantly Mormon fans, who would hopefully become my fans too. I, Super Mormon Jeff, would become the voice of the Mormon Church. Or at least the McLean family singing mascot.

What does it look like for a Mormon father and son to tour their record? From October to December, we folded the album promotion into the annual tour for *The Forgotten Carols*. That year, I sang a song from *Father and Son* before each show and during the revue section at the end. Then we would sell copies of the album in the lobby along with all of the Christmas merchandise. It was genius. *The Forgotten Carols* reaches sixty thousand people each holiday season. (The show's success was why we could move to Malibu, why I could study with Seth Riggs, and why my parents were able to pay off the Heber house.)

From January to September, Dad and I toured weekend by weekend, traveling almost every Thursday through Monday. We typically organized the tour around visiting different stakes throughout the church. Over two thousand stakes dotted the globe during the 1990s, so we weren't in danger of running out of places to visit. Let me re-create for you here one tour stop in North Carolina, a location that would soon become significant in my life.

We had been invited to perform at the Kinston Stake. The stake budget paid for our flights, and the stake president and his wife, President and Sister Deaver, met us at the airport. As we cruised the hour to their home, lounging in the back of their sleek BMW, we became fast friends.

Sister Deaver was beautiful, with delicate hair haloing her petite features. President Deaver spoke with an appealing Southern accent and proved to be wildly charismatic and fun. Their house was stunning—huge and brick, with a Southern flair. They had exquisite taste in fine antiques. I stayed in a room that was like something out of a picture book, with its four-poster bed and painted landscapes of vistas in France.

Sister Deaver had prepared a gorgeous dinner, chicken cordon bleu with phenomenal cheesy potatoes, and some delectable dessert, all of it served on fancy china. In short, Dad and I were pampered and treated like kings. And like, kings, we held court. President and Sister Deaver had invited various local Mormon leaders—the stake Young Men and Young Women presidents, the stake Relief Society president, and a few bishops. We chatted throughout dinner, retiring afterward to the living room to keep the conversation going. It was always like this with our hosts and their guests. These were our people, and we always found things to talk about (and inevitably discovered mutual acquaintances from the small Mormon world).

The next morning, the exquisite Sister Deaver prepared us a phenomenal breakfast, and we headed off to the stake center. In this roomy church building that held the stake offices and a chapel, we gave the first of the weekend's three performances.

Our audience comprised two or three hundred missionaries who were gathering for a zone conference (Mormons are really into conferences). We shook hands with all the missionaries and met the mission president. We often performed for the missionaries serving in whatever stake we were visiting. But sometimes our Saturday performances would be for the stake's youth or for the Relief Society sisters. Dad had twenty albums of material, so we had an ample library to draw on, making every performance special and unique for each audience. For the missionaries, he sang songs that he'd written on his mission so they could feel that he related to their current situation. Dad peppered the performance with easy monologues about his work on commercials and movies for the church, focusing specifically on the movies he'd created specifically for missionary work. And of course, since we were touring *Father and Son*, he made sure to include a few songs from that album.

After the missionary conference, we were shuttled to a small Mormon bookstore, where we signed albums and books for a couple of hours. With minimal rest afterward, we began the evening's extravaganza. Thousands of youth from miles and miles around gathered for a youth conference (yes, yet another conference), and we performed in the cultural hall (the all-purpose recreational wing of a Mormon church building, always with basketball-court-painted floors and flanked by hoops on either end). The whole performance was a little louder and more exciting as we sang all of Dad's most entertaining, youth-oriented songs—fun and even funky. Dad infused the evening with humor. We also sang songs from Dad's musical about Noah and the flood, *The Ark*. I had worked with Dad as he'd workshopped the musical in New York, and its songs appealed to kids. After the performance, we mingled and chatted with the audience, and then it was back to the Deavers' to bed.

On Sunday morning, we went to stake conference, a semiannual spiritual meeting for the area's congregations. Then that night we were back in the spotlight, this time for a sacred fireside with more spiritual, worship-heavy songs (Mormons like firesides—Sunday evening gatherings a little less formal than regular services—as much as they like conferences).

Dad and I did weekends like this so much that we did everything in tandem so easily. Sure, sometimes the details would vary. Sometimes we built Scout camps and did other service projects in between performances. No matter what, I knew what Dad was going to say, and he knew what I was going to say. We never had to rehearse. The seamlessness of our interactions and the way we complemented each other were really meaningful to me.

All told, Dad and I were on the road for a grueling forty-six weeks that year. It felt like an initiation into how my life would be from then on. Although all the traveling was rough, Dad and I had a blast. Dad knows how to have fun on the road. When we weren't staying with a family, we went to movies, ate delicious restaurant meals, and saw the sights. And as I listened to Dad speak for the crowds, I became even more converted to the Church of Michael. Dad is a truly gifted and inspired performer and speaker. He elevates everyone's spirits and helps them feel less alone. I look back on the *Father and Son* tour as a magical time.

17

Jeff

When you are a McLean, you serve a Mormon mission. There's no question, even if you are on the cusp of fame and fortune. So through all of the touring, I kept myself "worthy" to serve a mission—meaning I followed all of the good-Mormon-boy rules (no sex, no drinking, no swearing, no you-name-it). And the fact is, I was a true believer. I read the Book of Mormon all the time. I prayed every night. In high school, I'd gone faithfully to daily seminary class (seminary is religious education for Mormon high schoolers). I was seriously engaged in spiritual work, and I had had confirmations from the Spirit that supported my beliefs. When I was eighteen and attending a vocal camp at Marymount College in California, I felt overwhelmed because someone told me that I didn't have any emotion in my voice. It really challenged my perception of my singing voice. Did I only know how to sing pretty? Could I really not connect to songs? Feeling very overwhelmed and distressed, my impulse was to turn to God. I went into my room, knelt down, and pleaded for guidance. In response, I felt a powerful and undeniable connection with the divine, which was the ultimate catalyst for my going on a mission.

When you reach mission age—nineteen in my day—you send in your application, vaccination records, proof of wisdom teeth removal, and the like, and then the church assigns you to a mission location. You don't have a say in where you end up. Sure, the application form has a question about where you might like to go, but I've never heard of those preferences being taken into account. The assignment process is kept a mystery.

Missionary service was supposedly optional, but it felt mandatory to me and my peers. If you didn't go or if you came home early, you were a social outcast. To avoid this fate, thousands of young men went on missions reluctantly, feeling forced to do a job they had no desire to do. These were not happy kids, and they did not do good work. I would say that about 80 percent of missionaries fell into this category, and they made life challenging for the 20 percent of us who served with real conviction.

Women rarely went on missions back then. Those who served were somehow "special"—meaning they were strong and devout or had something to prove. Or, as suggested in shaming whispers, they were too ugly to get married. When my sister got her mission call, people said things like, "You're so pretty. Why would you go on a mission when you could get married?"

I was in Malibu when I got my call. Opening the letter revealing your mission assignment has become almost ceremonial in Mormon culture. The whole family gathers—Grandma on one phone, your second cousin on another—and you read aloud where you will be spending the next two years.

I was convinced I would go somewhere cool. Meggan got to go to Madrid, and Scott to Norway. My dad had gone to South

Africa, for heaven's sake. With hands trembling, I opened my letter, and (drum roll, please . . .) I was called to serve in North Carolina! What!? The USA? The SOUTH?

I could have spent the next two years learning Chinese or Italian or Spanish and living somewhere I'd never been before. Nope. Here I come, North Carolina Raleigh Mission. Land of the Piggly Wiggly. Land that I had just barely visited on the *Father and Son* tour and that held no mystery for me! No new language—just a southern drawl.

Off to the uniform store to get my suits, white shirts, and ties. And then to buy a bike. I'll have you know that I hate biking and I hate suits, white shirts, and ties. But the truth is, I loved my mission.

My month in the training center was a dream. The rigid schedule agreed with me—running every morning and having regular mealtimes left my body feeling strong and healthy. My gregarious self also loved the crowds and bustle. Apparently, every boomer had kids my age, so an insane number of missionaries crammed into the training center in the summer of 1998. I immediately bonded with my training group, and I am friends with many of them to this day.

A couple of things bothered me. The first was the script. I can make conversation with a tree, but I wouldn't be able to use my own words when I taught people. I had to essentially memorize lines. The second thing that bothered me was the communal shower. I felt like I was back in sixth-grade gym. I wasn't nervous about popping a boner, which is what every straight man thinks when I tell them how much I hated being naked with everyone. No, I was still carrying around my terrified sixth-grade self, who was really uncomfortable with his body. I've always had some degree of body dysmorphia, and suppressing my sexuality had turned my body into a source of shame in any context, especially when it was naked in front of other people.

An ongoing joke in Mormon culture is that if you serve a mission, you are then entitled to talk about it ad nauseam for the rest of time. Many a lengthy tale begins, "On MY mission I learned . . . " or "When I was on my mission . . . " I have decided to break from tradition because, as wonderful as my mission was, it was not and never will be the apex of my life. I'll just give the bullet-point version of my years wearing a name tag in North Carolina:

- I loved my mission and being a missionary. I don't apologize for representing a church that didn't want me to exist. I made the best choice for my circumstances, and I learned how to do hard things. Some of my experiences instilled self-love in my soul, while others fed the gluttonous Unlovable Monster.
- I love my mission president, Max Esplin, and his incredible wife, Cheryl Esplin. They treated each missionary like their own child. They knew me personally and encouraged me to be a better version of myself, inspiring me to do and give what only I could. Beyond that, they showed me that my unique gifts were valuable, and they allowed me to use those gifts in somewhat nonconventional ways. They even supported me as I created a mission boy band!
- The vast majority of my bad mission memories are related to riding a bike, helping people move, and doing yardwork.
- The people of North Carolina, especially the members of the church, are my heroes. They held me, cared for me, and loved me. And I loved them. I will always be grateful for their kindness.

Okay, I can't resist. I'm going to break out of the bullet points to get sentimental and a little wordy about a couple of my mission experiences that do maybe count as life highlights. You can't always take all of the Mormon out of the boy, even if the boy can take himself out of the Mormons.

The first experience has to do with a poignant message from God that comforted me after some cruelty from one of the other missionaries. Now, some of the missionaries I served with are still in my life, and I love them dearly. But I did get flak from other missionaries who decided that my gayness was their business. Flak is a very mild word for some of the abusive treatment I received. Luckily, this bigotry was limited to just a few of my fellow missionaries, the most blatant being one Elder Hussey.

Luckily, I didn't have to spend much time with him, but one day, my companion, who was a zone leader, wanted to shake things up. A zone leader is in charge of a number of districts, which each also have a leader. So my companion wanted to work alongside some of his district leaders. I got stuck with the companion of one of those leaders for the day. Elder Hussey. He revealed who he was right away, refusing to knock on doors with me or even to walk next to me. He said in a withering tone, "You're gay." Behind his words was an accusation.

I wasn't a chaste young man who happened to have same-sex attraction. No, I was actively gay, and I'd obviously had sex with other boys. I'd felt and heard this tone before in the halls of junior high and high school, even at church. But it hit harder here in the mission field. I had worked so hard to serve a mission worthily, and here this kid was basically insinuating that I'd lied to become a missionary.

Somehow, I got through this nightmare pairing. I prayed to God that night and asked if I really wasn't worthy to be a missionary. I knew that I hadn't lied, that I'd never looked at gay porn, that I'd never so much as held hands with a boy or man. I didn't even find myself attracted to any of the other missionaries. Soon, I felt a pure, loving inspiration from Heavenly Father: *Jeff, you are worthy to be on your mission. You belong.* Suck it, Elder Hussey.

The second formative experience involves a little less drama. North Carolina, if you've never been, is like the tropics in summer. Hot, sweltering sun, 80 percent humidity at least. And we were expected to go door to door in way too many clothes, knocking at houses that had definitely had at least seventy other pairs of Mormon missionaries come by unannounced over the years. Everyone in the South has already been saved anyway, so tracting—what Mormons call this house-by-house approach—was a huge waste of time. But we had to do it. Luckily, I knew a trick.

Picture this: Elder McLean and Elder Smith trudging down the road in the blistering heat, dark clothes, hot, dark shoes. They slowly ascend some unsuspecting stranger's porch while the dog (there was always a dog) starts losing its shit. Knock knock. Annoyed face appears from behind the door, leaving the screen as a barrier. Now, any fool can say, "Hi, I'm Elder McLean," and get a slammed door in the face in return. But what would happen if you *sang* that introduction?

Singing is a higher level of communication—it opens hearts and, for me, feels purely honest. And it certainly caught people off guard and kept doors open longer. And what would singing a whole song do? "Let me leave you with a song . . . " I'd say to every adamant rejection. Dumbfounded, people would say, "Um . . . okay." I can't think of one person who said no.

I always sang the same song, a sweet message of love (all of you graduates of Primary, join in):

Whenever I hear the song of a bird or look at the blue, blue sky,
Whenever I feel the rain on my face or the wind as it rushes by,
Whenever I touch a velvet rose or walk by our lilac tree,
I'm glad that I live in this beautiful world
Heav'nly Father created for me.[9]

By the time I finished, a loving spirit would have descended, and I would say, "Thank you so much for your time. Have a blessed day." Tracting became more about leaving messages of love and hope wherever we went and less about trying to get people to agree to our lessons or to join the church. I'd already known the power of music before these experiences, but this was something I was doing on my own, not with Dad. It showed me that even among people who had no idea who my father was, I could make a difference with my voice.

I returned home from my mission in the summer. Being set free from all of the mission rules was jarring. In two years, I hadn't seen a television or talked to anyone on the phone. I'd masturbated once the whole time. The reentry experience was like the wedding day of a couple who've saved themselves for marriage (not that I have personal experience with this, ahem): one minute everything is off limits, and the next minute anything goes. Add to this off-kilter feeling an extended amount of time that I would have to fill on my own. It was too late to apply for the fall semester at any college, and I would be starting rehearsals for *The Forgotten Carols* in October. In this lull, I decided to live in my parents' basement and spend my time on creative pursuits. *Father and Son* had sold well, so Deseret Book was pushing for a second album.

---

9 *Children's Songbook*, 228.

I would start working on some new songs. Sure enough, by the time we headed out on the Christmas tour, we had a few brand-new songs to add to the preshow and the end-of-show revue.

I also booked a role in *Joseph and the Amazing Technicolor Dreamcoat* at a Salt Lake City theater. I played Zebulun, one of the brothers, and I was reminded of how much I loved theater life—the rush of performing, the backstage antics, and intrigue. I had done a bunch of plays in high school, and, of course, had been doing *The Forgotten Carols* for several years by then. My experience in *Joseph* sealed my decision to audition for the acclaimed Music Dance Theatre (MDT) program at BYU for the winter semester.

I'd never wanted to go to BYU or any church school, but a friend from my mission convinced me to go. I figured I could keep living a life similar to the one I'd lived for the previous two years in North Carolina. At least at BYU, I wouldn't have to wear a suit and tie or ride a bike.

First, I had to get accepted. Admission to BYU is competitive. Every overachieving Mormon tries to get in, and, as you may imagine, such a high-demand religion produces a lot of overachievers. I had a good high school GPA and worked hard on my admissions paperwork, gathering some excellent letters of recommendation. But my highest ACT score fell below the 26 that BYU required. I applied anyway.

After I submitted all of my paperwork, I stopped by the admissions office to see if they had received everything. I got the attention of the clearly indifferent receptionist and asked about my application. Without looking up from her computer, she muttered, "What's your social?" I gave her the number. Still no eye contact. After about three seconds, she full-on gasped. She looked at me and then back at the computer. "Are you THE Jeff McLean?"

Finding the question a bit odd but not wanting to seem rude, I said, "Yes, I believe I am THE Jeff McLean." She smiled and said, "Oh, you don't have to worry. It's all been taken care of." Then she winked at me. This is how I learned to drop my surname into conversations when it might open a door. That name got me into BYU despite my ACT score.

While I was writing songs and playing Zebulun and leveraging my privilege to get into BYU, I had a new hidden life as well. Down in my parents' basement, I had my own massive TV with a vast array of channels. And there it was: PORN! Soft-core porn, sure, but still porn. Porn is a serious taboo in Mormonism. In fact, remember the missing bronze medalist from the Sin Olympics? I think it is for sure Watching Porn.

Besides those homemade solo efforts with my childhood camcorder, my only other exposure to porn had been when my cousin brought a *Playboy* to my grandparents' house the summer I was eleven. It didn't do for me nearly what those 1990s underwear and Abercrombie ads did. Man, those were hot.

And now porn had found me again via Cinemax or Showtime or whatever channel played soft-core stuff after nine o'clock at night. I watched and masturbated and felt terrible—the same cycle I'd felt every time I'd masturbated since I'd found out it was "wrong." I went running to my dad.

"You have to cancel these channels!" I cried. "They are really tempting." It wasn't a totally reasonable request, given what we all know about convoluted cable packages and interminable wait times on the phone. I would just have to deal with the content lurking on the TV. And maybe I could, I thought. Dad didn't seem to be in a panic. I don't think he meant to help me toward the following insight, but his cool head suggested to me that maybe porn isn't that big a deal. Now, I know that porn is embroiled in a lot of real-life issues—betrayal, addiction, human trafficking, pathological objectification of other humans, etc.—but I also think that some antiporn rhetoric is based in shame and can breed self-loathing. For me, the second I stopped feeling shame around porn was the second it lost its allure. (Frankly, I think the Unlovable Monster was a little disappointed.)

18

BRAD

Shoulds and Shame

Jeff's feeling that going on a Mormon mission was mandatory (even though it technically wasn't) serves to illustrate that parents or other adults don't have to verbalize their expectations for children to internalize them as mandates. A wish, a smile, or a nod is all it takes for a child to take up a task. If a parent shows approval, playing soccer or singing can transform into a *should* for a child.

When parents find out that their children have felt "forced" into these pursuits, they are often incredulous. "I just wanted them to be happy," they may say. "I thought they played tennis because they wanted to."

Questions for Brad

How can I tell if I am living my life by shoulds that aren't really shoulds?

It might take working with a trained therapist for a long time to help you unpack such issues. For years, I remember my therapist making comments and observations about my parents and my upbringing. I often thought she was overreaching. Now, so many years and therapy sessions later, her observations seem obvious.

You may not initially remember specific things about your upbringing—the origins of the should. But if you take stock of how you feel *today*, those childhood experiences and expectations may eventually reveal themselves. You may find insights into your past in offhanded comments from the grocery store cashier; somehow, you've encountered some old, familiar energy. It happens before we can register it with the conscious mind. We find ourselves in the emotional soup we were cooked in, the air that we breathed as children. And as a fish is the last to discover water, it is often only when we see our story from a different perspective—for example, a therapist's—that we see things clearly.

Clinical psychologist J. D. Gill says it this way: "The experience of seeing one's base from a different perspective can be profound. One way this happens is by allowing ourselves to be honest and open with someone who does not react the way our parents did. For example, what was 'very bad' at home is now 'nothing.' This difference in experience allows for the realization things could be different. One's assigned position in one's past is not necessarily one's assigned position in the universe."[10]

I relate to Jeff's love of structure during his mission service—and the unsettled feeling when the structure was gone. What is behind this?

Jeff's comments regarding the benefits of structured mission life and the return home feeling disjointed are common themes for

10 J. D. Gill, *Forms of Life and Other Essays*, rev. ed. (CreateSpace, 2014).

people who grew up in strict-father families. *Strict-father family* is a term coined in the literature that describes situations in which parents impose their values onto their children at the expense of the children's development. In Jeff's case, the "father" included his grandfather and his religious community. In any case, when adults impose their understanding of truth on a child under coercive means or the threat of rejection, the cost is the undeveloped self in the child; the child doesn't know who they are. In such cases, structure—being told what to do—is a comfort, and the absence of structure causes intense anxiety. How are children who have been defined and held in place by someone else's ideas supposed to know what to do, who to be, and how to survive if those constraints are lifted?

It's important for parents to have some capacity to step out of the parameters of the strict-father model. Children need support in developing enough of a self to meet changing circumstances with resilience.

Jeff talks about releasing all shame around porn. Shouldn't we feel some shame about things that may harm others?

Many people view shame as necessary. We have sayings like "he has no shame" and adjectives like *shameless* to describe despicable individuals. There is even talk of something called "healthy shame." To be clear, there is *no* healthy shame.

There is a higher law than shame—the law of love. Once when I was teaching a Sunday School lesson about the unhealthy effects of shame and guilt, one of the students talked about a prison visit he'd made during law school. He had a conversation with a young inmate who had killed someone at a convenience store for a couple hundred dollars. The student said, "I asked him what he did after the robbery. He told me he went home and slept." The student was aghast. "No shame? No guilt? No remorse? This inmate was clearly a sociopath," he reasoned. He concluded his comments with a question: "So, Brad, if not for shame and guilt, why would we do anything right?"

I answered simply, "Love." I then explained how guilt and shame lead us away from God and cause us to hide and betray ourselves. It was shame that inspired Adam and Eve to cover their nakedness and hide from God after they ate the forbidden fruit.

Reflection Questions

1. Are you carrying around any *shoulds* from your early life? Consider whether they are still serving you or whether they can be modified or discarded.
2. Do you have any shame-driven habits? What can you do to look at the issue through love—love of God, yourself, and humanity?

19

JEFF

The Brigham Young Experience

After I was accepted into BYU, I applied for the MDT program and got in, placing in the top five. This accomplishment had special meaning for me because I'd admired the program for years. The Young Ambassadors, my old friends from my cassette-peddling days at Promised Valley Playhouse and from Singing Entertainers Workshop, were considered the crème de la crème of the MDT program. It was a dream come true when I was also accepted into Young Ambassadors soon after I started in MDT.

We had a hugely talented Young Ambassadors group. Some of our BYU boys and girls eventually became Broadway *Jersey Boys* and girls, Paul Canaan of Broadway revivals *La Cage Aux Folles* and *Kinky Boots* cut his teeth there in the Harris Fine Arts Center's studios and stages, Tia Altinay would play Jasmine in *Aladdin* in the famed New Amsterdam Theatre, and Clark Johnsen would one day land a spot in the original cast of *The Book of Mormon.*

I fell in "love" with the beautiful Lisanne, a fellow Young Ambassador who looked just like Barbie. I fell in love with her for the same reason I've ever fallen in love with anyone for most of my life: she was going to save me. I was highly incentivized to make myself believe I was in love with her—my immortal soul was on the line. I knew I couldn't live with God in the hereafter unless I married a member of the opposite sex in a Mormon temple. I had to make it work.

To convince Lisanne to love me, I drew on the same tactics I used to get anyone to love me: I worked hard, overdid everything, and lied a little. For nearly two years, I exerted tremendous energy in wooing Lisanne. I took her on amazing dates and plied her with romantic dinners. Most of the songs on my second album were written for her. I dedicated poetry to her. When she had to go to Pittsburgh for an extended time, I flew out to see her.

I assumed that my dedication to Lisanne must mean I was attracted to her. I didn't know what attraction actually felt like because I'd never allowed any hint of it to take hold. But the reality is that I couldn't even bring myself to kiss Lisanne. (Eventually, Lisanne would marry a man also named Jeff.)

In the MDT program at large, it seemed as if every man I knew was gay. But because homosexual relationships are against the rules at BYU, everyone had to lie about being gay or risk getting reported and potentially kicked out of school. And it was a real risk. One of my fellow Young Ambassadors thought he could have an innocent relationship with another boy, but some student informed on him. My friend was expelled.

In overt and covert ways, my sexuality was challenged every day. Everyone who was struggling with homosexuality and coming out assumed I was in the exact same place. No one wanted to let me have my own experience. As I reflect on it, I can understand how lonely everyone was and how desperate we all were to find words for our struggle. But at the time, I was annoyed with the men who seemed hell-bent on discussing the topic at every opportunity. Annoyed and a little jealous. If I didn't have permission to be myself, how could they? Where did they get the balls to be so open and, in some cases, to break the rules and have relationships?

I regret that I was hard on those people. I had unwittingly adopted a bit of Elder Hussey's attitude. If you acknowledged your gayness, that meant you were a vile sinner. Being judgmental allowed me to keep lying about myself. No, not consciously lying. Gay didn't exist, of course, so I couldn't lie about being gay or not being gay. When reality is relegated to the unutterable reaches of your mind, you can believe insane things. For example, I believed that I wasn't tempted to break sexual rules with women because I was so virtuous—more virtuous than my peers, surely. Yes, it was superior spirituality, not being gay. Hiding your true self definitely brings you closer to God, you know.

I want to acknowledge how contradictory this may seem to other things I've shared, like that I knew I was gay in the womb. It's somehow also true that I didn't know I was gay. Any inkling of attraction was stuffed down and locked up with the Unlovable Monster. The monster and my unruly, unspeakable desire made pretty decent cellmates for each other—both were unacknowledged, and both wielded tremendous power from below. Willful ignorance was my survival mechanism. Without it, I would have been abandoned—or something unimaginably worse. I shuddered to think of the many dreadful ways to finish the sentence "If I came out . . . " So I turned it off, as described in the song from *The Book of Mormon.*[11] Simple as that!

---

11 "Turn It Off," from *The Book of Mormon*, music and lyrics by Trey Parker, Robert Lopez, and Matt Stone, 2011.

While still a student at BYU, I went in to record my second album, *Something's Changed.* I had been taking lessons with Seth all along. Seth told me that if I wanted to get a record deal outside of the religious market, I would have to learn how to make my voice less vanilla. This became painfully obvious to me when I listened back to the *Something's Changed* tracks. I hated what I heard. I felt like my voice—clear, beautiful, and soulless—had no connection to any of the songs. I was humiliated. How could I, the son of a brilliant lyricist, come across as so wooden when trying to interpret a song's words?

I asked to push the album release date by a year. Sheri Dew, the CEO of Deseret Book, was super supportive as I rerecorded all of my vocals. I brought in voice teacher and manager Jackie Poth, who had recently signed an artist to Capitol Records. We had three-hour sessions a few times each week to develop my vocal riffs. On my own, I meticulously studied other artists' voices, integrating vocal stylings I thought were cool. Jackie also helped me forge a link between my voice and the songs. I didn't know it at the time, but finding that connective tissue among my soul and my voice and the songs brought me closer to coming out because it put me in touch with my most authentic self.

After releasing the new and improved *Something's Changed*, I started to get antsy. Sure, part of this restlessness came from not knowing what to do with being gay at a church school. I didn't want the powers that be to investigate my sexuality. But I was also worried about my career. I knew instinctively that if I came out, it would ruin the following I already had in the Mormon music world. Every Mormon artist and musician I knew who came out in the eighties and nineties had lost everything—career, family, community.

I couldn't acknowledge these gay-related worries, but I could acknowledge and talk about general career anxieties. How could I capitalize on the taste of success I'd had before my mission? It was time to at least try to reclaim the opportunities I'd missed out on during those two years. (One example: While I was serving the lovely people of North Carolina, Seth called to see if I could sing "The Prayer" with Céline Dion at the 1999 Grammys rehearsal because Andre Bocelli couldn't do it. That gig went to a seventeen-year-old Josh Groban, another of Seth's students. You might have heard of him.)

I strategically auditioned for *American Idol*. It was a much bigger deal back then, and it would have catapulted my career. When I didn't get chosen twice in a row ("Your voice is too Broadway," they said), I moved on from that dream, gathered some funds, and self-produced a twelve-song demo called *American Idol Reject*. In these recordings, I incorporated everything I'd learned from Jackie, and I felt confident that the songs and my voice were interesting and a little edgy.

Satisfied with my demo, I decided to leave BYU and move to LA. I'd transfer to UCLA, work with Seth, get a record deal, and take my place in the Mormon rock-star pantheon. Before the big move, I was hired to do a show at Utah Valley University. This is where I met Clay, the first guy I ever loved. He was playing the villain, and I was the hero. He had a voice for days and was the most handsome man I'd ever seen. He also didn't have all the hang-ups about himself and his sexuality that everyone at BYU had. It's funny to call him experienced, but he was, compared to me.

Being near Clay was intoxicating. One night we decided to watch a movie at a friend's house. I remember lying next to him for the first time, completely startled by what my body was doing. I had been so successful in shutting down any and all attraction for so long, but now the floodgates burst. This new feeling wasn't exactly pleasure, or at least not exclusively pleasure. Lying in Clay's force field, my body went into convulsive, uncontrollable shaking. It lasted so long that I almost thought I was having a panic attack. And it didn't happen only this one time at movie night. Whenever I was with Clay—which was as often as possible because I could not get enough—the violent shaking would precede any contact.

My conditioning had never allowed me to entertain sex as a real-life possibility. And now I knew it was within reach. To be sure, Clay and I never had full-on sex, but we sure danced on the line. The first time we fooled around, I had an orgasm. Once he fell asleep, I went into the bathroom and dry heaved. Clearly the eruption of attraction had carried along with it the guilt and shame I'd also been suppressing. These negative feelings had no real effect on my actions. I would tell Clay, "No, we can't," and then I would capitulate and find myself in his arms, his lips on mine. When he was near me, resistance was nowhere in my power.

I had been judgmental of gay Mormon men for so long. With Clay, I learned what all the fuss was about, to put it mildly. I didn't quite know how to own it at the time, but there was no turning back. Now that I'd experienced the attraction explosion, I could never again act superior to my gay Mormon peers.

I wish I could have just fallen in love and been able to enjoy it. Instead, I wrestled back and forth between wanting and loving this man and trying to live the "right" way. This wrestle was bigger than Clay, of course. I knew I would need to leave him behind soon to become an international singing superstar. But the larger gay question lingered. I talked to my bishop. He basically said that one encounter didn't determine my whole life.

As I engaged in the repentance process with my bishop, I couldn't muster the necessary remorse. Now that I'd been physical with a man and opened my heart to the idea that I could be sexual, I knew who I was. I could not deny it, and I certainly could never marry a woman. But it would still take me a few more years to officially come out. All of this new self-knowledge had to contend with a lifetime of conditioning.

✢

After the play was over, I was off to LA I hadn't seen Seth in about six months when I arrived at his studio, and I was excited to show him *American Idol Reject.* The first track on the demo was "If You're Not the One" by Daniel Bedingfield. The song is high—like singing-in-the-stratosphere high. To tackle those challenging sections during the recording session, I had tried out using my falsetto to make my voice more airy. This was a technique that Seth decidedly did not teach. When I played the song for him, he shut it off after less than two minutes and said, "This is shit! What were you thinking?"

I didn't do his technique on one song, so he dismissed the whole demo. He didn't even listen to any other songs. I realized that Seth was more interested in my being his perfect disciple than he was in my creative exploration. With this realization, an important thing happened: my mentor fell off his pedestal. I had asserted myself, and I could suddenly see him more clearly: he was big on overpromising and underdelivering. I left that day and never went back. I love Seth and what he taught me, but I don't regret my decision. I had to find my own way and reject the notion that other entities—the church, Seth Riggs—knew better than I did. However, the Unlovable Monster clearly did not appreciate my little act of self-love, and a rough time followed.

I'd moved to LA in hopes of having Seth's support—and now it was gone. Then my manager disappeared. She'd helped me create the demo, and now she wouldn't even return my phone calls. I was alone. No manager. No mentor. I'd moved to LA to get a record deal and soar to new heights, and all I'd done was fall on my face. I didn't even get in to UCLA.

I was fortunate to have some safety nets. My dad's friend and frequent collaborator, John Batdorf, is a studio singer in LA, and he helped me get some gigs singing for commercials. I've never seen better musicians than professional studio singers. I even got to sing with the woman who lent her voice to the mousy little nun who lets loose at the end of *Sister Act.* I was in awe of her chops.

Another safety net was provided by Garth and Gina Vincent, one of my favorite couples from my old Mormon congregation in Palisades. They let me stay at their house while I figured out my next move. I started taking classes at Santa Monica College. It was never my intention to give up on school. Since my dad never ended up getting his bachelor's degree, I felt compelled to finish to complete his legacy.

My plan was to stay with the Vincents for a couple of months, which turned into almost a year. Failure often brings hidden blessings. I bonded with the Vincents as if they were my own family, and they proved to be a conduit for a new opportunity. Gina told me about a nearby performing arts school and suggested I introduce myself to the principal and ask for a job. So I did just that.

I walked into the Adderley School for the Performing Arts and told the principal that I would love her to hire me. Janet Adderley is a magnetic, over-the-top, boisterous woman, and we bonded immediately. She hired me on the spot. I would work with big groups of kids after school, preparing them for their end-of-semester shows, which were children's versions of big

Broadway musicals. The skills I'd acquired before dropping out of the MDT program came in handy, and I loved my work.

It was at the Adderley School that I met one of the most important people in my life. Simone. A New York City soul living in LA. My second divine-feminine guide.

Elegant and surprisingly powerful, she taught ballet at the school. In the future, she would literally write the book on female empowerment and seducing men (it's called *Smitten*[12]; check it out).

She became my dearest friend and soul mate, my confidante. I knew I could trust her with anything, and one day at lunch I whispered, "I think I'm gay." I had said this aloud maybe twice before.

She handled it perfectly. "Oh yeah? Cool, great," she said. "Do you want some ranch with that? Are you eating your fries?"

Simone was the first to know who I am—a gay man—and love me exactly as I am. Over the years, Simone would show up for me in endless ways. She passed away a few years ago. Some wounds, some heartaches, you never get over. She always said I should write a book. I've dedicated this one to her.

During this time, I had some tentative experiences with dating boys and not-really-dating boys—kissing them, crying about it. One of these boys offered me my first drink of alcohol, taking me one more step away from my upbringing. This slow coming-out process felt like how it felt to be Mormon: I was sure I was doing it all wrong.

---

12 Ariel Kiley and Simone Kornfield, *Smitten: The Way of the Brilliant Flirt* (San Francisco: Chronicle Books, 2013).

20

BRAD

The Value of Failure

A master therapist once explained that if you want someone to grow, give them a task where they will fail. Failure, and other detours on the road, ask us to give up our old ideas. Joseph Campbell taught that "We must be willing to get rid of the life we have planned so as to have the life that is waiting for us." Failure seems to be a universal impetus for change, for asking new questions, and for accepting new answers.

Jeff's departure from BYU was followed by what felt like failure after failure. But the unintended path led him to new friends like Simone, who gave him space to begin expressing himself authentically, almost for the first time.

Question for Brad

I felt pressure, like Jeff, to finish school because my parent never had. How do you keep from taking on this pressure (or giving your own kids pressure to fulfill your dreams)?

The unlived life of a parent can settle as a burden on the shoulders of their children. Not only did Jeff feel like he had failed, but he was also crumbling under the weight of his father's life. If we want to support our children to get where they need to go, we must accept that we do not know their path. We do not know their truth.

One of my favorite stories in this vein is about Bob Dylan. A reporter asked him, "Your son Jakob and his band have a number-one album. How do you feel about his success?"

As I remember it, Dylan simply responded with, "It's irrelevant." At the time, I just chalked it up to Dylan being Dylan. He could be a little cantankerous and objectionable with the media. But as the years have worn on and I reflect back on that story, I understand it in a much different way. Our children's success is not our success. If we are going to support them, we must aspire to not knowing what they *should* do. I believe in my heart that Jakob Dylan knows that his father loves him. I believe he knows this feeling is independent of any of his successes or failures. I don't have any confirmation from Bob Dylan on this, but I've come to feel this way about my own children.

Reflection Questions

1. Consider your personal "failures." Can you see how they made way for the life that was waiting for you? If you are just starting out in life, ask a parent or other trusted elder about their own supposed failures.
2. Did you feel pressure from your parents to live their lives for them? If you're a parent, are you currently passing along this pressure to your children?

21

Jeff

After I'd been living with the Vincents for nearly a year, architect Bruce Bolander, a good family friend, was just about to finish building a home on his property in Malibu. Mom and Dad missed living in Malibu and didn't want to live with my grandparents in Heber anymore. They decided to rent Bruce's house once it was completed. Dad loved the idea of Scott and me helping him produce all of his works, and both of us were living in California then. The Malibu move was perfect for the family business my dad had always dreamed of.

Dad was also planning his Broadway debut. Dad's musical, *The Ark,* was going to be produced off-Broadway with the hopes of eventually moving to the Great White Way. I had been part of the original workshop cast when I was sixteen and seventeen. We'd traveled multiple times to New York City to learn from and collaborate with the illustrious Stephen Schwartz—writer and composer of *Godspell* and *Wicked.* All of that work was on the cusp of paying off, and we McLeans were abustle over it.

I left the Vincents in the Palisades and moved into the newly finished house in Malibu—a tiny, modern house with an expansive view of the Santa Monica Mountains. It was breathtaking. We felt so lucky to be there. This would be McLean home base for the next several years.

Scott and I were working on an album at the time. We hired a hot producer in Vegas, but we broke a cardinal rule: never let anyone convince you that they know more than you do about what you want creatively. I thought I'd learned this lesson when I cut Seth out of my life, but so often these tough lessons take a while to sink in. I decided this big shot knew better than Scott and I did. Our vision was to populate our album with duets we'd written ourselves. Mr. Fancy Producer's vision was for us to not sing together at all and for someone else to write the songs. It was a disaster.

In the wake of the album debacle, I decided to change careers. I was demoralized, and taking a different path seemed a wise choice for another major reason: my existing fanbase was largely Mormon. I was on the verge of coming all the way out and would no longer be viable in that market. So I chose to do what many other gay men had done before me: I would go into musical theater! Of course, this was hardly out of the blue. I had been involved in my father's forays into musical theater for years and had a growing understanding of the business—as well as a lengthening list of contacts.

To be taken seriously, I knew I would need an Equity card (basically the actors' union's stamp of approval, earned by doing shows at theaters that follow Equity rules—paying fairly and not working actors to death). Every musical on Broadway has to have an Equity chorus call every six months. I decided these

Equity-only auditions would be my best shot for success in my new career. The hunt for my card began.

I went to all the auditions I could find in LA, and I met and fell in love with a casting director. He was fond of taking me to plays about coming out. The Unlovable Monster did not like this cozy situation, and it started to convince me that I was too fat for auditioning. This was not the first time I'd been dissatisfied with my body. Far from it. I had grown up in what can only be called a fatphobic household. My dad, like his mother before him, was obsessed with body weight—his own and others'. I'd been given a gym membership at the age of ten, and I was lectured as early as twelve about the importance of performers staying skinny. I had once been threatened with exclusion from *The Forgotten Carols* if I didn't get some weight off.

So there in LA, I decided that cutting open my skin and liquifying and removing my fat—a.k.a. undergoing liposuction—was going to save me. God forbid I implement healthy eating and exercise habits. I had always gone to extremes as far as my body was concerned: It was total neglect or borderline violence. Middle-way consistency was not my thing. When I'd lost weight for *The Forgotten Carols*, for example, I'd essentially starved myself. Getting lipo was simply a natural next step.

Emerging from the procedure with a newly svelte abdomen, I learned that Tuacahn, an Equity theater in Southern Utah, was doing a production of *Joseph and the Amazing Technicolor Dreamcoat*. My first chance for Equity points! Off I went to audition, but I didn't get cast. So much for lipo. A few weeks later, though, the producer called and asked if I could replace their Joseph for the last two months of the run. The pay wasn't going to make me rich, but I negotiated for a valuable perk: I would take the job if they would give me my Equity card. They agreed.

Nestled in red-rock country near Zion National Park, St. George, Utah, is a geological masterpiece. It's a spiritual place. My grandparents had a vacation condo there that they weren't using, and I moved in. I started the summer semester at Utah Tech, where I would finish my associate's degree and do the show later in the fall.

Being alone in St. George was wonderful and traumatic all at the same time. I was able to sit with myself and ponder the important questions that had been simmering just under the surface. What does it mean that I'm gay? What is my path forward? At that time, church leaders were still advising men who "struggled" with homosexuality to marry women. God would take care of the rest. I knew in my core that this approach was wrong—disastrous, really. It was not the answer for me.

I was still attending a Mormon congregation for singles from time to time, but I knew that my time in the church was coming to an end. With each guy I dated, my feelings grew stronger. Early on, I'd experience the same uncontrollable shaking I'd had with Clay. Over time, though, along with the guilt and shame that had emerged when I'd been with Clay, my eruptions of attraction unsurfaced anger—rage, really. Rage that I'd had to stifle my orientation so I could feel accepted and loved in my family and culture.

Eventually, the shaking began to subside. As the panic receded, in its place was a steady and unquestionable attraction to men. I felt myself slowly opening up to the possibilities. But I couldn't quite give up on how I'd been raised. I knew I could not be attracted to women, but could I find a middle way?

One day, I called my dad and told him I was never going to be happy because I couldn't marry a woman. I also couldn't live a gay life because I didn't know what that would even look like. I told him that I was weighing my options but that I was in no place to make a decision.

Dad listened to me and cried with me. He was exactly who I needed him to be. I have given him a lot of crap about not showing up, but the truth is that he's showed up for me many times throughout my life.

I hung up with Dad, still depressed and despondent despite his support. I decided that I needed to pray and ask God what to do. Some part of me had been holding back from directly addressing the Father of the Universe when it came to these questions. But I had come to a point of crisis, and I couldn't avoid God any longer.

One of the bedrooms in the condo had this weird offshoot that was like a long closet, big enough to fit a twin bed. I went into that strange closet and got to my knees. With all my heart, I poured out my predicament to the heavens. And I had what I like to call my Joseph Smith experience.

The story goes that when Joseph Smith was fourteen years old, he went to the forest to ask God which church to join. God and Christ appeared to him and told him to join no church but rather to restore Christ's true church.

So I followed Joseph's pattern. On my knees in the closet, I began, "Heavenly Father, I'm never going to be happy." Then I asked God the most purely authentic questions I'd ever asked: "What am I supposed to do? What's the point of living?" I didn't feel suicidal—I just had no idea how to exist outside of the world I'd been raised in.

As I knelt there with my eyes closed, I became aware of two presences in the closet with me. I knew them. I'd known them my whole life. Something told me not to open my eyes, but I knew that these two beings were God and Jesus. God said, "The Mormon Church is not true on this, Jeff. They are wrong, and they don't know."

I was stunned. All of those crazy things I'd heard for nearly three decades were wrong. And the most important message came resounding into my heart: God said—crystal clear—"I am bigger than gay. I am the creator of all, and I DON'T MAKE MISTAKES."

I knelt there as it sank in. "I'm not a mistake?"

"No, Jeff, you are not a mistake," was His reply.

22
BRAD

Limitless God

Jeff's prayer experience was a breakthrough. He began to have a relationship not with his projections of God but with God Himself. Some people may think Jeff's experience is illegitimate because it is not in line with their view of God. But it is illogical to teach people to seek answers from God—the Mormon Church emphasizes personal revelation—and then tell them which of the messages are from God and which are not. Jeff learned about prayer in his upbringing, and that foundational practice helped him to reach God despite what he had been told about Him and His supposed limitations.

Religionists spend so much time debating whether a camel can pass through a needle's eye or which denomination has the most truth. What we truly need from religion is support as we walk through the most difficult times in our lives. We need a God, a religion, or a higher power that helps us to know we are not alone. We need a place where it's safe to come and talk about our horrible, rotten selves. We need a hospital for the soul.

Questions for Brad

I've come to a place where I struggle with the idea of God. How else can I find solace through difficult times?

Begin the gentle work of finding and knowing yourself, and you will find a deeper connection with something larger than yourself. Don't rush it. The poet Rumi wrote, "I searched for God and found only myself. I searched for myself and found only God." When people lose connection to a higher power, it is often an indication that they have lost connection to themselves. You must disentangle yourself from the programming of your childhood so that you can connect to God without the filter of your wounds.

The biblical book of Genesis states that humanity was created in God's image. In psychology, we also see that the reverse is true. The characteristics of our fathers, mothers, and other caretakers shape our ideas about God. How could it be any other way? These are the first authority figures we know. If our caretakers are fearful, controlling, and desperate to prevent bad things, we come to believe that God is also fearful, controlling, and desperate. If this was your experience, it is small wonder you struggle with God.

One beneficial concept I like to borrow from the Twelve-Step world is that God doesn't have to be the kind of God we were raised with. I've heard people in Alcoholics Anonymous (AA) refer to God as "good orderly direction" or even "group of drunks." In short, we don't necessarily need to throw the baby out with the bathwater. You can still find solace in God—a reimagined God.

Therapy can also be a place to have our spiritual needs fulfilled. It can help us to hear the voice of God or our inner child, separating these divine voices from the voices of our parents and the other authority figures who raised us.

Jeff says that Michael listened to him and cried with him. I am impressed that he didn't try to talk him out of his feelings.

Michael was not always the perfect father for a gay son coming out in a Mormon context, but he sometimes shows remarkable instincts. In this conversation, he didn't try to shield Jeff from pain. Although often well-intentioned, trying to prevent pain is harmful. The only way through pain is to feel it all. As parents, it's important to allow children to learn how to confront and experience so-called negative emotions. Walking through grief, disappointment, and anguish is the work of becoming who you are. It is the work of finding God.

Reflection Questions

1. Has someone shared a spiritual experience with you that you felt dubious about? How did you react then? Would you react differently now?
2. If you have gone through a faith crisis, have you found God on the other side? What did that look like for you?

23

MICHAEL

God Is Bigger Than Gay

When Lynne and I were raising our kids, most of our family's gospel study sessions centered on Jesus and how he took upon himself the sins and agonies of all people. But when Jeff was struggling with coming out, he said that if Jesus *did* give His life and die on the cross to pay for our sins, it applied to everyone but him. "The Atonement doesn't work for me," was his refrain.

Hearing him say that broke my heart and drove me to my knees on his behalf. I prayed that God would intervene somehow to show my son love, forgiveness, and hope. No matter how the church may have failed, shamed, or bullied him, I begged God to speak to my Jeff in a language he would understand. That prayer was answered, but not in a way I expected.

I went to see Jeff in a show, and afterward we spent time catching up. Jeff told me he'd had a revelation. He had felt an answer to his prayers about how to move forward as a gay man and about whether or not God could ever love him. The heavenly message had taken him completely by surprise:

Jeff, you've been dealt a tough hand, and whatever choice you make, it's going to be difficult. If you marry a man, you'll have challenges. Being a celibate single man in the church comes at a price. But whatever YOU choose, it must be your choice. It can't be the choice your musical theater friends would make, or the choice your family or the church has pressured you to make. No matter your choice, I want you to know that I'm your Father in Heaven, I love you, and I want to help you learn to be happy.

With tears in his eyes, my son said, "God's bigger than gay. He loves me and wants me to be happy."

Maybe that's what I needed to learn about my role as Jeff's earthly father. Maybe I needed to honor his choices and find ways to help him to be happy and successful in his journey.

24

BRAD

Rebirth

Michael's comments on Jeff's transformation and rebirth suggest that Michael is also undergoing a rebirth. He has new eyes and ears to see and hear things that he couldn't before. He was blinded by dogma, by the traditions of his parents and his community. But as his former understanding and skills fall away and a new sensibility emerges in him, he can see what is important: Jeff. Jeff is important.

Michael's connection to the heaven right in front of him reminds me of something Alan Watts observed: "The meaning of life is just to be alive. It is so plain and so obvious and so simple. And yet, everybody rushes around in a great panic as if it were necessary to achieve something beyond themselves."

It's important to note here that Michael's journey is just as important as Jeff's. In fact, his transformation supported Jeff's and still does to this day.

Reflection Questions

1. Consider the tandem transformation that Jeff and Michael experienced. Have you experienced something similar as a child or parent?
2. Do you think it is possible for your own parents to transform?

25

JEFF

I Picked Gay

I had God's acceptance, so I thought I was done and good. But as the stories show us time and again, the most difficult challenges come after prophets receive their visions. My journey had just begun, and the Unlovable Monster was yet to have its heyday.

I finished my summer semester and took over the role of Joseph. The fall semester began, and I was doing shows at night and school during the day. I was two months away from graduation when a fantastic opportunity presented itself.

One day, I was perusing the various notices and announcements on the backstage bulletin board, and something caught my eye: a world cruise line was looking for singers. They'd held auditions in LA, New York, and a few big cities in Europe. Now they were in St. George, of all places; the director and producer had ties to the area. I decided I could use all the audition practice I could get, so I went. I was expecting to see a large group of auditionees, but it was a ghost town. I was the only singer who showed up. My audition lasted an hour; I sang all the songs they threw at me, and the director and I had a great conversation. I got the job. Rehearsals started in three weeks—in Italy. I decided to drop out of school and go on an adventure.

Over the course of six weeks, I learned six different hour-long shows. Many of the songs were in different languages. When rehearsals ended, my castmates and I all took a train from Italy to Marseille, France, where we got on our ship, a seven-hundred-passenger luxury liner. I had my own tiny room—with a porthole! We set sail for Spain, stopping in Portugal before crossing the Atlantic to the Caribbean. We tooled around Mexico and Central America and sailed through the Panama Canal. We crossed the Pacific to Japan, China, Thailand, and Malaysia, then looped around to Singapore, Sri Lanka, and India. From India, we went to Dubai and other ports on the Arabian Peninsula. Then it was up through the Red Sea to Egypt and Jordan and through the Suez Canal to the Mediterranean. We crossed the Mediterranean, sailed around to the North Sea, and ended up in Hamburg. We'd hit more than fifty countries in seven months.

During this time, I learned that I was one little person participating in the magical, astonishing world. I drank sangria in Spain. Scuba dived in caves near Guam and in the Red Sea. Skydived in Hawaii. Swam with dolphins in the Philippines. Danced on the Great Wall. Rode elephants in Phuket and camels in Cairo. Shopped at the markets in Shanghai and Mumbai and Dubai. I ate all of the food in all of the places—and still managed to look super hot in my mermaid-scaled spandex leggings and plunging sequined sports coats. (Our costumes were gloriously outlandish.)

In my experience, everybody who works on a cruise ship seems to be running away from something. Nobody is grounded. Everything is free and open. I met some remarkable, beautiful people. I made out with a guy or two. I was also open to making out with girls if I wanted. I fell in love with a photographer. I lived seven full months of being undefined. I didn't want to say I was gay or straight or Mormon or non-Mormon. I just wanted to be Jeff without labels. I wanted to find out for myself what I wanted and who I was. I wasn't Michael McLean's son. I was just a guy nobody knew, figuring things out while singing in the middle of the ocean.

While being exposed to this beautiful, broken, unimaginably varied world, a new anger started stirring within me. The myopic culture I came from—less than 0.002 percent of the world population, by the way—was trying to put chicken wire around a God of infinite magnitude. It was laughable. Of course God could handle gay—and anything else, for that matter—and I was livid that I'd ever been taught otherwise. My experiences kept confirming what I'd learned in my Joseph Smith prayer.

I knew I had to come out. But I knew it had to be a beautiful, honest choice. So I had to deal with my rage first.

When I was back in the States, I chose to enlist the help of our family therapist, Ken Rodgers. During my first session with Ken, I talked about my anger, mostly toward my dad. Ken asked me why I was so mad at my dad. I could barely say it out loud, but I began to whisper about tingle fingers, about how I'd wondered if it was molestation, about how I wondered if I'd interpreted it as molestation to explain why I was gay. I waited for Ken to tell me I was insane and to tell me that my dad could never molest anyone. Instead, he simply said, "Okay, let's talk about it." All I could do was curl up in the fetal position and cry.

In our next session, Ken explained the importance of intention versus message received. Our psyches react to the messages we receive, not to the intentions behind those messages. We are not always privy to those intentions, and we certainly are not responsible for them. This was a life-changing concept for me. My job was to process only my lived experiences, but I hadn't been doing my job. I'd been internally defending my dad's intentions for years and belittling myself for the messages I had received. This is a form of self-abandonment. With Ken's help, I finally gave thirteen-year-old Jeff the understanding he had always needed and wanted. I learned to honor myself rather than defending my dad or anyone else who had wounded me. And, counterintuitively, my anger began to dissipate.

Ken started me on the road to forgiveness, love, and grace. The road was not short (a blowup or two is yet to come), but as I write this years later, I can tell you that the rift with my dad has been healed.

As we continued meeting, Ken also provided a shame-free space for me to deconstruct my false gay origin story so I could embrace what I already knew: I was born gay.

One day I said to Ken, "So, we know I'm gay. What should I do about it?"

He gave me three options. He said I could become asexual. Or we could manipulate my soul to figure out how to not be myself. Or I could be gay.

I picked gay.

I know many people struggle with telling their parents. I was not one of those people. The very next day after my breakthrough with Ken, I drove straight to my sister's house, where my parents were visiting. I came through the door and into the living room. I didn't even say hello. "Everyone," I said, "be prepared for me to bring a man home for Christmas someday." And I walked out, closed the door, and left.

26

BRAD

Self-Discovery and Impact vs Intent

When we venture into the forest (the road to self-discovery), we often feel both liberated and terrified. The fear comes because we have left the known. We also leave behind the shackles of *should* and *should not*. We get lost. We make some wrong turns, make some *bad* decisions, but all the while discovering who we are outside of a context that told us who we *should* be.

Questions for Brad

Seeing my child go off into the world and make terrible mistakes is the most harrowing experience of my life. How can I come to peace with this?

You are not alone. Parents often find this part of a child's journey frightening. They may cite the child's mistakes as evidence that the known path is the more virtuous. But the story of Moses in Abrahamic traditions recounts the value of stepping into the unknown—as well as the fear that accompanies this choice.

Moses leads the formerly enslaved Israelites through the desert for forty years, braving detours and questioning, but their lengthy wandering is not in vain. It prepares them for the gift that lies ahead: a new homeland. Your child is journeying toward their own Promised Land. And so are you. This difficult experience is part of your own enlightenment, which is ultimately about undefining and unlearning.

Spiritual teacher Adyashanti puts it brilliantly: "Enlightenment is a destructive process. It has nothing to do with becoming better or being more or less happy. Enlightenment is the crumbling away of untruth. It's seeing through the façade of pretense. It's the complete eradication of everything we imagined to be true."[13] And in her now-famous talk on shame and vulnerability, Brené Brown describes her own forty years in the desert: "I call it a breakdown. My therapist calls it a spiritual awakening. A spiritual awakening sounds better than breakdown, but I assure you it was a breakdown."[14]

Ken tells Jeff that Michael's intentions regarding tingle fingers don't matter. I don't understand why my good intentions as a parent are worthless if my child considers my actions harmful. Can you explain this a little more?

The simplest analogy I can offer is this: If someone drops a hammer on your bare toe, you will probably cry out, feel intense pain, and develop bruises on your skin. You will likely feel anger or

---

13 Adyashanti, *The End of Your World: Uncensored Straight Talk on the Nature of Enlightenment* (Boulder, CO: Sounds True, 2010).

14 Brené Brown, "The Power of Vulnerability," June 1, 2010, TEDxHouston, video, 20:03, https://www.ted.com/talks/brene_brown_the_power_of_vulnerability.

annoyance toward the person who dropped the hammer. You and your body will have these reactions whether the person dropped the hammer on purpose or by accident. If it was an accident and the hammer dropper apologizes, that is certainly better than if they ignored your pain or laughed at you. They at least didn't add insult to injury. However, you will continue to feel pain, you will persist in wishing Mr./Ms./Mx. Butterfingers had paid better attention to your foot's whereabouts, and your toe will still be purple tomorrow.

The truth is that one of the most common ways to invalidate somebody else's experiences is to focus on the intentions of those who hurt that person. When a person who wounded another centers the conversation on their own intentions, they are protecting their fragile ego. The intentions beneath behavior are often in service of protecting our feelings, anxiety, ego, or some other uncomfortable experience. These motivations are not good or bad. Our intentions just *are*. We protect others so that we can protect ourselves against what I call our empathic pain: It hurts me to watch my child hurt, and I definitely don't want to be the cause of such suffering. So I try to prevent their pain and, subsequently, my feelings too.

A mature adult acknowledges the impact of their behaviors without needing to shelter their ego. It is wholly appropriate for a child to realize, as Jeff did, that he was defending his father at the expense of his own healing. Children often carry their parents' wounds when they sense their parents can't handle it.

Like Ken, who listened to Jeff without correction or judgment, therapists are ideally positioned to listen to how we feel wronged, abused, and dismissed. With a safe place to talk and feel, we can move through our feelings rather than living in them forever. This process can help prevent children and parents from cutting each other out of their lives.

Reflection Questions

1. How many spiritual awakenings/breakdowns have you experienced? Consider the value that each one brought.
2. How have people with good intentions impacted you in harmful ways? How have you protected your own good intentions over another person's pain?

27

MICHAEL

Relationships Trump Rules

Of all the prayers I'd offered in my life up to that point, none were as urgent as my prayers for Jeff after he came out. If ever a father needed help from heaven to reach his son and to heal a broken heart, I did. And what I got was nothing.

Silence. Emptiness.

No comfort from the God who had blessed me with a sacred mission that I'd fulfilled. Nothing from the God I'd trusted.

At first, I thought I couldn't get answers to my prayers because I was in shock or denial over Jeff's revelation. Surely everything would make sense in a few months.

But two years of heavenly silence passed. I found out during this time that Mother Teresa had experienced a spiritual drought for forty-nine years. Only her inner circle knew about it. I understood why she'd kept her crisis quiet. I had the same inclination. Who could I tell? What could I do? Put out an apology album and call it *Just Kidding, You Are Alone*?

With Mother Teresa on the brain, I had a dream about her. We were on a stage together. She sang the story of her life while I played the piano. I remember only one number, "Keeping Promises":

I choose to pray to One who doesn't hear me
I choose to wait for love that He conceals
And though God's chosen now not to be near me
I'm keeping promises my heart no longer feels

At the end of the song, I woke up in tears. I quickly wrote down the lyrics in the early, still-dark morning. I felt an urgency to decide whether to trust in God or to give up. I decided to follow Mother Teresa's example and keep the promises my heart hadn't felt for two years.

I promised God that I'd trust Him to tell me why He hadn't been speaking to me. Was I unworthy? Was I a disappointment? Did He love me? Had I gotten everything wrong?

Now for an embarrassing confession: as I made this promise, the theatrical part of me thought, *This is a really, really great prayer. I've made a grand gesture, and the answer's gotta be coming in seven weeks—tops.*

It would be seven more years.

Things got worse in the meantime. The silence from heaven continued. And people started to criticize me—people I had thought would lift me up.

One gloomy day, I sat brooding over the frayed ends of my faith.

In all the movies I've ever seen about heavenly experiences—from *Heaven Can Wait*, to *Always*, to my favorite, *It's a Wonderful Life*—a messenger from the other side breaks through from the spiritual realm just when the main character reaches a crisis. Sitting alone seven years after my unanswered grand-gesture prayer, I was surely in crisis.

And in that moment, my messenger arrived. He was John the Baptist, I swear. Only in jeans.

John the Baptist. I know how you're feeling. I had a pretty severe crisis of faith myself.

Me. No, you didn't.

John the Baptist. I did.

Me. How could the man who baptized Jesus ever wonder if he'd gotten it all wrong?

John the Baptist. Exactly. I was in prison waiting to be killed, and Jesus didn't rescue me. I asked my friends to find him and ask if he was really the Messiah. Had I wasted my entire life preparing the way for the wrong person?

Me. And then what?

John the Baptist. My friends returned, and they told me they'd found Jesus and asked him my question. He invited them to stay a while. He performed miracle after miracle and told my friends to tell me everything they'd witnessed. I realized that the Lord had sent me a perfect and personal message. The miracles Jesus had done in view of my friends were the same miracles that the prophet Isaiah had said the true Messiah would perform. He communicated to me, a prophet, by fulfilling prophesies. Do you get it?

Me. Get what?

John the Baptist. If the Lord sends prophesies to prophets, he sends songs to songwriters. You've been writing songs all through your crisis, haven't you? Well, those songs contain the answers your heart most deeply needs. The ones you didn't even know you were looking for.

This insight left me speechless. I looked at all I had created during my crisis, and just like John the Baptist in jeans had promised, I did find the answers I needed to help me build a new kind of faith.

Other answers came through more traditional means. Lynne has always taken strength from going to the temple, which is a place where Mormons perform our most sacred ordinances and where we express our highest form of worship. While we were living in California, we would have what Lynne called Temple Tuesdays. We'd gather all of the widows in the congregation together, and I would drive us all to the Los Angeles Temple. Lynne went because it gave her peace. I did not have the same experience. The whole thing was torture for me, especially during those dark, silent years. The church's idea that worthy family members can be together in the afterlife was painful. Being in the temple was a reminder that this didn't seem to be happening for our family. All of our children had been through the temple and had served full-time missions for the church, but now Jeff and Scott were both out of the fold.

One Tuesday, as we sat in the temple, Lynne said, "We think our children are supposed to learn from our experiences, but they can't. Our experiences can only help them to know who we are. But they must live their own lives. Jeff is having an experience that is unique to him. It's a gift from God—not a punishment or a test." This was an insight I could understand.

I started asking God to let me in on some of these aha moments that Lynne had so frequently. I admit I was still a little tentative because the nine-year silent treatment was fresh in my memory. But one Temple Tuesday, I had a breakthrough.

I was thinking about the Garden of Eden and what I could learn from Adam and Eve's experience with the forbidden fruit. I'd been troubled by the idea that God would give Adam and Eve conflicting directions: Don't partake of the fruit from the tree of knowledge of good and evil, but also multiply and replenish the earth. When Eve ate the fruit, she would have to leave Eden. Adam had to decide if he would eat the fruit along with Eve so they could stay together and start multiplying and replenishing. Adam chose Eve. Sitting in the temple, I had a thought I'd never had before:

Could it be that relationships trump rules?

I felt like I was getting more of the direction from heaven that I had been craving. But could I accept the idea that the rules and commandments I'd tried to keep all of my life are trumped by relationships? I started to think that I had to accept it, though. It became clearer to me that my preoccupation with rules and commandments had distracted me from keeping another commandment of higher importance.

I needed to commit to my relationship with Jeff. There could be no more finger wagging about the rules he was breaking.

Since then, my spiritual life has continued to ebb and flow. But I keep going to the temple every week, not to show off my righteousness but to see if maybe, just maybe, I will hear more.

28

BRAD

Fighting Dragons

One day in church, I heard a father describe a dream he'd had about his son. His son was standing in the middle of polluted and treacherous water and began calling for help. The father felt helpless because he could not immerse himself in the toxic water.

In real life, this father's son had fallen into drugs, which led him to homelessness and near death. The father considered the filthy water to be a symbol of the profane world, and his son's immersion in that world made it impossible for the father to both save his son and remain pure. The only solution—which was no solution—was to go back in time and convince his son not to swim into the ways of the world to begin with.

My interpretation of the dream is different. In my version, the water symbolizes the father's own rejected unconscious, full of things that terrify him. To save his son, the father must be willing to get dirty—look into his own past, confront his dragons, and heal his wounds. Only then could he traverse the water to reach his son.

If you want to save your children, you'll have to step into your own poisoned pond. But you don't need to go it alone. Find a therapist or a support group or another parent who is already in the deep end. Reading Michael and Jeff's story is a good start. In the previous chapter, Michael shows how he started to confront his fears.

Questions for Brad

How exactly did Michael wade into this poisonous water, i.e., his unconscious fears?

Michael asked questions and had to learn to be honest with himself and to be honest with God. He had to confront difficult truths like how disconnected he felt from God for long periods of time. He accepted that he needed new skills, that it was HE who must change if he was going to be able to help his son and draw closer to him. Michael became willing to sacrifice something small—his idea of what life should look like—for something much more profound: a loving and connecting relationship with his son.

I love Michael's insight that relationships trump rules, but I think some people in my family might find it a little blasphemous. What is something I might say to support Michael's idea?

We can't always change people's minds, but you can point out that Michael's epiphany points to the true nature of religion: love. All the stories and metaphors and parables point to this one concept. Religion comes alive when it prioritizes love over dogma. Otherwise, the symbols and stories remain empty, vain worship. This is what we can understand as the sin of idolatry.

When I hear what a hard time Michael had with his son coming out, it makes me angry. Why does it have to be such a big deal?

Ideally, parents would not blink when finding out that a child's sexuality differs from what the parents consider the norm. The reality is that being gay was a taboo for a very long time and still holds that entrenched status for many. Sadly, I must admit that some parents have told me they would rather their children be dead than for them to identify as LGBTQ+. My license, my heart, my humanity, and my conscious tell me that this option is beyond unacceptable.

Even a slightly less hideous reaction does not work. Parents may tell their gay children something like, "I love and accept you despite your same-sex attraction. You just cannot act on it. And also, please don't talk about it around your younger siblings or cousins." These same parents often wonder why the child experiences this response as rejection.

In my therapy practice, a young adult woman who grew up Mormon reported to me such a response from her parents. She was admitted to my program for self-harm, depression, and suicidality. After I met with her and validated her experience, she wrote a letter to her parents: "I have met with Brad, and after sitting with what he said, I don't want to kill myself anymore. But if you are not able to see the harm you did, I will not have you in my life going forward." The parents were upset and confused and, on our next call, confronted me about their daughter's assertion.

"How dare you give her such ideas?!" they said.

I listened compassionately and then shared with them their daughter's version of her coming out. She'd heard that her parents loved her, but she also heard that she must not act on her feelings or share them with her younger siblings.

They struggled to see this response as unaccepting. I explained what I already mentioned earlier in the book: sexual orientations (and gender identities) run so close to our notions of who we are that the idea of *hating the sin and loving the sinner* doesn't quite work.

In the end, I offered the following explanation of what had happened in therapy: "You sent your daughter here because of self-harm and suicidality. According to her, those problems were fixed in a couple of sessions. She turned her anger from herself to you, and that will make all the difference in the world. As she sees it, either she or you must bear this pain. If you are not willing to stretch yourself and grow enough to hold her truth, she may have no choice but to let you go. And this letting go is how she will preserve her life."

Gratefully, these parents did their work and, over time, were able to shed ideas they had been taught about being gay. This gave way to a greater love than any of them had known.

Reflection Questions

1. Consider your own reaction to Lynne's words from the previous chapter: "We think our children are supposed to learn from our experiences, but they can't. Our experiences can only help them to know who we are. But they must live their own lives. Jeff is having an experience that is unique to him. It's a gift from God—not a punishment or a test."
2. If you are a religious person, how can you center love more than dogma as you practice your faith?

PART 3

Supergay

29

JEFF

Sin City

After I came out, I had a recurring daydream:

I'm deep in a crevasse. At the top of the hill to my right is Mormonville, full of beige houses like the Salt Lake suburbs. Up to the left is Gaytown, full of gorgeous naked men like West Hollywood. Mormonville can never be my home again, but I am not quite ready to take the train to Gaytown. So I remain in the crevasse, homeless and exposed. Nothing my parents taught me is relevant here. Unfamiliar tools are strewn about the ground, and I scavenge them to start building a home.

Here come Mom and Dad Mormon to visit my little shanty. "You know," they say, "there's plumbing where we live." I get wildly defensive. "You're the reason I'm living like this! You kicked me out, and none of the tools you gave me work here!"

As I moved out of limbo, this daydream faded, and I found I didn't have to choose between Beige Wonderland or Naked Hollywood. I could make my own path. And, as I have frequently experienced, I found some helpers on that path.

On the cruise, I had met a pair of German twins, Judith and Esther, who had been living in the States for a long time. They got on the ship in Singapore and stayed all the way to Dubai, which took about a month. We fell immediately in love and were inseparable. In contrast to our generally elderly clientele, Judith and Esther infused fun and joy into everything. Did Esther conduct a shipboard romance with one of the chefs? Indeed, she did. Were these women there for me in a totally profound way as I found myself on the high seas? You bet they were.

My final port on the cruise was Hamburg, where I met up with Judith. Esther happened to be hiking in the Grand Canyon, so Judith and I flew to the States together to meet up with her. We stayed at my grandparents' house in St. George and explored red-rock country together. I would be starting the summer term at Utah Tech right away to finish my associate's degree.

I decided I would audition for every show in Vegas, so I drove the ninety minutes to Vegas as often as possible, all the while taking math and studying voice. I got callbacks for two shows: *Spamalot* at the Wynn and *The Phantom of the Opera* at the Venetian. Of course, they were at the exact same time, so I had to make a choice. I thought *Spamalot* might be a little more fun. By the time I finished school, I still hadn't heard back yet, but I needed to keep progressing in my career.

Esther and Judith to the rescue! In addition to their horse farm in upstate New York, they had a flat in Manhattan, and they invited me to stay in it *for free* while I did some auditioning in the city. Sometimes I have a truly charmed life.

I auditioned for everything I could in New York. I was still learning the musical theater business, but I had my Equity card and excellent friends—including my dearest Simone, who was from New York and had an apartment there.

In early fall, I booked a small Gershwin revue that paid next to nothing. We performed in this tiny church auditorium, and I was one of the least experienced people in the ensemble. One day in the dressing room, about an hour before curtain, I received another one of those life-changing phone calls: I'd been cast in the original Las Vegas company of *Spamalot.* I was floored. So were my Gershwin castmates. They'd been around a lot longer than I had, and they couldn't quite believe I'd booked a show.

Rehearsals didn't start until January 2007, so I had a few more months of living—really living—in the city. I could breathe free there. I was going on dates and feeling embraced by my new community in a way I'd never experienced. Though, of course, I discovered that being out did not solve all of my problems. Being gay was not all there was to me, no matter how successfully I took on the persona of Jeff the Super Gay.

In November, I returned to my old world and did *The Forgotten Carols* tour with the family. Everything seemed amiable enough on the surface, but it was weird. When I'd come out earlier that year, Scott had been the most supportive, giving me a simple, "Great, I love you. You're the best." I'd expected Meggan to be cool too. But she was wildly weird in a way I never would have guessed. She said she had to mourn the loss of her brother ("Um, I'm still right here," I might have said if I'd thought she cared to listen). Luckily, she eventually came around, but it was hard for me to get over her response for a while.

Grandma McLean had taken my coming out in stride, but Grandpa McLean never acknowledged it. He'd taken in the information and apparently deemed it unworthy of his comment. Mom's response had been the most fearful. Almost the first thing she'd said to me after I came out was, "You can never tell my parents." She was convinced they would disown me in horror.

As the tour for *The Forgotten Carols* went on, Mom was always secretly crying, and dad completely ignored it when a guy I was dating brought flowers backstage after a performance. In this needlessly gloomy atmosphere, I sang my songs, did my thing, and let my family do theirs. It would be my last McLean tour for a long time. Weeks before it was over, I was already mentally in Las Vegas.

For me, Vegas had always been just a city to drive through on the way to California. Now it was going to be my home. In January, Scott and I drove down to the new furnished apartment that the company provided. I put Scott on an airplane back to California and kept the car—which gave me the distinction of being one of the few people in the *Spamalot* cast to have a car.

Rehearsals began, and I was in a heady new world. I'd always believed that if I didn't stay true to the gospel, nothing good could happen to me. But here I was, making more money than I ever had, sitting at the feet of masters—Monty Python cofounder Eric Idle, legendary director Mike Nichols, and superstar choreographer Casey Nicholaw. And no one cared that I was gay! In fact, a huge number of the delightful ensemble and cast were gay too.

I felt at home with these luminaries because being around famous and important people was not new to me. I'd met a lot of legends through my dad, and my brother dated Ryan Gosling's sister, Mandi, for a long time. When I was in New York, I spent a lot of time hanging out with Ryan and Mandi. One crazy night, I ended up singing "My Way" at a karaoke bar with Ryan and none other than Dave Matthews. So when I got to know Mike Nichols, I had no problem treating him as a peer, showing him pictures of my newborn nephew, Bucky. He was so gracious, and throughout our time together, he always asked for updates. This level of comfort was great, but it had its downsides too. For one,

I was oblivious to the fact that I was actually in a pretty hierarchical environment. As a member of the ensemble, I was not Mike Nichols's peer. I wasn't Eric Idle's peer. And I was not Casey Nicholaw's peer.

I had never been in a full eight-shows-a-week production before. I had a lot to learn, and I wish I could say I was receptive. But I was a headstrong, cavalier, entitled boy. If someone called me out, my go-to response was some variation of "Don't you know who I am (i.e., Michael McLean's son or Seth Riggs's student)?" or, worse, "Who are YOU?" Let's just say this attitude was not an asset, especially when combined with a strange piece of misinformation I got from a powerful source: Peter Lawrence, our associate director and a major player who had worked on huge shows in New York like *Miss Saigon* and *Les Misérables*.

Our rehearsal space was in an industrial part of Vegas. Despite the usual lack of life you see among the warehouse sector in any town, there was a bar next door (in Vegas, there's always a bar next door). We'd go into this dive bar after almost every rehearsal, and one day we had a cast meeting there with Peter. After the more formal discussion, people started to head home, but three or four of us stuck around and got some face time with Peter. I took something he said as gospel truth: "You know, this is just Vegas. You should be able to call out of the show whenever you want." Given my inexperience, I had no reason to doubt Peter. I started calling out whenever I wanted, leaving the swings (understudies who cover the ensemble) to do my work. If a friend back home was throwing a big birthday bash, I'd call out and fly to Utah. If I had a vague tickle in my throat, I'd call out sick. Why not? Peter Lawrence himself had basically given me permission. It took me a much longer time than it should have to realize I was the only person calling out regularly. I was totally oblivious. I'm still unsure of why Peter gave this advice, because it completely contradicts everything I've ever heard since, which is basically that you don't call out of a show unless you are literally dying.

Casey Nicholaw choreographed the project. He's truly masterful—the epitome of old-school musical theater. A beautiful example of someone who has dedicated his life to his craft, he'd worked his ass off to get to where he was. I was petrified of screwing up in front of him. Of course, while we were learning our first dance number, I was placed in the front row next to Julie, a.k.a. the Legs of Vegas. Why couldn't I be in the back next to someone who was a little less excellent at every dance she ever tried? My mind began to race.

Donotfuckthisupdonotfuckthisupdonotfuckthisup.

After a few minutes, Casey called me out from the front of the rehearsal hall: "Jeff, find your purpose in this number. You're standing out." Now, if there was ever a time to shut the fuck up and say *yes, sir*, this was that time. But no. I panicked. All of my lessons in respect and etiquette flew out the window. I adopted a snarky, juvenile voice and said—to one of the most successful musical theater choreographers of our time—"We're hitting each other with fish. How deep would you like me to go with that?" Yikes. This gaffe would come back to haunt me years later.

So I'd gotten off to a rocky start. But then *she* walked into my life. Divine-feminine guide number three: Semhar.

I saw her for the first time in the hall as we waited for a meeting to start. She wore massive sunglasses, held a latte in one perfectly manicured hand, and cradled on her hip a purse from some big-deal boutique. She was, and is to this day, the most beautiful woman I had ever seen. And unlike this virgin, she knew exactly how her body spoke and why. I looked at her and thought, *She will be mine.*

I approached and said, "I'm Jeff. We are gonna be best friends." She smirked and, like in the movies, pulled her sunglasses down just enough to peer over the top and look me up and down. She put her sunglasses back in place and turned her head slowly to look out the window. She inhaled slowly.

As she exhaled, she uttered, "Okay."

And just like that, I had the most thrilling, ride-till-we-die friend anyone could hope for. An inseparable pair, we would drive to work together, blaring Danity Kane and *Dreamgirls* and singing along at the top of our lungs. We tried our luck at slot machines between shows and after every pull of the lever, we would sing full voice, "Big money, no Whammies!" She won a thousand dollars once, which I remind her of at the close of every phone call to this day: "I only love you for your thousand." She laughs and replies, "Don't they all." My heart fills with unconditional love when I think of her or get to be around her.

A sweet interlude came when my aunt Tracy and my cousins Kari, Jane, and Maren drove hundreds of miles to see me in *Spamalot*. Though my mother was still carefully shielding her parents from the news of my gayness, these extended family members had learned the truth. One evening, we strolled around the Wynn and sat down by a fountain. Every single one of them hugged me and said in one way or another, "We love you so much, we support you, and we're proud of you for coming out." Unbelievable. I wished my younger self could have known that people I knew and loved would still love me even after my "terrible secret" was out.

As a Mormon, I'd been part of a tribe with very specific norms and mores. When I joined a new tribe, I looked to adopt new behaviors that would help me fit in right away. If the thing to do in Mormonism was to engage in quiet reflection and maintain strict celibacy, in the gay tribe, the thing was to drink heavily, do recreational drugs, and have lots of sex. The great thing is that both the Mormon rules and the gay rules brilliantly suppressed the Unlovable Monster.

Oh, but I did have fun. Herself a gay man in female form, Semhar became my guru and gave this newly out gay the knowledge I needed most: I am beautiful, and life is meant to be fun. With Sin City as our backdrop, Semhar showed me that the no-nos of my earlier life—no sex, no drinking, no swearing, no you-name-it—didn't have to define me anymore. I learned how to treat a bouncer, how to skip a line, how to really flirt, how to move on a dance floor without spilling my drink. My teacher was Semhar, and my classrooms were dives like Krave and the Piranha. To this day, I will take a seedy bar that smells of cigarettes and latex over some pristine and chichi cocktail lounge.

I also found ready teachers in other *Spamalot* castmates. One number featured an all-male ensemble dressed as Orthodox Jews. (This may seem peculiar if you haven't seen the show. A showstopper called "You Won't Succeed on Broadway" follows up the title with the line "if you don't have any Jews.") After we changed into our massive hoiche hats and blue-and-white tabards, we had a rare opportunity in a very busy show: a minute to sit and talk. During these chats, the older and wiser gays would tell me everything I needed to know about sex. Any question was allowed. We covered everything from anal bleaching to waterworks, often ending up in uncontrollable laughter and creating inside jokes that we'd quip at each other for weeks. Those racy conversations among ersatz Hasidim are some of my fondest memories. These were my people.

With its constant flow of visitors, Vegas is the perfect incubator for a newly out and proud gay guy. I tried to date a few locals, but they always ended up saying the same thing: "You just came out. Go play the field for a while." They were right, but I didn't understand quite yet. I merely felt rejected. I was still dating the way I'd been raised to date, the way I had dated Lisanne: with serious intent. I tried hard to convince guys to love me, and I'm a compelling salesman. I could fool anyone for about two weeks before my self-loathing became noticeable.

Eventually, I ran with my fellow gays' advice. Soon, I was playing the field to the point that I had to give each new love of my life a nickname instead of using his real name. (No, I won't share those nicknames. My mom is reading this!)

⁜

I instinctively knew Las Vegas would not be good for me in the long term. I could never live a balanced life there. And since *Spamalot's* run was limited to eighteen months, I was already plotting my move out of Sin City.

I got my next job partly because I was so willing to call out of *Spamalot* performances. I had to fly to New York five times for *Legally Blonde: The Musical* first national tour callbacks (brutal!). I met the show's director, Jerry Mitchell, during the audition process. Jerry, a brilliant artist who surrounds himself with other brilliant artists, has won a couple of Tonys for his choreography—no big deal. Eventually, I was cast as a lead: Warner, the ultra-handsome and condescending ex-boyfriend. It was unreal. Booking a lead is a heady kind of drug.

Another reason I got my next job is that I had started doing regular assistant work for the Tesley Office, the casting company my friend Rachel Hoffman, who had worked on *The Ark*, belongs to. They hold auditions in Vegas for upcoming Broadway and touring shows. (For reference, saying Rachel works with the

Tesley Office is like saying she works at the Mayo Clinic if she were a doctor or she dances at American Ballet Theatre if she were a dancer. They are the big time.)

I agreed to help with auditions during the day, when I was not doing *Spamalot*. I am meticulous and obsessive about details, and with my etiquette training, I was a natural at making higher-ups feel as if the coffee I'd brought them was in fact "Oh, my pleasure" to retrieve. I built relationships and felt comfortable asking for an audition when I heard they were casting the first national tour of the musical *Legally Blonde*. I wanted in.

Sometime after I'd been cast as Warner, Rachel called me up and said, "Hey, can you help us with auditions for *Peep Show*?" This was another Jerry Mitchell project, a burlesque show he'd done for years in New York. He wanted to bring it to Vegas for the first time. Jerry is always giving back. He created Broadway Bares, which has raised millions and millions of dollars for Broadway Cares/Equity Fights AIDS.

On the first day of *Peep Show* auditions, I was stapling headshots together in the studio. Rachel walked in, and behind her Jerry Mitchell rounded the corner. He called out to me, "Hey! There's my Warner!" and enveloped me in a big hug. Jerry is all charisma and fun—and genius, of course. Jerry was a blast to watch as he directed the dancers through the combinations. I also loved observing Rachel and her fellow casting directors—all masterful professionals—do what they do best.

From this experience and my time in *Spamalot*, I was really beginning to feel that I was a part of the small world of musical theater. I was so excited to start working on *Legally Blonde* because I knew that any team led by Jerry would be spectacular.

30

BRAD

Magical Helpers Redux

When we look back at our lives and recall all of the chance occurrences, small decisions, and people we met along the way, it all merges together to create a wonderful and obvious picture of our lives. But when first stepping across the threshold, we are sure that certain death or annihilation awaits us. We cannot imagine anything different. In fact, we consider dead bodies at the threshold crossing to be evidence that everybody who has tried to cross this way hasn't done well. But I'm here to tell you that magical helpers appear where there was once nobody at all, just like Semhar showed up for Jeff when he had just met with humiliation during rehearsal. Doors appear where there were walls, just like *Spamalot* rescued Jeff from the dead-end Gershwin revue.

People with experience are waiting for you, and they will provide you with the support you need. Finding your tribe is not an easy task. But it is worth it.

Question for Brad

Isn't Jeff just self-medicating in Vegas, not finding true connection?

Both can be true at the same time. It might be helpful to know that everybody self-medicates. Life is very difficult, and staying present in our lives can be exhausting. Sometimes self-medicating is obvious: drugs, alcohol, food. And sometimes our drug of choice is less obvious: gambling, shopping, helping others, financial or career success. A drug is simply something you can't get enough of that you don't really need.

Success is actually the most ubiquitous and hard-to-spot self-medication of all. While we are seldom enthusiastically encouraged to take on alcoholism or heroin addiction, others routinely reward a hyperfocus on success. But showering accolades on somebody who self-medicates with success, money, power, or accomplishments reinforces the medicine and mesmerizes the person the same way that complimenting an anorexic for being thin encourages them on the path of destruction.

Jeff's referring to booking a lead as a drug indicates that the pursuit of success is something he's hooked on. Of course, there's a difference between following your dream of singing on Broadway and becoming intoxicated from the praise and admiration of others. At this point in his story, though, Jeff is intoxicated, wandering through life trying to discover what will make him feel alive. Unconsciously, he is hoping that the praise and admiration of others will erase the rejection and the shaming messages he received from his family of origin and his church-based community. When he gains success and receives praise, he feels temporary relief from the Unlovable Monster, but he must still go further on his journey to find real and lasting peace.

Reflection Questions

1. Do you self-medicate in ways that go easily undetected? How can you show yourself compassion?
2. Have you noticed your parents or children self-medicating? How can you support them without taking ownership of their problem?

31

JEFF

Your Tour of Tours

Soon *Spamalot* closed, and I headed for New York City. A special enchantment comes with doing theater in New York City. It's Mecca. We rehearsed in a new space on storied 42nd Street and had costume fittings in the private section at Saks Fifth Avenue—not to mention that these costumes were created by the genius Gregg Barnes. I really gave my parents something to brag about. I'm sure it was fun for them to talk to their friends about their son Jeff, the lead in a national touring company—definitely more fun than trying to dance around the subject of Jeff the wayward gay.

I felt even more ensconced in the musical theater world in New York, of course. Soon after I arrived, Jerry invited me to dinner with some of his friends. Everybody was super sweet and complimentary to me. I was young and cute and fun, starting out my theater life in earnest. They must have wanted to eat me with a spoon. On the way home, I shared a cab with Jack O'Brien since we both lived on the West Side. I said, "So, Jack, what do you do?"

He responded, "Well . . . I'm a director. Jerry and I worked on *Hairspray* together." I pushed past a little embarrassment that I hadn't known who he was, and I asked him all about his process and his favorite part of his job.

I did have to deal with how insecure I was in my acting abilities, and I proved myself correct during one horrible rehearsal. I had to say one line—"Elle, what are you doing here?"—and I could not say it in any way that felt natural. We tried over and over, but I just couldn't get it. Humiliated, I was sure everyone thought I was just the sexy lead who couldn't act.

I will be forever grateful for the other two male leads in the show, D. B. Bonds and Ken Land. Two consummate professionals, they took me under their wings and taught me how to act over the course of *Legally Blonde's* run.

Before I knew it, we were on the road. It had its challenges, but overall, I loved tour life. And I soon found an energetic, buoyant, beautiful soul in the ensemble: Josh. The quintessential musical theater actor, he lives for performing and will never do anything else. As with Semhar, I said in the back of my mind, *he will be mine.*

And then, suddenly, he was. He was my first official boyfriend. Together twenty-four hours a day, we were bound by our common work. We fell in love with each other and with the counterfeit world of tour. It felt like my cruise life in some ways—we moved around so frequently, it was like we were on the run. Just as a city started to feel a little like home, we were off again. Josh and I didn't settle into the mundane or familiar, because there was no mundane or familiar.

We knew how to have fun together. During some tour stop or other, Josh and I created a mock art gallery. Josh and our friend Leslie had done a photo shoot featuring life's seedy underbelly. We put sheets up around our room to hang the photos on. I played Hans, the gallery owner—over the top in a silver lamé jacket—and Josh played the photographer. We made our friend Brian don a Speedo and pass around cucumber squares and bits of cracker while whispering "Sustenance?" The big reveal was Leslie behind a curtain. She lay on a bed in the fetal position, dressed all in white, mascara smeared all over her face. When you'd open the curtain, she'd look up at you and say, "Subterfuge." Tour was a blast.

And I was finally partnered! The best thing about having a steady boyfriend is that you start to understand intimacy. I for sure mean sex, but I also mean the intimacy that comes from letting someone really see you. It's like your partner is holding a mirror up, reflecting back everything you do—even the things you might not want to see, even the things you've been hiding in order to keep yourself safe.

Feeling intimate with Josh, however, didn't mean I knew how to be in a relationship. I'd spent my formative years in a church that had no place for me, and I was part of a family that couldn't see me. I had no template for knowing what I needed or wanted, and certainly had no idea how to ask for those needs and wants to be met.

The first issue that arose in our relationship was Josh's jealousy. He was convinced I would leave him for someone else. He came by this fear honestly. He'd grown up in a family where cheating was more normal than fidelity—and I am a bit of a flirt. One time in Buffalo, New York, a bunch of the cast went to drag night at a gay bar. A guy from a different show was there, and I had a crush on him. We flirted pretty hard, and we kissed on the dance floor. Josh saw, and I saw him see. He ran out, and, feeling intense shame, I chased him. We ran and screamed through the streets of Buffalo. The drama! When we were finally face to face in our room, I promised that nothing like this would happen again. I chose Josh. Cheating isn't my thing anyway.

After that, we got along well enough. But I didn't love Josh as he was. I wanted to fix him. I decided—out of love, of course—to reveal to him his key flaws. For example, I once spent two hours explaining to him that he was loud and that it was inappropriate to scream in the dressing room. He was stunned by the feedback, and he spiraled, quickly descending from mere embarrassment to believing he was the worst person in the world.

We had conversations like this frequently. It was volatile and exciting, and I felt right at home.

Josh is so much like my dad—the loudest and most talented, charismatic person in the room. Josh has lots of Lynne in him too: if he couldn't control something or make it perfect, it didn't exist. Basically, I'd found a man to love me in the same ways my parents had.

Though we both had issues from our childhoods, our backgrounds were very different. I didn't blend well with Josh's family. Our interactions felt sterile. I was used to over-the-top family lovefests, but when I visited Josh's family in New Hampshire, I could hear crickets during dinner.

Beyond our different backgrounds, Josh and I had incompatible core beliefs. To me, family is the center and purpose of life. For Josh, work plays that central role. With these huge differences, our relationship seemed to be heading for an inevitable conclusion. But a new solution soon presented itself.

I'd experimented a little with drugs in Vegas, but I trace the real beginning of my drug life to the *Legally Blonde* run in Detroit, when Josh and I started doing ecstasy together.

The drug is known to tear down walls and help couples reach deeper levels of intimacy. It worked on us for sure. The impending end of our relationship was kicked down the road a few years. How we felt on ecstasy became the new standard against which we judged our relationship even when we weren't high. Consequences would follow, as they do.

About six months into tour, Josh was cast in the revival of *Ragtime* at the Kennedy Center—and he was also hired as the assistant choreographer. We were in Austin, Texas, when it was time for him to leave. Instead of breaking up, we decided to keep things going long-distance. Anything less would have meant failure to me, and failure was not an option. Not when it came to the most important thing in life (being partnered, of course). We bought promise rings for each other on Guadalupe Street, vowing to visit each other every three weeks. *Ragtime* was a huge hit, and Josh was elated when they began the process of taking it to Broadway, even though it would mean more time apart.

One day, while talking to Josh on the phone, I was absently thumbing through a catalogue. I saw an ad for the coolest David Yurman engagement rings, and a thought popped into my head. "Want to get married?" I asked.

"Wait, what?" was Josh's reply. So I asked again and made a short, compelling argument for the prospect. A few minutes later, he said, "Sure."

A while later, I paid him a visit in DC, and we officially proposed to each other on the steps of the Lincoln Memorial.

A lot of people were curious about the logistics of gay marriage. "Who proposes?" they'd ask. The answer is that when little precedent exists, you create your own rituals. In our case, I asked Josh, and then Josh asked me.

This was 2009. Gay marriage was legal in only a few states, and it wasn't recognized at the federal level. But Josh and I had the audacity to think we could get married. We were two clueless boys in love (or was that unbridled codependency?).

Where did our audacity come from? Well, for me, it came from growing up Mormon. I was just doing what practically every person I knew had done: marrying the first person who would marry me.

Marriage to a man also meant that I would be truly, officially out. My parents and my McLean grandparents wouldn't be able to keep this in the dark any longer.

My mom revered her parents, Grandpa Jack and Grandma Joyce Eggington, and had persisted in keeping the truth about me from them. With my engagement, though, I had rendered continued silence impossible. Mom finally made the trek to her parents' house in Layton, a suburb about twenty-five miles north of Salt Lake City. Sitting in their comfortable kitchen, she addressed herself to her mother (incidentally, the most beautiful woman in the world), "So, Jeff got engaged." She couldn't bring herself to say *gay*. She simply added, "He got engaged to a man."

Grandpa Egg (gorgeous, tall, stunning singing voice—I take after him, obviously) said, "To a man? Jeff got engaged to a man?"

Finally, Mom could say it. "Yes. He's gay."

Grandpa Egg surprised everyone with a casual, "Oh yeah, I have always known." He opened the fridge door and asked, "Do you want a Pepsi?"

Stunned at this no-big-deal response, my mother took the proffered soda in a daze. Grandpa wasn't done surprising her: "Make sure he knows that we will always love him and accept him for who he is."

So Colonel Jack Eggington of the Air Force, this epitome of masculinity who had looked down the barrel at a grizzly more than once, showed up the most beautifully for me. Soon after my engagement, I had some leave from *Legally Blonde* and was playing cribbage with Grandpa Egg. He said to me, "Hey, I just want you to know that some of my best friends on the planet are men. Well, all of my best friends on the planet are men. I was never attracted to them, but I understand how your connection to men would be so strong. I did know some men in the military who were gay, which is not an easy thing to be. I'm proud that you are being truthful and speaking up for yourself."

He also told me about a burlesque show he'd seen in Paris. He said, "These were the most beautiful women I had ever seen. And then at the end of the act, they popped their bosoms! They were all men!"

Now, Grandpa Egg didn't stop twitting me for voting Democrat, and he still wouldn't let me live down the time I'd lost a bet that I could eat a full order of pancakes at the Ranch Hand Trail Stop in Montpelier, Idaho. But he fully accepted my gayness with total love and acceptance.

32
BRAD

Loving Without a Map

Falling in love is a blind madness, and Jeff is a pro. Connection has been so elusive for him, and his longing for it so strong, that he is quickly drawn into relationships by a planet-sized magnetic force, especially when these relationships promise to assuage the unrequited love from his childhood and early romantic ventures. For many people, this is true. That's why our language has such phrases as *madly in love* and *crazy for you.* However, the hard work comes after the delirium and projections of new love wear off. There is work to be done, no matter how good the chemistry or how powerful the attraction or how seemingly compatible we are in the first stages of courtship. Joseph Campbell taught that in marriage, the facts will eventually break through, destroying the projections of the early stages of a romantic relationship. What comes next is *love.* In marriage, he taught, we must transform our passion into compassion.[15]

---

15 Joseph Campbell, lecture 1 from *Mythos: The Shaping of Our Mythic Tradition.*

Questions for Brad

When I read about Jeff wanting to fix Josh, I recognized my own behavior toward my partner. Why do we do this?

The urge to fix other people is a powerful one and can be understood in the context of childhood. We often seek out those we think we can make better, happier, or more whole. Unconsciously, we think that if we can solve *this* riddle, make *this* person happy, then we will have finally solved the puzzle we were asked to work on our entire young lives. Therapists and laypeople alike talk about "marrying your father or your mother". In these cases, the similarities in the relationships don't have to be exact.

Instead of solving this riddle, what we need to do is work our way through the feelings caused by the original childhood wound. The wound must be felt and grieved so it can be integrated into a larger version of ourselves. And just like in childhood, we fear that if we are unable to make someone happy, they will leave us. Renowned psychologist Alice Miller says it this way: "We have feared and struggled to ward off something that really cannot happen any longer; it has already happened, at the very beginning of our lives while we were completely dependent."[16]

What is the danger of pointing out someone's flaws?

Anxiety and a need to control other people may lead us to attack somebody's flaws and call them on their bullshit—all in the name of love. But those flaws and that bullshit are this person's crutches, their defenses. A mentor once taught me that taking away people's crutches is not an act of love. We may be able to see how

16 Alice Miller, *The Drama of the Gifted Child: The Search for the True Self* (New York: Basic Books, 1981), 101.

somebody else's protective tools are preventing their growth or keeping them isolated, but the child inside of them holds onto these tools as if to a stuffed teddy bear or a life raft. If we assault someone's defenses before we consider the cost, we are re-creating their childhood abuse. Our job as parents, partners, friends, or therapists is merely to love. And if we love well, then we might create the kind of safety that allows the other person to lower their defenses—that is, recognize and address their own flaws—because the threat has been removed.

Reflection Questions

1. If you find yourself struggling with a loved one's coming out or simply choosing a life different from your own, how could you follow the example of Jeff's Grandpa Eggington rather than his parents and other grandparents?
2. Has it been helpful for you when others have pointed out your flaws? If yes, how did they approach the issue?
3. Do you contribute to romantic notions about marriage and committed partnerships? How can you speak more realistically about what people can expect from such relationships?

33

JEFF

A Real Boy

I was genuinely in love with Josh. Absolutely. But I have to acknowledge that part of my excitement around matrimony had to do with finally becoming a real person. For Mormons and McLeans, you're not real until you're married. Deep down, I still wanted the approval of the very people I was trying to differentiate myself from.

My family wanted to meet Josh. Dad was the first to have that honor. *Legally Blonde* was doing a run in Houston, and Dad was at a conference nearby. Josh went to the conference, experiencing Michael McLean in all his glory.

Dad was lovely to Josh and immediately treated him like part of the family. This is how my dad is. He's good at connecting with new people. But seeing how freely he showed love to Josh bothered me. Why couldn't he act this way toward me? I felt rage rising, and it was about more than being jealous about Josh. It was about tingle fingers. We hadn't spoken about it since I'd first confronted him—when he'd denied any wrongdoing and I'd defended my own experience.

There in Houston, I said to him, "Here's the deal. I don't want you involved in my life ever again. Don't comment on how I live or who I love. Don't even show up at all."

And then Dad surprised me. He said, "If I had done the things you are accusing me of, I would hate me, too. I have to believe in a God who would forgive me, because I could never forgive myself." At these words, I was entirely overcome. In a moment of unbounded gratitude, I fell to the floor and wept. It was clear that Dad's experience of tingle fingers had been completely different from mine, but it was also clear that he was willing to allow me my experience, no matter how hard it was for him. Though he and I would have plenty of drama and disagreement over the coming years, this talk was a big turning point in our relationship.

When *Legally Blonde* came to Salt Lake, Josh managed to come for a visit. Instead of living in tour-provided housing during the run, Josh and I stayed in Heber, and I commuted forty-five minutes to the Capitol Theater every night. On one of our days off, I rented vans to bring the whole company up to Heber, where we made chili and had a bonfire. I loved merging my two worlds.

Just like my dad had earlier, the whole family embraced Josh. They may not have known what to do with the big issue—Josh and I being engaged—but they knew how to be hospitable to a newcomer. It soon became clear, though, that my coming out was still a very tender issue.

On the night my family and Josh came to the show, Kathy, a dear family friend, came along. I love this woman. We had spent many sacred and fun hours touring through Israel together when I was younger. Backstage after the show, Kathy gave me a big hug, touched my face, and, looking into my eyes, said, "I'm happy as long as you're happy." It was so sweet, but it also raised some defensive hackles for newly out Jeff. Was she patronizing me? In the moment, I gave her nothing but love back, but later, as I drove home with Mom and Josh, I scoffed, "It's so dumb. 'I'm happy as long as you're happy.' What does that even mean? If I'm not happy, she can't support me? I bet she thinks there's no way I can even be happy if I'm not Mormon."

Lynne McLean turned to me, beet red, and screamed in my face: "Well, well, well. How dare you suggest her kindness isn't enough, seeing as how you are living in disgusting sin?" There went Josh's warm welcome.

My mother has never been able to own this incident. I know that sometimes when we are triggered, we can say and do things we don't remember. Maybe the trauma she felt around the situation overtook her. But she had revealed herself, as people eventually do. These feelings—and this ability to let all hell break loose—had always hidden beneath my mother's loving, calm demeanor. My instincts had been right all along.

When she stopped screaming, I said, "Now I know how you feel."

And then my mother said what Mormon mothers are apparently allowed to say to their gay children: "I don't know who you are anymore. Why are you so angry?"

Well, you know what happened, Mom? I just stopped pretending to be the person you taught me was acceptable to you. And I'm angry because you are my mother and you didn't protect me or love me unconditionally.

✣

A year into the show, our contracts were up. Everyone was renewed except me. The producer pulled me aside and said, "Here's the deal: you didn't get renewed because you're too fat. If you can lose the weight by the time we get to LA, we'll sign you again. If not, we'll need a new Warner."

I'd fallen in love and gone soft. It turns out you can be fat and in love in real life, but you can't be fat and cut a romantic figure on stage. These higher-ups had clearly been talking about my weight for months behind my back, just waiting for my contract to end. Nice.

The whole situation illustrates how unable I was to consistently take care of myself, to devote time to myself instead of to whomever I was in love with or trying to impress in some way. I had swung into neglect territory, and it was time to swing back to the other extreme: starvation. My old trick still worked. I lost the requisite weight by the time we hit LA, and I got to stay in the show.

About two days after the fat talk, I had another odd encounter. The stage manager (who had also been the stage manager for *Spamalot*) was leaving to do another show. He came into my dressing room and closed the door. He said, "I need to make amends to you."

"Okay," I said. "What is it?" I had no real idea what amends meant at that point, but I had a vague idea that it had something to do with AA.

"I need to apologize to you," he said. "I've come to learn over the years that you are actually a really good person. And I've blamed you for a lot of things that you didn't do. I am sorry." And he left.

What? I had no idea what he was talking about. I found out later that during *Spamalot*, he had written awful things about me in his weekly reports. Maybe my relative inexperience had made me an easy scapegoat when his addiction led him to make mistakes. The things he wrote definitely warranted an apology and would end up wreaking some havoc on my career down the road.

✢

When Josh and I first got engaged, we set a wedding date more than a year out. We made as many arrangements as we could during our long-distance engagement. I asked my friend Bryan if we could get married on his property in Iowa, one of the states with legal gay marriage. He was so sweet, but said his family was too homophobic. They would never allow it. Then I asked the illustrious John O'Hurley, who had played King Arthur in *Spamalot*, if I could get married on his property in Vermont, another haven for gay marriage. He graciously said yes. His house is on a private lake—with a floating gazebo. Oh, this wedding would be worthy of a Tony Award for sure.

Josh came back to *Legally Blonde* for the last six months of tour. We could finally plan our wedding together in person. As we traveled from city to city, we gathered delectable details and touches. We also scoured the internet for goods to import for the occasion, flying tartan material in from Scotland, which we used to handmake the invitations for seventy-five of our favorite people.

To top off our perfect life, Josh and I got a dog together, a champion Samoyed puppy from the Vincents, my surrogate family from the Palisades congregation. Josh and I gave her the gayest name possible: Princess Samantha, the Ruby Jewel of Manhattan. Why so much name? Because of the legendary animal trainer Doug Seus, who lived near my family. I grew up listening to his wolves howling, and I saw the eminent movie star Bart the Bear all the time. Doug's family dog had the distinguished name Beauregard of the Rockies, and Doug explained to me that naming pets is an opportunity to show them deep respect. Hence, Princess Samantha, the Ruby Jewel of Manhattan—Ruby Girl for short. She made everything better.

In August, we had our last performance in Toronto. Our marriage date was in September, so we had a month to put the finishing flourishes on the wedding of the decade. I made our table runners out of the same tartan as our invitations, and as the day neared, I also made our wedding cake.

Mormon boy that I was, I devised the rituals, creating a veritable temple on the water. Everyone congregated in a tent on the lakeshore before heading out to the floating gazebo. I asked my friend Kristin to offer a prayer and then directed everyone to take a few of the several hundred origami swans Josh and I had made. Each swan was connected to a blank piece of paper, where we directed people to write their fears and anything that would keep them from being present at the wedding. Before people could go to the gazebo, they had to burn their fears in a fire we had lit.

And then Simone officiated our marriage as we floated on a lake. The radiant Katie Thompson sang. It was perfect.

After the wedding, we all adjourned to an old library-turned-pub in Hanover, New Hampshire. Josh and I soon became too exhausted to keep the party going. We got to our room and collapsed into bed. I turned to Josh, and all of a sudden, I had an intense sinking feeling in my gut. The show was over. We had spent over a year curating it and putting it up, and now it was over. And even though we had said our vows mere hours before, I knew our relationship was over as well. It was clear to me then that I'd used Josh—and spent tens of thousands of dollars on a meaningless wedding—to validate myself and my gayness. What could I do? I did the only thing I was then equipped to do: I faked it. We had a honeymoon to go on.

We traveled around Maine and then back to New York. It was beautiful, but the second we got home, Josh left to do a show. I didn't have anything lined up yet, so I took Josh's departure hard. I turned increasingly to drugs and alcohol. A little ecstasy here and there would help me feel connected to myself at least. Sometimes I'd drink at bars and flirt with bartenders, just enough to feel less lonely. I didn't think any of this was serious, but looking back, it's clear I was developing a very real drinking habit.

I hadn't minded the time apart when we were dating and engaged, but I expected marriage to be different. A husband should make sacrifices to be with his husband. He should put the relationship first and foremost. Independence and alone time were for single life. Josh clearly had no idea how to be married in the way I defined marriage. Josh's adult life had always been molded around "the show," whatever the show was. Marriage was really too long-term a proposition for him to really conceptualize. I couldn't see his short-term approach to life for a good while, though, because from the beginning we had always been in a show together—whether it was *Legally Blonde* or our own wedding.

34

BRAD

Approval

Jeff says that as he began his engagement with Josh, he still craved the approval of those he was differentiating himself from. Put another way, some part of him wanted to follow the path he'd been raised to follow, even as part of him was rejecting that path. The difficulty of letting go of the familiar is understandable. The well-trodden path is comfortable and well-populated. The most difficult paths we must walk in life are the ones we walk alone. Joseph Campbell explains, "You enter the forest at the darkest point, where there is no path. Where there's a way or path, it is someone else's path."[17]

Those who have wandered into the forest know that it is a frightening journey. No signs show the way, no guides warn you of the monsters. Both parents and children may find themselves in the forest. For parents reading this book, the forest might be a support group for the parents of LGBTQ+ youth. It might be a

---

17 Joseph Campbell, *Pathways to Bliss: Mythology and Personal Transformation*, ed. David Kudler (Novato, CA: New World Library), xxvi.

therapist's office. Or it just might be learning to love and support your child without understanding. For the teens and young adults reading this book, the forest may be sharing your truth—your anger, hurt, or sadness. In any case, the journey into the darkness requires courage. And for most of us, the loneliness is the most chilling aspect of the voyage.

Questions for Brad

Why was Jeff so angry about his family friend who said, "I'm happy as long as you're happy"?

The difference between *I'm happy as long as . . .* and *I'm happy that . . .* is a subtle one. The former has a bit of condescending energy, while the latter is an expression of deep connection. *I'm happy as long as you're happy* is like saying *Even though I know what you're doing is wrong, I am happy if you say you are happy.* In contrast, *I'm happy that you're happy* communicates a nonjudgmental approach.

Language matters. Language is how we connect to each other, and it informs how we learn to understand ourselves. If you make a mistake in your language, please listen to your loved one's ensuing hurt and anger with deeper understanding. The person correcting you is trying to be seen. If it feels like you can't get anything right, your ego is being threatened. My advice would be to find a support group or therapist who can help you. One of the biggest mistakes we can make in this process is to ask the LGBTQ+ person to support us in our journey. They simply can't. They are going through their own process, which is riddled with shame, pain, and other trauma.

The confrontation between Lynne and Jeff was intense. Can you unpack it a little more?

Some readers may think that Jeff is too critical of Lynne in this section of his story. He says that she has not protected him, that she always had this anger boiling under the surface, and that she doesn't love him unconditionally. Jeff is not being too critical. He's just revealing the greatest secret he was ever asked to keep—for that matter, the greatest secret all children are asked to keep: their true feelings toward their parents.

When a child tells us they are angry, or when they tell us they don't trust us, we would be wise to respond with, "I'm so glad you're telling me now. Please keep talking. I want to understand you."

In contrast, when parents are incapable of hearing their children's hurt or anger, children learn to doubt themselves and to hate themselves. They become different people altogether to hide from or appease their parents. So when Lynne says that she doesn't know her son, it is not an accusation. It is a *confession*, an acknowledgement that she hasn't been willing to see and hear her son. And because Jeff wanted to survive childhood, he colluded with this wound of hers. Their unspoken conspiracy kept Lynne in a place where she was incapable of hearing and seeing things that would threaten her sense of self.

During the confrontation with Lynne, Jeff is learning to connect to the unconscious themes and feelings that had always been present in his family and in his community. In his mother's response, Jeff finds threads of the themes he'd been tacitly asked to deny, the dysfunction that had him doubting what he'd seen and heard and felt.

As we uncover similar covert feelings and harms, we don't have to throw up our hands and give up on our families and communities. We can learn to listen to the hurt that those we love experienced. It will require more capacity than we have ever needed before, but it is a worthy endeavor.

Can you explain why Jeff was so willing to fake it in his marriage?

Jeff's acknowledgement and insight that he was equipped only to fake it is profound. So much of what we know and what we are equipped with is an echo of patterns we learned in childhood. These patterns run deeper than our behaviors. Our very selves are forged by the context of our early childhoods. If we were asked to ignore our feelings in childhood because they were considered "fake," this is what we will do in adulthood.

In contrast, if we were allowed to confront authority when we were young, we can keep doing it when we are older. Being seen and welcomed as we are sets us up to know ourselves, whereas being asked to deny or ignore who we are leaves the scar of not knowing what we want and need. Our ability to answer even the simplest questions—*what do you want for dinner?*—relies heavily on whether we were seen in our early contexts and whether the big people around us welcomed the goings-on of our internal worlds. If we were seen, then we would eat when hungry. We would sleep when tired. If our internal worlds were not seen, our minds became cluttered with myriad voices telling us what we *should* do, regardless of what our bodies or souls may have needed.

When Jeff fakes it, he is simply doing in his marriage what he learned to do as a child.

Reflection Questions

1. Are there contexts in your life in which you feel you have to fake it? Why might that be? Can you imagine telling the truth in that place instead?
2. Were you free to express yourself in your family of origin?
3. If you are a parent, how do you react when your child reveals their true feelings? As a child, how did your parents react when you expressed yourself honestly?

35

JEFF

An Ideal Husband

We'd all been hearing about *The Book of Mormon* musical for the past three years or so, and it intrigued me. I thought the auditioning ship had sailed, but then I heard they were still looking to fill a few smaller roles. I was thrilled. If I got the gig, I could merge my Mormon life and my theater life. In my mind, it made so much sense for the show to hire the out son of a prominent Mormon musician. When the character breakdown came out and it fit me to a T, I asked a friend to get me an audition (yes, after five years in the theater world, I was still a maverick without an agent or manager).

At the last minute, the creative team replaced the original director, Jason Moore, and hired Casey Nicholaw, the brilliant choreographer I'd worked with on *Spamalot*. Perfect! I thought our having worked together could only help my chances. I went through several callbacks and made it to the final with five other guys. This time, we auditioned for the whole creative team, including Casey, and I felt like I killed it. Everything was coming together for me. I was married, and soon I'd have a job in my first Broadway show. The next day, though, the breakdown for my character was released online again, meaning they were still casting it. I hadn't been chosen. My agent friend called the casting director and said, "I thought it was a done deal. He was perfect for it!"

The casting director said, "We all thought he was perfect for it, too."

"Then why didn't he get it?" my agent asked.

The casting director paused for a moment and asked, "What did Jeff do to make Casey hate him so much? After the audition, we were ready to hire Jeff, but Casey said, 'There is no way in hell I will ever work with Jeff McLean again.'"

I was not prepared for this. The director of the biggest show on Broadway said he would never work with me again. I mean, I knew I'd made mistakes during the run of *Spamalot*, but I had also devoted nearly two years of my life to that show. I loved the people I'd worked with and had tried to be a positive contributor.

I felt blacklisted and ashamed, and I wanted someone or something to blame. Enter the *Spamalot* and *Legally Blonde* stage manager! He must have poisoned Casey against me. Now his amends made sense. He had scapegoated me for his failures. In turn, I scapegoated the stage manager for the unraveling of my career.

The truth is that I deserved the blame. Beyond my unfortunate sarcastic question about how deep Casey wanted me to go with hitting my castmates with fish, I had frequently shown up late, forgotten rehearsals, and called out of performances. It hadn't occurred to me that people wouldn't always give me the benefit of the doubt. It took a while after the failed audition for me to recognize that I was not the victim here. I was the common denominator. I lived a reckless life and had been reckless with my career. I wanted to take back everything I had ever done.

A more philosophical me could have shrugged off *The Book of Mormon* incident and said, "So Casey doesn't want to work with me. So what? There are other directors." But at the time, it felt like everyone hated me. Moreover, the whole situation proved my upbringing correct. I had been taught that if I did everything right, God would reward me. If I didn't do everything right, He would punish me. And now I was reaping the punishment I deserved because I'd chosen to live a life of sin. These feelings were hounding me years after I'd left the church. The conditioning was deep.

I slipped into a deep depression. I sat alone in my apartment, trying to figure out how to audition for anything else. Or that was what I told myself I was doing. Mostly, I was appeasing the Unlovable Monster with drugs and alcohol, much in the same way I had used righteous superiority to keep the monster at bay back in my Mormon days.

I was in this state when Josh came home after months on tour and said, "Jeff, I have been doing some thinking, and I realized that I have been confusing sex for love. I don't want to have sex with you anymore. I'll do it if I absolutely have to, but I just don't want to. I'll let you know if that ever changes."

"Ummmm . . . okay." That was all I could say for a minute, my heart slamming in my chest. Then, "Do you want to sleep with other people?"

"Maybe," he said. "Just not you." End of conversation.

Why would Josh drop this bomb at a time when I desperately needed the courage to get back out there and book something? He had intended to hurt me deeply, and I knew it.

Deep in my soul, I felt the Unlovable Monster's size and

restlessness increase. Its three words—*you are unlovable*—contained a truth I had known as long as I could remember, but I couldn't allow them to be uttered. I'd tried everything to keep the monster quiet—drugs, marriage—but these shields were losing their potency. My husband, who was supposed to be my biggest advocate, had confirmed my lifelong belief that I was disgusting.

I kept auditioning, but I was not booking anything. Two things had sucked the theater spark right out of me:

One, I didn't believe in myself anymore. If Casey thought I was uncastable and my own husband thought I was gross, who would ever book me again?

Two, I felt desperate. If I didn't have a job in theater, what would I have in common with my husband?

I had to find a way to prove my worth as a spouse. With no theater work on the horizon, I found a new obsession. Josh had this fantastic rent-stabilized apartment in Washington Heights, and I spent most of my days trying to make it a home. I replastered the walls, scraped off old paint from the window frames and doors, redid the whole damn kitchen. In a rental. Why? Because Josh and I were going to raise children here, and it needed to be nice. In fact, it needed to be perfect. Just like my body needed to be a paragon of gay beauty to hide my self-loathing (thank you, Botox and obsessive gym time), my home had to reflect a certain (nonexistent) inner flawlessness. When I replastered those walls, I was plastering over the Unlovable Monster.

Josh was offered a part in the hottest new show on the musical theater scene: *Tales of the City*, based on Armistead Maupin's book series. Jake Shears of the Scissor Sisters and collaborator John Garden wrote the music and lyrics. When I heard this, I was immediately taken back to a close, hot room at Sundance Film Festival in 2000. Not out yet, not ready to admit to myself I was gay, I'd watched and listened, entranced, to the Scissor Sisters perform a set. They were openly queer and over-the-top magnetic. They sang very risqué yet smart songs and dressed in very risqué and smart costumes. I knew any musical by these forces of nature was a spectacular opportunity for Josh.

The American Conservatory Theater in San Francisco was producing the show, and all the big names were attached, including Jason Moore as director (yes, the original director of *The Book of Mormon* that Casey Nicholaw had replaced). He'd been the resident director for *Les Misérables* on Broadway, and right after *Tales of the City*, he directed the first *Pitch Perfect* movie.

Josh would be in San Francisco for at least six months. I asked if I should come too, and he said he didn't care, that I should do whatever I wanted. This lack of concern was alarming to me, and I started to realize that he was never going to stop. For the rest of my life, he'd be gone—and totally disconnected—for months at a time.

I made a decision. Instead of staying in New York and trying to further my own career, I followed Josh. Being near my husband was my job.

The company put us up in a knock-out of a studio apartment in the heart of Nob Hill, right across from Grace Cathedral. I was seeing San Francisco, one of the most beautiful cities in the country, if not the world, for the first time. We had our Ruby Girl, and Josh was working (i.e., Josh was happy). I didn't have to worry about him. But what the hell was I going to do with my time? Enter Frank!

My brother from another mother, Frank is married to Kathleen, a woman in the *Tales of the City* cast who had also been in *Legally Blonde*. Frank and I would wake every morning, say farewell to our spouses, and meet for coffee. We'd walk our dogs around the city and go to the gym together. He introduced me to cold-brew coffee and American Spirit cigarettes.

Hold up. Did I just say American Spirit cigarettes? Oh yes. After thirty-one smoke-free years, I decided to just casually pick up smoking. But, of course, it was hardly casual. It was a calculated play for my husband's attention. Josh hates smoking. In case you were wondering, no, my nicotine habit did not save my marriage, but smoking served as my *fuck you* to the world. I was such a rebel and cared so little what anyone thought of me that I switched from Frank's American Spirits to Camel Crushes because they were Jake Shears's brand. (By now, I had met Jake and was even more convinced than I had been before that he was the coolest man alive. And he somehow managed to also be down-to-earth and sweet as can be.)

I was instantly addicted to both the nicotine and the fuck-you power. I knew I had to quit. Not only was I a singer, but cigarettes had killed my great-grandfather. From the very first day, though, I started to feel normal only when I was smoking. I think underneath it all, I felt like smoking would keep me safe from anyone who might want to be with me.

I smoked for ten years.

Frank is also an actor, and we had both made plans to attend the theater's summer acting program while our spouses were in the show. Before the program started, though, *Tales of the City* fired an actor during rehearsals. The swing took the vacated role, and they asked me to be the swing. I was honored and accepted the position, leaving Frank to do the summer program without me.

As the swing, I would be covering nine parts, one of them a leading role. I never had to go on—thank God!—but I was a basket case. I felt really lucky that the *Tales of the City* cast was much more committed than I'd been back in *Spamalot* days. I immediately had so much love and respect for the swing who'd had to go on whenever I'd called out. Being a swing is the hardest job in theater, and I am in awe of those who can do it.

The show's team and community were lovely to be part of. They made me feel like I belonged, even though I never went on. All of us ended up meeting and even visiting Armistead Maupin. This gay icon invited the cast over for tacos from the taco truck that was a permanent installation at his San Francisco home. We rubbed shoulders with Laura Linney and Olympia Dukakis as well. They'd starred in a miniseries version of the show and came to the premier party, which was one of the most chic parties I've ever attended.

I thought that being part of the show with Josh would fix the marriage, but it didn't. We kept growing further apart.

36

BRAD

Seek Grace

Jeff's maturity allows him to see the connection between his past actions with the director Casey Nicholaw and Casey's current rejection, but something darker is at play. His catastrophic thinking—*And now I was reaping the punishment I deserved because I'd chosen to live a life of sin*—speaks to the unforgiving world in which he grew up. We learn about God through the way our parents show up in life. How could it be any other way? Jeff's version of God at this time of his life reminds me of Grandpa McLean: he was a grandfather of punishment rather than an earthly representation of a forgiving God.

Many Mormons share this harsh view of God. The Mormon Church does not emphasize God's grace as His predominant feature. God's justice is frequently prioritized. This is a complicated topic because Mormon doctrine does not state that heaven is earned by works, but in practice, the culture embodies this belief. The same focus on justice and works above grace can be found in other high-cost orthodox religions.

Question for Brad

Jeff thought that his move to San Francisco would save his marriage. I've had similar thoughts before. Why doesn't that kind of "geographic cure" work?

Entering into or ending a marriage isn't the solution. Joining a church or leaving one isn't the answer either. The answer is deeper. The answer is in learning how we see ourselves and understanding how the relationship we have with ourselves impacts all of our other relationships. When my therapy patients seek clarity or advice from me about major life decisions, I explain, "It doesn't matter if you take this new job and move across the country or if you get married to this guy. The work is the same. The work is about knowing yourself and knowing who you are. The answer to your questions will arise out of that discovery."

Reflection Questions

1. How was the concept of grace discussed in your family of origin? What role does grace play in your life today? (Even if you are not Christian, you can think in terms of a pliant, forgiving God or Universe.)
2. How can you prioritize your relationship with yourself? Was this concept ever modeled for you by parents or other caretakers?

37

JEFF

The F-Bomb

Mirroring my relationship with Josh, my relationship with my parents was also steadily declining. On the rare occasions we even spoke, my mom would call me up and say, "I have figured it out."

I would say, "What did you figure out, Mom?" And then she'd say, "I received a revelation in the temple that you are like someone who has severe spina bifida or Down syndrome. You don't have accountability, so God will let you back into heaven."

She would say this shit with so much conviction, utterly confident that she was expressing her love for me—and utterly unaware of her words' dehumanizing effect.

I would simply respond, "Thanks, Mom. That's wonderful for you."

And my dad. He'd made all these commercials with the tagline "Family: isn't it about . . . time?" But now he had no time for me. Mr. Fix-It couldn't fix me, and he wouldn't or couldn't acknowledge things he couldn't repair or heal. He gave the appearance of showing up by checking boxes. He was kind to Josh, check. He came to our wedding, check. He answered the phone if I called, check. But it was all a veneer. He wasn't actively creating or nurturing real connections. Of course, I didn't know that my dad was in his own dark night of the soul during this time. I wouldn't hear about this for a few years yet.

I deeply resented that they hadn't offered to pay for my wedding like they had Meggan's. But what truly rankled was their attitude toward the wedding, and all of these months later, I couldn't stop thinking about it, especially since my marriage was a failure. I had done what they'd always told me to do—get married—and they hadn't stepped up. They thought they were so cool because they'd deigned to show up to my gay-ass wedding at all.

No, you're not fucking cool. It doesn't take that much to show up to your child's wedding, especially for marriage-and-family freaks like you. You let the Church of Jesus Christ of No Gay Love loom over the whole affair and keep you from being fully present.

The fact is that Michael and Lynne had been acting strangely for years before my wedding—really from the second I'd come out. For one thing, they'd started talking to me through Meggan, as if they were afraid of me. This is from people who had always taught me to be direct. They were clearly on their own journey, but I couldn't manage it because I was managing my own.

I had plenty of time to stew over their behavior as I orbited my husband in San Francisco. I finally got fed up with waiting for them to get used to the facts of my life. I called them out on it. Well, *called them out* is maybe too mild a term.

What actually happened is I told them to fuck off and that I didn't want to see them again.

That's right! For the first time in my life, I said, "Fuck you, Lynne McLean, and fuck you, Michael McLean. You don't deserve me as your child. I'm fucking done with you." I had to protect myself, and carrying them and their issues was beyond my capacity.

I didn't call my parents out of the blue to share my profane sentiments with them. No, the *fuck you* was a reaction to one of my increasingly rare phone calls with my mother. These weren't her exact words, but the essential message was, "Because you're married and monogamous, you're one of us. I know how to talk to you now." I couldn't take it anymore. Her love for me was conditional upon my being married? And she couldn't pay attention enough or talk to me enough to see that my marriage was failing? The Unlovable Monster was triggered, taking on more heft and unleashing my wrath.

My parents didn't understand why I was so angry, which was part of the problem. They couldn't face the fact that they had been slowly disowning me from the second I'd decided to be truthful about myself. They couldn't face their actions because it went against who they thought they were. If you believe that family is everything, but then disown your child, your cognitive distortions are on par with the physical twistings of a world-renowned contortionist.

Saying *fuck you* was the best thing I ever did for myself—and my parents. Their conditional love and vile behavior required it. They couldn't hide how much my gayness disgusted them. You know what's really disgusting, though? The way so many Mormon parents treat their gay children as a result of what the church teaches. Kicking your children to the curb in the name of God is much more disgusting than any gay sex kink I ever learned from my *Spamalot* castmates.

After the *fuck you*, two things happened: First, I was freed from my parents' expectations. Just like that. Second, my relationship with Meggan became strained for a while. She called and reamed me up and down about how selfish I was to disown our parents. I was angry, but it didn't take too long for Meggan and me to find our way back to each other.

⁜

Somehow while I was having the time of my life in San Francisco with smokes and jokes and being in denial about my unraveling marriage, I had also become strong enough to look for my next theater job.

After the run of *Tales of the City*, Josh went to LA to work with his mentor, the brilliant director Marcia Milgram Dodge, whom he'd worked with on *Ragtime*. I also headed to LA, but not just for Josh. I was auditioning for two shows: the second national tour of *Jersey Boys* and the Reprise Theatre Company's production of *Cabaret*. The *Jersey Boys* audition didn't go well (I was apparently too gay), but I booked the role of Cliff in *Cabaret* (my gayness level was apparently just right since Cliff is bisexual). This was a huge win for me—I felt like being cast had broken the Casey curse—and it also meant Josh and I would be working together. He'd been hired as the assistant choreographer and would also be in the ensemble.

We had a month's lag time between the close of *Tales of the City* and the start of *Cabaret* rehearsals. We couldn't go back to New York because we had a subletter. Going home to Utah was impossible since I'd dropped the f-bomb. Finding our own short-term place was out of the question. How could we deal with deposits and sky-high rents? Josh and I had been in debt ever since the wedding and seemed incapable of living a consistently responsible life. Our success with budgeting was about on par with my brilliance at taking care of my body.

I asked my friends Russ and Sarah in Glendale, California, if we could crash with them and their roommate, Gina. Thank the saints they said yes to cramming five adults and one dog into a tiny two-bedroom apartment. Josh and I stayed through the run of *Cabaret*. God bless Russ and Sarah!

Those weeks in LA felt like what I'd always imagined marriage to be. It was sort of mundane—we watched a lot of *True Blood* and ate a lot of Cheesecake Factory—but also sweet and sublime. I hope that when I'm an old man, these golden weeks are what I recall most about the Josh years.

Cabaret was summer stock, which is when a company puts up multiple shows in one summer—four shows in Reprise Theatre Company's case—so you have to learn a role at warp speed. Everyone in the show was a rock star, while I felt like I was winging it. I was always self-conscious about my lack of formal training as an actor. I'd never done summer stock before and was used to the luxury of rehearsing for months. For *Cabaret*, we had two weeks. It was grueling. And fun.

The artistic director of the theater company was true genius Jason Alexander (George Costanza on *Seinfeld*). He stopped by to watch the first run-through, which was held after just five days of rehearsal. I was barely holding on. Afterward, Jason pulled me aside. I am a huge fan, so I was geeking out while trying to listen. He said to me, "Jeff, I've never liked Cliff in any of the *Cabaret* productions I've ever seen. Not even in the movie"—where the character, renamed Brian, is played by the legendary Michael York—"I've never bought the fact that he is into Sally. And I'm not buying it with you."

"Okay," I said. "I'll figure out how to sell it." No matter that some of the best actors ever haven't been able to make this role believable and I had less than two weeks to outdo them all. No pressure.

I did the best I could, but I'd always believed (aided and abetted by a certain Unlovable Monster) that even my absolute best was never enough. I felt like I'd never done a good job in any of my shows. I couldn't live up to the unspoken McLean motto: *Do it perfectly and make everyone happy.*

When *Cabaret* was about to go up, Josh got a call. His mom had cancer. It was advancing so quickly, they didn't know how much time she had left. She ended up passing away that week, and Josh couldn't leave the show to go to the funeral. I will never understand why Josh's family wouldn't postpone the funeral until he could attend. No matter what issues my family had, I knew none of them would pull something like that during a time of loss.

On our next day off, Josh and I went to Disneyland to celebrate his mom's life. I sat in the park thinking about the time I'd spent with my own mom at Disneyland. We hadn't spoken in two months, and I realized that she or my dad could be gone at any moment. So I called her right then and said that she, Dad, and I had to go to therapy to figure out how to move forward. She gratefully said, "Absolutely!" We agreed to book a session with Ken soon after *Cabaret's* closing date.

Josh and I finished out the run of the show, said a profuse thank-you to Russ and Sarah for saving the day, and began the ten-hour drive from California to Utah. And then Mom called.

"You can't come home," said Mom.

"Excuse me?" I said as Josh and I passed through Mesquite, Nevada.

"You have to go to Grandma Eggington's house"—three hours out of our way—"and wait for your uncle's birthday party to be over. Then you can come home."

"You mean I get to sneak into the house in the middle of the night?"

Ah, more evidence as to why I'd had to say fuck you to my parents. Grandma McLean—with my parents' support—had insisted that I not be invited to my uncle's party because then it would be about me and my gayness. I was upset but completely unsurprised. This was just how Mike and Lynne kept the fifth commandment (you know, "Honor thy father and thy mother and give them whatever they want even if they are batshit").

So we went to Grandma Eggington's and waited it out for a few hours. Once the sun set, my husband and I got to slink into Heber under the cover of darkness. And it was against this backdrop that my parents and their gay son intended to start therapy.

Ken Rodgers, you may recall, has long been our family therapist. He is the guy I went to when I was coming out, and he knows my parents well. He's helped us get through many situations, but we don't usually see him between crises. For our current issues, Mom arranged ten sessions.

The three of us sat down at our first appointment, and Ken asked, "So, what's up?"

My response, in essence: "I've ruined my parents' dreams. I've destroyed my mom's idea of an eternal family, and I've totally devastated her. And I've destroyed my dad's career, and I can't further his legacy."

Their response, in essence: "We ruined our child's life by raising him to be straight when he is gay. And we destroyed his chances of happiness because we weren't able to see what was right in front of our faces."

Ken took this in and said, "You all feel responsible for each other." He turned to my parents. "Mike and Lynne, has Jeff ruined your lives? Mike, has he ruined your career?"

"No," said Michael.

"No," said Lynne.

"Are you strong enough to handle your own lives? Does Jeff, in fact, have the power to destroy your lives?"

"Absolutely not! We can handle our lives, and we are okay. We're really strong, actually."

Ken turned to me and asked, "Jeff, have your parents destroyed your life by not raising you gay?"

"No. It may have made things easier, but none of us were in the position to handle gay. We all did the best we could."

"So nobody has ruined anybody's life here?"

"Nope," the collective answered.

And twenty minutes into our first therapy session, we were done. Go team go. Within a week, I was back in New York.

38

BRAD

The Power of Anger

The pain from our trauma must go somewhere. It will either be directed inward, manifesting as suicidality, self-harm, and destructive behaviors, or sent outward through aggressive acts or through our verbalizing the pain to someone who can *hold it* with us. Jeff's expression of anger toward his parents helped him find a way out of his pain. Confronting your parents, even when it is less than graceful, can be a lifesaving act. Wise and capable parents will develop a capacity to honor the anger directed at them. Wise and capable parents will intentionally connect with a child's anger because sometimes that anger is the only window into the child's world.

Questions for Brad

I take the fifth commandment seriously, but I can see why Jeff struggled with how his parents prioritized their

parents over him. How can I honor my parents without accepting harmful behavior?

Obedience to the fifth commandment can be problematic. Generational transmission of trauma, mental illness, and addiction are all legacies that happen in the shadow of this edict. We would be wise to follow the example of the great revolutionaries (Moses, Christ, Joseph Smith, etc.) and depart from the status quo, confronting the patriarchy, the matriarchy, and any other oppressive regime that asks children to bear abuse and mistreatment with respectful, silent deference.

Why not interpret *honoring* as telling the truth about the ways in which our parents hurt us? Why not honor our parents by healing the parts of us that they have dented?

Why did Lynne share with Jeff her theories about why he was gay?

If we were to ask Lynne about her intentions, she would explain that she was just trying to make sense out of something. She would suggest that she was trying to support Jeff. But her real intention was to soothe her anxiety in the face of Jeff's sexuality, an essential threat.

Her intentions weren't good or bad. They were just her intentions. The real harm was the disconnect: she thought she was acting for Jeff's benefit but was really acting in her own best interest.

This is a very practical example of how parental anxiety passes to children. Because Lynne could not own and work her way through her anxiety, she passed it on to Jeff. But Jeff wasn't having it, and the Unlovable Monster, his protector, was unleashed.

I was surprised that Meggan called Jeff selfish. Is it normal for siblings to take the parents' side in disputes?

This is common practice. When we exceed the bandwidth of others, not just our parents, they will label us selfish. This is their attempt to get us to shrink and fit inside the limits of their capacity. Instead of owning their inadequacy, they attack us and identify us as the problem. Anyone escaping old patterns or working on boundaries would be wise to anticipate this kind of backlash. They are inevitable when we grow out of our old contexts, out of our old selves.

Jeff says that the McLean motto is "do it perfectly and make everyone happy." This mirrors my own family's attitude. Why do so many of us get this messaging?

Most parents believe that the job of a parent is to raise a *good* child. But since there is no such thing—we are all good and bad and everything in between—the child is destined for failure and shame. The idea of raising a good child, a good athlete, a good student, a good such-and-such leaves many seemingly successful and accomplished young people with a sense of dread.

I teach parents that the goal of parenting is to raise a healthy self, not a good child. A healthy self is messy, imperfect, and much more difficult to manage, but taking this approach fosters resiliency in children. Since being a self includes all the messy parts and being good does not, children raised to be themselves are more able to deal with setbacks and mistakes. Children raised to be good have little experience with navigating failures gracefully.

When we hear about the captain of the team or the valedictorian struggling with depression or anxiety or even dying by suicide, we take a collective gasp and utter *why?* The answer may be in this notion of self versus good. The CEO of Spanx, Sara Blakely, tells how her father would go around the dinner table and ask everyone about their tales of failure for the week. At each failure shared, her dad would lift his glass in salute, teaching his children that failure is inevitable and not shameful.[18] Not only that, he was teaching them to be candid with their loved ones, friends, peers, and coworkers. Taking the shame out of failing gives children a pathway to becoming their highest selves. If failure is seen as an enemy, shame and self-hatred will be sure to follow.

Were the McLeans' problems really solved after twenty minutes with Ken?

Definitely not. But Ken helped the family to see that they are each responsible for their own lives and that this personal responsibility makes the path to connection available. Without this clarity, each member of the family could sit in their corner pointing the finger of blame, preventing them from taking responsibility for their life.

That is not to say that others aren't accountable for how they have hurt us or that we aren't accountable for how we have hurt others. But two things can be true: you have valid hurt and anger at another person, AND the feeling is yours to deal with. In essence, we must sort out our own injuries for ourselves, regardless of who may be responsible for injuring us.

---

18 "Spanx Founder: My Dad Encouraged Me to Fail," CNN Business, video, 3:59, March 30, 2018, https://youtu.be/_TeV9op6Mp8.

Reflection Questions

1. What tenets from your religion seem to have caused trouble for you? Before abandoning them outright, can you look at them from a different perspective and see how you might lovingly reinterpret them to your benefit?
2. Can you think of your anger as a teacher and protector? What have you learned from anger in the past?
3. When the McLeans go to therapy together, they discover that many of their fears are unfounded. Is it possible that your own fears may also lose their power when you share them?

39
MICHAEL
Heaven Enough

At Jeff's wedding, Lynne and I felt that we'd been cast as the curious (somewhat homophobic) Mormon parents who were there (somewhat reluctantly) to feign support for a marriage they (probably) considered illegitimate. We felt our every move being watched closely for any signs of disapproval, but I thought we did a pretty good job of accepting and even celebrating the wedding. But Jeff came at us with a tsunami of anger afterward, saying we had not supported him or accepted him the way we had Meggan when she'd gotten married. It's true that we hadn't footed the whole bill for Jeff and Josh, but we had chipped in. We'd also driven from Utah to Vermont with all the sound equipment.

But now Jeff was done with us and never wanted to speak to or hear from us again. I have to admit that, in some ways, it was a melancholy relief. It was exhausting to believe that we had gone above and beyond to connect with him, only to find that every move seemed to be the wrong one.

During that time of estrangement, I found ways to frame myself as the victim of an ungrateful child's rants and raves. I told myself that Jeff's anger was the darker side of his being gay. It had nothing to do with me.

When Jeff called and asked Lynne if we could all go to therapy together, Jeff made it clear that he wanted his mother in his life again, not me. Though he felt it was important for all three of us to attend sessions together, his issues with me were so deep and complicated that he wasn't sure any amount of therapy could bridge the gulf between us.

Before our first session, I knelt in a bathroom stall in Ken's office and blubbered something about how I believed God could do miracles, but that this miracle—a reconciliation between Jeff and me—would probably be a long time coming.

With that prelude, I entered Ken's office with Jeff and Lynne. Though we had all worked with Ken separately, this was our first session all together. Ken set some ground rules before we started.

First, we couldn't tell others how they felt. Second, we needed to listen to *understand* rather than to respond and defend. The second rule revealed to me that oftentimes when I "listened" to my son, I was actually looking for flaws in his reasoning.

At one moment during the session, Jeff was shouting about his anger and pain. The veins in his neck bulged, and his face became almost unrecognizable. Then he went silent, withdrawing into a very private space.

"Wait," he said, breaking the silence. "I just realized something. My whole life, I've been carrying the burden of ruining the lives of everyone in my family. I broke my mother's heart by not getting married to a Mormon girl and having three kids and a picket fence. I ruined my dad's dream of our singing together to help people find hope and happiness in Jesus. I can't carry this burden anymore. It's too heavy."

Ken asked Lynne if Jeff had ruined her life. "No," she said.

He then asked me if Jeff had destroyed my life. "No."

Ken asked if we loved Jeff. "Of course," we replied.

The floodgates opened. Jeff poured out his thoughts, feelings, and insights, continuing as we drove home and on into the night.

Lynne, exhausted, eventually went to bed, but Jeff kept talking. I occasionally chimed in with a nod or a smile or a knowing laugh. Jeff said he didn't want to go to sleep. He wondered what I'd been watching on television.

"Have you seen *Sherlock* with Benedict Cumberbatch?" I asked.

"Not yet, but I want to! I'll make the popcorn, Dad."

Watching movies or television series and then deconstructing them has always been a McLean family pastime. Jeff isn't shy about expressing his feelings during a film. Watching anything with him is sort of a show within a show, and I was thrilled to experience it again after so long.

As we watched *Sherlock* that night, something changed in me that revolutionized how I think about heaven. For Mormons, the highest and happiest place in eternity is the celestial kingdom. Being there forever with our families is the goal of existence. But that night, as we talked and laughed, I realized that the celestial kingdom was *here and now*—eating popcorn and watching *Sherlock* with my son.

That was enough for me.

40

BRAD

Heaven Now

Joseph Campbell explains that prophets speak of the soul, which is to say they talk about the depth of human experience. “Mythology,” he observes, “in other words, is psychology misread as biography, history, and cosmology.”[19] The prophets don’t talk about history or predict the future. Campbell posits that the prophets’ lessons are vertical (rooted in the here and now) rather than horizontal (rippling along a timeline pointing to past and future).

The prophets teach about transformation to another plane, another way of seeing the present world. They talk about heaven not as a literal place but as a way of being in the world and perceiving the world. A rebirth takes place the moment Michael is able to shift and see what is important. Experiencing transformation is

19 Joseph Campbell, *The Hero with a Thousand Faces* (New York: Pantheon Books, 1949).

sublime and may be described through metaphor and poetry—it might be understood only by naming it *heaven*.

Questions for Brad

How could Michael really have thought that Jeff's anger had nothing to do with him?

He had told himself a story that supported his personal goodness. He *had* to be good because he'd been told that being good is the purpose of life. In his reflection, we see the wisdom Michael has gained from his journey. We see the evidence of his work: he has developed a deeper love for his son and has learned to admit his own mistakes.

It is so important for parents, mentors, therapists, and other authority figures to model being human, which includes owning limitations, mistakes, and harm done. Demonstrating these behaviors is even more important because we have few-to-zero examples of deities—the ultimate authority figures—making mistakes or apologizing. We're on our own here, but since we're human, we make mistakes every day. Owning and apologizing without a clear template from God is a heroic human endeavor. As my oldest daughter suggests, "One of the most loving things a parent can do is remain willing to be cast as the villain in their child's story."

I never want to find myself sobbing in a public bathroom stall like Michael. Can this be avoided?

Your experience will not be identical, but we must experience the pain and hopelessness of the old way—we must see its futility—to be open to transformation. Our lives until this point of anguish taught us that the old way is the only way to survive, and indeed, those timeworn practices did (for a time) protect us from pain, from greater suffering. But when our circumstances change so dramatically, the old self must make way for the birth of the new. Desperation, as well as the hope hidden within it, creates the fertile soil that brings new seeds of action to life. Prominent Trappist monk Thomas Keating says it this way: "The spiritual journey is not a career or a success story. It is a series of humiliations of the false self that becomes more and more profound."[20]

I recognized myself in Michael's description of realizing that he never really listened to Jeff. Can you give more information on how to stop that habit?

An insight like Michael's about listening versus defending is clearer in the rearview mirror. It reminds me of a clever contrast someone once shared with me: the opposite of listening is *waiting*—waiting to reply, rebut, and clarify. True listening, the kind that does not involve merely waiting your turn to speak, is called *deep listening*, or *listening to understand.*

Deep listening is a communication skill taught by virtually every therapist and every program treating any kind of disorder. Why is deep listening so important and ubiquitously promoted? Because when we really listen or are really listened to, the experience creates a place for pain and other emotions to be felt. And in feeling our pain, we are able to move through it. In the absence of being heard, we communicate our pain through symptoms.

Deep listening is a hallmark of those who have made peace with themselves and their demons and dragons. They are not

---

20 Thomas Keating, *The Human Condition: Contemplation and Transformation* (New York: Paulist Press, 1999).

threatened by the people they listen to. Mahatma Gandhi explains that "a coward is incapable of exhibiting love; it is the prerogative of the brave." Psychoanalyst James Hollis expands on this, stating that "projection, fusion, 'going home,' are easy. Loving another's otherness is heroic. If we love the Other as Other, we have heroically taken on the responsibility for our own individuation, our own journey. This heroism may properly be called love."[21] Through their willingness to explore themselves, the McLeans found the path to experiencing deeper love. This truly is heroic.

Reflection Questions

1. What do you think of Michael's declaration that he is living in heaven with his son now?
2. How willing are you to let go and allow change to come into your life?
3. How often are you able to truly listen to others? Do you wait instead of listening?

---

21 James Hollis, *The Eden Project: In Search of the Magical Other* (Toronto: Inner City Books, 1998), 57.

41

JEFF

Monster Unleashed

For Josh and me, it was a constant struggle to make our relationship function. Our marriage had all but failed. *I* had undeniably failed. But I wouldn't be a McLean if I didn't keep trying in the face of the impossible. So when we got back to New York, it was time for therapy with Josh.

Our therapist was straight out of Central Casting—nondescript and forgettable. I was happy Josh agreed to show up, but he couldn't acknowledge that he had done anything wrong. On the other hand, I assumed I had done everything wrong. Ultimately, our sessions were useful only in that they proved one thing: our marriage had been over for a while. Josh didn't seem to want to be around me at all, let alone touch me. To me, that meant that he didn't care if I lived or died. And that's what I deserved.

I decided to see a new therapist on my own, someone a friend highly recommended. The therapist's super-chic SoHo office sat on a secluded street, the kind of street where you are bound to see not one but several celebrities sitting outside drinking coffee or having a cigarette—and you know to leave them alone.

During the first session, the therapist asked me question after question and carefully weighed my every answer. He was exactly how I'd imagined God in my childhood and young adulthood: stern, cold, and capable of brilliant, unquestionable judgment.

Him, regal: "How many drinks do you have in a week?"

Me, with fear and trembling: "Well . . . uh, I think like ten or maybe four. I guess it depends on the week."

"Do you cheat on your partner?"

"No. But kind of. Our relationship is sort of open right now, but not really. There was this one time—"

"Just answer the question. Yes or no?"

"Oh . . . um . . . no?"

"Do you think you're a good person or an honest person?"

"Uh . . . "

"Do you do bad things?"

"Doesn't everyone?"

"Just answer."

This went on for an hour. No empathy, no understanding, just a list of questions. Like my old God.

Session two was a week later. I entered the office and sat down. The therapist left for a minute and returned with some papers. He sat before me, leaving an eerie silence between us as he looked at the sheet in front of him.

Then he read forth his verdict: "Based on your responses and your body language, this is what I have determined: You're an alcoholic and drug addict. You are a liar and a cheat. You are totally responsible for everything that has happened to you, and IT'S ALL YOUR FAULT."

He waited for a response. I had none, so he pushed further and deeper.

"You are a failure in your life. You are an alcoholic because you drink more than four units a week. You are a drug addict because you use drugs for recreation and to deal with your relationships.

"You don't take responsibility for cheating because you say you are in an open relationship.

"You lie so much that you don't even know you are lying. It has become like breathing to you.

"You want to blame your parents for the failure of your life. If you didn't have them to blame, you would find somebody else.

"You are not a good person, and you don't know that you are as bad as you actually are."

He kept going, my ears and brain distorting his words for full minutes at a time.

He finished and sat there in silence.

I had been weighed in the balance and been found wanting.

I didn't say anything for a while. I just sat there. Eventually, "Yeah, okay," was all I could muster.

And the session was over.

As I walked out of his office, I felt like the earth was crumbling under my feet. The only kind of authority figure I knew how to give credence to at this point in my life had explained to me just how terrible I really was. No ounce of love or empathy or *Oh my God, tell me about it.*

Hearing it out loud was rough, but the truth is, I had been saying these exact same things in my head for years.

I walked to the subway, incessantly thinking, *It's all my fault. I deserve it.*

For years, decades, I'd kept the Unlovable Monster imprisoned so deep that I'd evaded the full measure of its message. But now its shackles shattered. The monster grew gigantic, tearing through all of the layers of protection I had meticulously built up. It snorted out its three words:

You.

Are.

Unlovable.

Now that I had submitted to hearing the words, I had to believe them. The words were true. I couldn't hide from the truth or deflect it. It was proven and written in stone.

On the A train from Spring Street to 181st Street, I stared at the yellow-and-orange subway bench in front of me and cried, but not in a sobbing, ugly-cry way. I'd never cried like this: staring blankly ahead, seemingly infinite tears pouring out of my eyes. I held my bag, my body numb, and repeated the truth over and over in my head for the full thirty-minute ride. *You are unlovable, and it's all your fault.*

When I reached 181st Street, I stood to exit the train. All at once, a sharp pain throughout my body overrode the numbness. I walked along the platform in a daze. Rode the elevator up to the street. Walked across the park and into my apartment. Josh was gone. He was always gone. But for once, I was grateful.

I put my bag down, and the sharp pain worsened along my right side and my right inner thigh. I walked into the bedroom and took off my clothes in front of the mirror. A red and blistery field blazed from my right knee to my armpit. I stood and looked at my body for I don't know how long. I swear I saw more blisters form right before my eyes. Some of them looked like pustules. I tried touching the rash, and I winced.

I'm a great one for physical manifestations, apparently. Just as the emergence of unmistakable sexual attraction had set me to shaking uncontrollably a few years before, the Unlovable Monster's dramatic arrival into my conscious mind seemed to have left its mark all over my physical body. What could this be? I turned on my computer and looked up my symptoms online.

Shingles. Shingles? The virus that plagues the elderly? I was barely in my thirties!

I went back to the mirror and stood there, covered in sores. Sores I deserved because it was all my fault and I was unworthy of love.

I knew two things in that moment:

First, I would never go back to that therapist.

Second, I wanted to die.

✣

I had always told Josh that I didn't want to have any deal breakers. I believed that deal breakers were just a crutch for people who are too cowardly to break up. The truth is that I did have a deal breaker: I wanted to start a family. And Josh stepped across the line.

We were on the phone one day when the end was so near it was almost tangible. Josh was in Florida doing *Hello, Dolly!,* and I was sitting on a slope in Fort Tryon Park in upper Manhattan. Josh said he didn't want a family. He couldn't provide for one. He'd crossed the line, but he still couldn't say the words to end it.

And then I felt something vaguely familiar, like the distant memory of a feeling. God's spirit. God and I weren't close then, and maybe that's why the feeling was so faint. But soon a voice spoke: *Let him go. Love him by letting him go.*

So I said the words Josh couldn't say. I presented all of the compelling reasons why divorcing was the best for us. Finally, I told him that if he didn't want to have a family with me, I was going to leave him, and he said, "Please do. I'm done."

After that day, God's spirit was drowned out by the crowing of the Unlovable Monster. I couldn't get out of bed. My mom flew out to help, but I was irredeemable. There I was, a pioneer in gay marriage, and I had failed. Mom went home without budging me.

It was Meggan who woke me up. She called and said, "Come home. I bought you a ticket because I need you to sing at a conference."

There was the faint feeling again, and the good voice breaking through the monster's noise: *Go home, Jeff. Go home.*

Then the voice came stronger: *Go home so you can heal.*

I told Meggan I would come. Five days later, I packed one bag and left everything else behind.

I never went back. I moved to Utah and started over.

42

BRAD

Hearing the Quiet Part Out Loud

The voices in our heads come not just from what our parents say to us or from the rules posted on the fridge. The inner voices we develop come from our parents' *feelings* and *thoughts* about us. We end up thinking and feeling about ourselves the way our parents do. A child whose parents are worried, upset, frustrated, or angry develops a sense that something is wrong with them, not with their parents.

We must undergo a profound awakening to the realities we experienced in childhood that led to our sense of self, or lack thereof. This awakening often comes from sustained exposure to a loving and empathic other—such as a good therapist—over a significant period of time.

Question for Brad

Jeff's experience with the last therapist is terrifying, but bad therapy might not always be that obvious. How can you tell if a therapist is good or not?

First, assess how the therapist makes you feel. Do you feel seen, safe, and listened to? Empathy isn't just the appetizer in good therapy—it's the main dish. Master therapists are master listeners, priding themselves on what they *don't* say. A therapist may be right or wrong with their diagnosis, their "verdict," but that's not where the gold is. The gold is in the therapist's creating a space where the client feels safe enough to lower their walls just a bit.

Second, confront the therapist on ways they have hurt you, upset you, or made you feel uncomfortable. An inadequate therapist will turn it back on you to preserve their "expert" position. An adequate or good therapist, however, will welcome genuine dialogue and say something like, "I am so sorry. Thank you for telling me that. It must take a lot of courage for you to say that, and I feel honored that you would be willing to share it with me. I will see if I can do better."

A good therapist will have the capacity to sit with us in our unsolvable problems. Yes, some problems are unsolvable. Most dilemmas have consequences regardless of which direction we ultimately choose. If these issues were simple, we wouldn't need therapists. We would just make a list of pros and cons, tally the ledger, and act accordingly. But that is not how life (or therapy) works.

Reflection Questions

1. Have you or someone you love had a bad experience in therapy before? Did you find a better therapist or eschew therapy altogether?
2. Do you relate to Jeff's experience with his Unlovable Monster? Have you even had physical symptoms from trying to repress the negative voices?

43

MICHAEL

What Kind of Father?

When Jeff's marriage and musical theater career came to an end, I could feel his sadness from 2,500 miles away. I wondered if I should fly back to New York so he wouldn't do anything permanently tragic for a temporary heartache.

I called him about scheduling a trip to the city, but when I heard the despair in his voice, I said instead, "Jeff, why don't you just come home?"

His two-word response broke my heart:

"Can I?"

It was such a heavy moment for both of us—heavy with fear for Jeff and heavy with regret for me. What kind of father raises his children to ever question if they can come home?

After a few beats of painful silence, I said, "What good is having a gay son if he can't come home and help his mom redecorate?"

I had hoped to hear a laugh. None came. But Jeff did come home.

When Jeff had asked, "Can I?" he wasn't questioning only whether he could come home to our family. He was asking if he could come home to Heber—the predominantly Mormon community he had abandoned because he felt like they'd abandoned him. But the good people of our little town rallied. At the market I'd hear, "Hey, I heard Jeff's back. Can't wait to see him." Their love for him was palpable. Whatever had happened in his life didn't change this. A well-known and much-loved Mormon hymn echoes Jesus's words, "As I have loved you, love one another." Even with all their flaws and shortcomings, our community kept this commandment beautifully.

44

BRAD

Safe Harbor

We (parents and children) have no instructions to go along with each of our individual paths. We have only our hearts, our souls, and love to guide us. So, what is your goal with your child? Do you want to be a safe person they can come to when they are in their most difficult and dark spots? That is a worthy and attainable goal. Despite all their problems through the years, Jeff still saw Michael as a somewhat safe harbor when he had nowhere else to turn and was considering ending his life.

Many parents would defend themselves against Jeff's implicit accusation that he is unwelcome, but Michael has developed the capacity to accept Jeff's indictment. It takes courage to see that our children's reactions to us reflect, in part, how we have treated them. I suppose that in the end, every parent must choose between being right (accepting their child only if they live "correctly") or being connected to a wonderful, beautiful, flawed, and lovable child. I am grateful for Jeff that his father chose the latter, and I am also happy for Michael that he discovered the meaning of God and heaven while still on earth.

Reflection Questions

1. Do you feel like your parents' home is still one you could return to? Why or why not?
2. If you are a parent, how will you let your children know that they are always welcome?

PART 4

Exposed

45

JEFF

Source

I pulled up to the McLean estate, back where everything had begun. It felt strange, but I knew it was right. Even before the voice told me in no uncertain terms to go home and heal, I'd heard gentler whisperings along the same lines while I'd taken contemplative walks around Washington Heights with my Ruby Girl. God had been guiding me home for a good while.

Although I knew I was supposed to be here, it did not make perfect sense. I'd learned to hate myself in this house. In the church down the street, I'd learned I was unworthy of God's love. How long would I have to be here? What would my healing look like? I started by simply getting up every day—even though I didn't want to most of the time. On good days, I even made my bed.

I was not sure what to do for work. I'd been singing nonstop since I was eight, and I had a PhD's worth of experience and training. But the singing had dried up. I couldn't do it. This seemed an impossible turn of events for someone who had sung day and night most of his life—I mean, I would sing in the grocery store without realizing it until someone would come up and say *You have such a lovely voice.* Those days were done. I was broken.

Maybe I wanted a "real" job—I could become a dental hygienist or a sensible X-ray technician. But as the days passed and I got ever so slightly stronger, I felt the pull of music again. I wasn't sure what to do with that, but I was certain I wouldn't be going back to musical theater or touring.

I started by giving Jann a call. It had been twenty years since she and Onstage had saved my life, but we'd kept in touch. She'd come to all of my shows through the years.

We met at her studio in Holladay, a suburb of Salt Lake City. I asked her a question I'd been asking myself the preceding few days: "Should I teach voice?" With no hesitation, she said, "Yes! You have more experience with Seth Riggs than anyone in Utah, so you can charge a lot. And you can teach here for free until you get enough students to afford rent."

And that was that. In ten minutes' time, I decided to teach, nabbed a studio, and set my price at $100/hour. Blessed, miraculous Jann had saved me yet again. She even helped me find my first students, and she continued to funnel kids my way.

As my vocal studio picked up steam, it became clear that I'd found more than just a way to earn money and spend my time. I'd found my purpose: I would teach people how to find their voices, even if I had lost mine.

I was informed enough to know that some flavor of depression had robbed me of my voice. *Have you lost interest in the things you once enjoyed?* asked the internet depression quiz. *Yes, indeed*, I replied. I needed the tools to get out of the despair, to keep the Unlovable Monster at a manageable size, and to find my voice again.

Just in time, along came another living example of the divine feminine: Kelly, my angel.

An inspired Google search brought us together. Kelly was preparing to audition for American Idol, and she wanted the help of a local voice teacher. The gods put me at the top of the search results.

Kelly arrived at her first lesson dressed like a magnificent Instagram influencer who had just breezed in from some exotic location like Tulum or Sardinia. I knew right away that I wanted to be more than just a teacher to Kelly. I wanted to be her best friend. Soon, my wish was granted. Kelly's husband was out of town doing sales that first season of our friendship, and we embarked on what would become the Kelly and Jeff Summer of Wonders. If Jann and Simone had taught me unconditional love and Semhar had taught me how to be unapologetic, Kelly taught me how to connect to myself.

Both at a crossroads in our lives, Kelly and I embarked on a spiritual journey together. Around the time we met, Kelly had seen a clairvoyant healer and shaman that she swore by, and I decided to go in for a reading too. In the upstairs of a Harmons grocery in Draper, Utah, the clairvoyant gave me a spot-on reading. Regardless of the unconventional space and my general skepticism, I was blown away. The shaman saw me so clearly that I knew I needed to learn more from her. She was going to teach an eight-week chakra class, and Kelly and I decided to take it together.

We learned new things about beautiful and ancient traditions, about energy and our bodies, and about tribes. The shaman told me that I had no connection to the root chakra, the one tied to family. Without a bond to this chakra, I was unrooted and tribeless. Over eight weeks, the shaman guided me to find a connection. During each session, she asked me to silence my mind, and she walked me through the process of feeling myself in my body. Depending on how busy my mind was on a given day, this process was sometimes easy and quick and sometimes decidedly not. When I managed to achieve mindful connection with my body, the shaman would ask me to envision a cord that started at the base of my spine. I imagined the cord as a bundle of fiber-optic cables emitting light. This cord reached into the earth and sprouted roots like a tree. Using my light-up roots, I could draw up the earth's strength and nourishment.

Of course, it took me a long time to feel like a glowing tree. The first several times I tried to stretch my cord into the earth, I felt keenly that the earth didn't want me. With my eyes closed, I'd say to the shaman, "I don't belong. Mother Earth will only reject me." I started to understand why I had bounced around so much in my life, never settling. I'd always believed in my core that I didn't belong anywhere. I was now learning that I had to heal the part of myself that kept me from a sense of belonging. The shaman helped me to see that Earth didn't hate me, that I *could* rest my feet on the ground and draw in power and love and abundance.

The first time my cord tapped into Earth, it was mind-blowing. Through the connection between my root chakra and Earth, I found I could also access Source. (*Source* is a woo-woo word I use to refer to the abundant power of the universe, the wonder that exists under our feet and all around us.) This shamanic experience was my first time practicing a new kind of faith and belief. No longer was God some white guy sitting up in heaven judging me. God was everything.

I was getting just a little closer to developing the spiritual tools I needed in order to deal with the Unlovable Monster. I had to build the case that I *was* lovable. These new meditative practices helped me fight the overwhelming conditioning from my childhood. I became glad that I'd been kicked out of the church so I could find something that worked for me.

✣

I had been teaching for six months when I got a call from my dear friend Kristin Hanggi. An accomplished and heavenly being, she is one of a handful of women to be nominated for the Best Direction of a Musical Tony (for *Rock of Ages*).

I met Kristin back in my early LA days through Rye Mullis, the casting director I had dated. Rye took me to Kristin's super-cool Silver Lake house. I walked in and immediately knew that this was the home of an enchanted person. We ordered pizza and watched a video of a play Kristin had directed off-Broadway, *bare: a pop opera*. It is a coming-out musical, like nothing I'd ever seen growing up in a family that had meticulously avoided anything with gay undertones, and I know Kristin and Rye were showing it to me to help nudge me all the way out of the closet. The two of them held my hand during that confusing time of my life, and I'll always be grateful to both of them. Rye died at forty-two in 2023, another dear friend gone too soon.

Soon after I met her, Kristin relocated to New York, where she's mostly been ever since. When she was working on a screenplay, I invited her to Heber for a week of mountain air and uninterrupted writing. We also spent several Sundance Film Festivals together (Heber is a hop, skip, and a jump from Park City, the epicenter of all things Sundance).

When Kristin called me six months into my return to Utah, she told me the screenplay she'd been working on in Heber was being produced—and she was the director too! It was a movie musical called *Dear Dumb Diary* and would be filmed in Utah.

Kristin invited me to meet with her and executive producer Janet Zucker. Janet is Hollywood royalty, along with her husband, superstar writer/director/producer Jerry Zucker. Over lunch at the Grand America Hotel in downtown Salt Lake City, Kristin and Janet offered me a job: vocal coach for the production. I took it!

The lead actor, Emily Alyn Lind, didn't have any official vocal training, so I took a month off of my regular teaching schedule, moved to LA, and gave daily voice lessons to Emily. It was like vocal boot camp.

I loved Emily instantly. She was bright and inquisitive and knew exactly who she was. I got to share my knowledge with someone who was hungry to learn, and the stakes were high. Did Emily and I make it? You better believe we did. We delivered big and then some.

The validation felt spectacular. I'd failed at marriage and my musical theater career, but I could do this. I was broken, but I could still give everything I had to this project and this breathtaking little person. If I wasn't sold on teaching before, I was all in now. I could see that Emily was teaching me as much or more than I was teaching her.

When I said I'd moved to LA to teach Emily, I left out a little detail: I stayed at Janet and Jerry Zucker's Mandeville Canyon home, a magical mystery land of lush moss growing on ancient trees, the air scented with rose, bougainvillea, and jasmine. The house was somehow both stunning and warm and personal, an incubator where I could be my best self. It's true that, at first, I was nervous to meet Jerry, but he was so humble, sweet, and loving that I soon forgot he was a Very Fancy Man, the mind behind some of my favorite movies: *My Best Friend's Wedding*, *First Knight*, and *Airplane!* After only a month in the Zucker house, I was calling him "Jair Bear." (Did he like this? I have no idea. But he and Janet would let me lie on their bed with them for hours while we talked about our dreams and aspirations.)

Mama Janet was that kind of mother who is bossy in the most beautiful way. "It's cold outside, Jeff, you need a coat," she'd say. And I'd be like, "No, Janet, I think I'm okay," and she'd be like, "No, no, I think you need a coat!" On would go my coat, of course. I can't help but give in to that variety of mildly domineering affection.

With Janet Zucker as my number one cheerleader, my parents were getting calls from LA friends, the common theme being, "Everyone is talking about Jeff! What's he up to?" So not only was I an excellent teacher, I was a mover and shaker to boot!

After a month, we all headed to Utah to begin production. On Team Emily, our first task was to record all of Emily's vocals before we started the three-month shoot.

I love being on movie sets. It reminds me of being a kid and visiting my dad when he was the big-shot director for church films. This time around, Kristin was at the helm, and I got to spend time with her and be in awe of her directing prowess. I also got to know Janet better. She took me under her wing and made it clear that she believed in me. On top of that, she was so much fun. I could listen to her stories of life in the film industry all day. Working with Janet is among my most treasured experiences.

⁂

Before working on the movie, I'd been commuting about ninety miles every day between Heber and Jann's studio to teach. After a few months of that, I decided to start looking at houses in Salt Lake so I could lay down some roots and have a mortgage like a real adult.

Dad helped me with the search (and the down payment). We were looking in Sugar House, a super-charming neighborhood in Salt Lake proper. We focused on fixer-uppers, but then a perfect turnkey home became available in what is called the ABC streets (the street names are in alphabetical order: Alden, Beverley, Chadwick, etc. Dearborn was my home sweet home). The house was gorgeous and refurbished exactly how I would have done it myself. I snapped it up! I figured it was worth the cost since this was where I would share a life with a partner and start a new family. So I went blithely into debt—hundreds of thousands of dollars' worth.

My neighbors were an eclectic mix of old and young, Mormons and non-Mormons. On my first day, a woman from next door came over and introduced herself to me and Meggan, who was helping me move in.

"Hi, I'm Charlayne," she said. (This is not her real name. But that's about how stereotypically Utah Mormon this woman's name was. If you know, you know.) Then, pointing at Meggan and taking on the tone of a Spanish inquisitor, she asked, "Is this your wife?"

"Nope, this is my sister," I responded. Now to blow her mind: "I just moved from New York after divorcing my ex-husband."

She smiled in a glazed-over way and left quickly. I had clearly rocked her world. I heard later that she went up and down the street spreading the news that A Gay had moved in. She had apparently been hoping to mobilize the troops against me, but luckily, my other neighbors had no time for her bigotry. Demoralized, she and her family moved away in three months' time. Over the next two or three years, the other neighbors would mosey up to me as I worked in my yard and thank me for moving in and driving out that nightmare neighbor. Apparently everyone, Mormon or not, had met with her disapproval in some way or other. I even received gifts and cards of gratitude for unseating the troll. That's Sugar House.

Salt Lake at large is an interesting world to live in, especially as a gay man. A lot of gay people live there, but no one is looking for friendship. In New York, people are looking for friends—because people in New York aren't from New York. But every gay man in Salt Lake is from there or connected to Utah in some way. They all have family nearby, and they've known their friends for twenty years. If you're not going to be their partner or husband, they don't need you. When I threw a housewarming party, only my divine friend Kelly showed up.

Kelly's influence was profound, and journeying with her had given me powerful insights and tools. However, I often found that I simply couldn't bring myself to use these tools. The Unlovable Monster, increasing in size again, was understandably resistant to anything that required me to poke around its lair too much. It much preferred my using drugs to find connection. As I met more people in Salt Lake, I partied with them, using love drugs like ecstasy and shrooms, maybe the occasional bit of cocaine. For every friend like Kelly I found in Salt Lake, I had five or six more who colluded with my monster, using drugs alongside me—or using *me*.

46

BRAD

Role Reversal

It's no mystery that the student is often the teacher. This is true in our professional lives as well as our personal lives. So many of us parents think that our primary role as a parent is to be the teacher, the guide, and the one with all the answers. But as in Jeff's experience with Emily, the roles are often reversed. *Our students and our children are here to teach us*, and we will be open to their lessons if we can see the journey for what it is. I often playfully point out to the parents I work with that if I were God and I wanted to teach them the lessons they needed to learn, I would send their children—with their specific issues—to be their schoolmasters.

Welcoming this role reversal suggests we are ready to adopt a perspective of radical acceptance, no longer focusing on the question "What SHOULD be happening?" This acceptance allows us to open ourselves up to the experiences that life's detours have to offer us. If, however, we think our children or students are *supposed* to get back on a certain track, we may miss important lessons.

Questions for Brad

Jeff wonders at first whether it was a good idea to go home to the place that had wounded him. What do you think?

One of my goals as a therapist is to create experiences that compete with a client's trauma and attendant shame. By going home, Jeff creates such a competing experience. He is back to where it all started, and he creates positive experiences in the actual setting of much of his trauma. This real-life rewriting can powerfully counteract the effects of trauma.

Jeff's competing experience works also because his childhood home is, in many important ways, no longer the same. It is different because Jeff is different, and so are Michael and Lynne. With the emergence of new knowledge and a deeper understanding of love and of their individual responsibilities in relationships, Jeff and his family can begin anew. It is in this atmosphere that Jeff rediscovers the most authentic parts of himself. This does not mean he is out of the woods or that he won't endure many more hardships. That's life. It simply means that he has been able to reprogram home and family as safe harbors.

Why did Jeff think that Mother Earth would reject him?

James Hollis explains, "The truth about intimate relationships is that they can never be any better than our relationship with ourselves."[22] Our earliest contexts and relationships set the patterns for all other relationships, and without intervention, we can expect these patterns to continue ad infinitum. Such patterns shape

22 James Hollis, *The Middle Passage: From Misery to Meaning in Middle Life* (Toronto: Inner City Books, 1993), 47.

how we come to see ourselves, so given Jeff's background and experience, what else could he expect but rejection?

Going back and finding the origins of our defense mechanisms provides us with a sense of safety and the experience of being seen, if only by ourselves. When a client comes in with a seemingly problematic behavior, I say, "Instead of thinking of this behavior as the problem, let's think about it as the solution." From there, we can ask, "What problem is it solving?" Taking this route effectively uncovers many of the patterns from which our problems originate.

This excavation yields new insights that form a foundation upon which we can build the skills suggested by our therapists or self-help gurus of choice.

I want to emphasize that we often can't do this work on our own. We are wounded in relationships, and we are healed in relationships. So much of our woundedness comes from the messages in the external world. In that context, the idea of picking ourselves up by our bootstraps is quite crazy. We need affirmations. But not affirmations about our pretty parts, the successful aspects of ourselves, or our accomplishments. We need somebody who can see all of us: the beauty and the horrible, rotten self. Healing happens in that kind of relationship.

Reflection Questions

1. Is it easy or difficult for you to accept others' less-than-perfect selves? How has your approach to others affected your relationship with yourself?
2. As a parent, what have your children taught you? As a child, did you ever feel that your parents learned from you?

3. What do you think about the idea that we are wounded in relationships and we are healed in relationships?

47

JEFF

Christopher

With Kelly and our explorations taking a back seat, it should come as no surprise that a certain recurring issue was back in control: I still couldn't value connection with myself and Earth and Source above the connection I could have with the "perfect" partner. The search was on. Josh was already in another relationship. It only made sense that I would find one soon as well. I looked ideal on paper and was even a little bit Utah famous because of my dad. This time, a relationship was going to work. It had to. I needed to shut the Unlovable Monster down, and partnership would prove beyond a doubt that I was lovable.

I got on Tinder for the first time since my divorce, and I matched with the drop-dead gorgeous Christopher, who lived in Seattle but was in town for a wedding. We agreed to get together at my place the next day. Since he lived out of town, I could let my guard down. I wouldn't be seeing him all the time, or possibly ever again.

I can still replay the scene when Christopher walked into my life. He showed up late (I would come to learn he was always late), shoegazing as he walked up my path and front steps. When I opened the door (yes, I'd been looking at him through a window), he finally looked up and pulled his long, dark hair away from his face. His beauty and charisma rendered the gregarious Jeff McLean momentarily speechless.

After a few hours, it became clear that this man was going to be my partner. He would fix all of my problems and slay the Unlovable Monster once and for all to prove that I was, in fact, lovable.

No pressure, of course.

To be clear, I didn't say any of this on our first date. How would that have sounded? "Oh hey, Christopher, it's nice to meet you. I'm excited for you to fix all of my insecurities and finally give me purpose. You are clearly the embodiment of everything I need to be happy." Yes, that would have driven him away—but it would have been honest.

Instead of saying the truth, we read tarot cards and talked for hours. He was the first man I'd ever fallen in love with who'd also been raised Mormon and lived a similar life. We got each other.

And just like that, nothing else in life mattered. Remember my cute house and my dynamite teaching studio? My profound spiritual progress? Irrelevant. I was in love.

Christopher invited me on his family vacation—a mere week after meeting—and of course, I said yes.

In gay culture, there's a perennial joke about how quickly lesbians move in relationships:

What does a lesbian bring on a first date? Flowers and chocolates.

What does a lesbian bring on a second date? A U-Haul.

Christopher and I were lesbians in disguise.

We bonded on vacation, and his parents and I also fell in love. After the trip, Christopher met Mike and Lynne. Everything was going swimmingly. Or so I thought.

With Christopher, I was on a mission to overdo it big time so I could silence the monstrous voice inside my head. I needed this man to make me happy and take away my pain.

About two weeks in, things start to slip. And the things that slipped with Christopher were pretty big red flags—like end-of-first-act–*Les Misérables* red flags. Filling-three-quarters-of-the-stage, impossible-to-miss red flags—such as the little fact that Christopher had a boyfriend back in Seattle.

Do you think this revelation registered with me at all? No, it did not. I couldn't hear it. How could any other relationship possibly compare to ours?

As we maintained a long-distance relationship, I agreed to some awful things, distorting reality to make room for one where Christopher and I were partners. I would visit him in Seattle, and we would fight endlessly. I put up with every cruel barb, every proof that I was not important to him.

On the other hand, I had expectations for him that no one could live up to. Anytime Christopher did something counter to what I wanted, I went crazy. For example, if he said he'd be somewhere at nine and then show up at 9:15, I'd lose it.

If Christopher called or messaged, I dropped everything. I had zero boundaries. Frankly, I had no idea what boundaries even were. He got married while I was in love with him, and I still didn't slow down.

I followed the same pattern I had since my time with Josh: I threw drugs at the relationship. When I got high with Christopher, we felt an intoxicating connection—which would, of course, start fraying as soon as we were sober.

Our involvement lasted for two years. When I think about those years with Christopher now, I am reminded of another two-year period of my life: my church mission. Here I was again, dedicating two years of my life to making something unworkable work. And if it didn't work, it would prove I was unlovable.

Unlike with my church mission, regular life had to go on during the Christopher mission. I taught singing and tried to build financial stability—and pay a mortgage—in a fickle business. Students came and went, and since a lot of them were school age, I could teach only from two to eight o'clock. I wanted a second job where I could work from ten to two. I asked the music chair at a nearby college if I could teach there. He said I could have a job after I finished my bachelor's, so I headed back to school. Classes cost money, of course, but I reasoned that tuition would bring dividends in the long run. While in school, I finished my basement and rented it out, one of the only sound decisions I made during this period.

Another career prospect arose: Janet Zucker helped me establish a studio in LA. For a while, I flew back and forth to maintain both studios. I had a problem, though. I was too distracted with trying to get Christopher to marry me to care about the kinds of opportunities my LA studio could have afforded me. Ultimately, I closed it down because I would have had to move to LA to make it really successful. I was too obsessed, too in debt, too riddled with self-doubt to go all in.

At the height of juggling the two studios, I was still going broke. How was that possible? Perhaps all the travel. The college tuition, sure. My increasing drug habit didn't help. That little bit of cocaine became a little *more* cocaine, and the intervals between parties were shrinking. The main culprit in my money situation, though, was my house, or rather my attitude toward it. My insecurity required me to make my house look perfect. I spent oodles on landscaping and lawn care because if my house and yard were beautiful, it would prove that I was worthy to live in my home. Just like so many of my decisions, it was about proving the Unlovable Monster wrong. But I couldn't fund everything for much longer, even with the rental income from the basement apartment.

To cope with the fact that I struggled with being an adult, I clung to anything Christopher offered, but these crumbs grew fewer and farther between. I needed more survival tools, more things to distract me. I filled my time with random sexual encounters, drinking a bit here, doing some recreational drugs there, ordering massive pizzas (if you know The Pie in Salt Lake, you know what I'm talking about), finding friends willing to keep me company along the path toward oblivion. Certainly not maintaining any kind of spiritual health.

The final straw was inviting myself to Christopher's birthday party. I'm almost certain that I lied and told him my trip was for some other reason. I bought a hot outfit but played it casual. It makes me so sad to envision myself during this time. The things I allowed myself to believe and cling to were flimsy and absurd.

The party was at a club you had to be invited into, so I waited outside for two and a half hours before the guest of honor and his entourage arrived (remember that Christopher is always late). Once everyone finally showed up, it was clear that not one of Christopher's closest friends knew of my existence before that night. I wished Christopher a happy birthday, and he said he was grateful I'd come. He went back to his other guests, which made me feel like I was disposable. I believed that if he cared for me at all, he should want to shower me with attention! I knew then that

I'd been trying to force something that wasn't meant to happen. I was convinced that I was an embarrassment to this man. I *knew* I was an embarrassment to myself. Of course I was. I told myself I'd always been an embarrassment to somebody—to my church, to my family, to Josh.

When I left the party, I thought I had never felt so empty. But I had felt this empty many times. It was so familiar. I was alone, and I deserved it. I had failed once again at making someone love me, because I was unlovable.

Sitting in the airport to head home, I ruminated over the whole two years. As with Josh, I'd betrayed myself in every way for the chance to be partnered. My behavior had been ridiculous and aggressive, but I couldn't help myself. I was like an automaton repeating a pattern over and over again. With a sinking feeling, I knew I was doomed to a life of unhappiness. I would continue to ignore every good instinct because all I wanted was to belong to someone.

I later learned that most of life is an effort to prove or protect. Instead of just living my life, I was living to prove that the Unlovable Monster was wrong. I overcompensated and tried too hard. At other times, I was busy protecting myself from any suggestion that the monster was right. I protected myself through manipulation, stopping at nothing to prove that I was worthy, even though I didn't believe it.

48

BRAD

Burden of Proof

Trying to prove to the world that you are worthy requires a tremendous amount of energy. If we could escape childhood with the sense that we are okay, we could use that energy to give a gift to the world, to give love to the world. But most of us aren't so lucky. Jeff was not lucky in this way. If the legacy of our childhoods is that we are not enough or that who we are is not worthy of love, we pursue avenues that make us *seem* enough and worthy: Education. Professional success. Money. Being invited to the coolest parties. Again, all of that requires energy.

When I was going through one of my midlife crises, a friend gave me the book *Death of a Hero, Birth of the Soul: Answering the Call of Midlife.*[23] It describes the point in life when people surrender the project of trying to be good, of trying to save the day. This surrender is the *hero death*. After this—and only after this—can the hero embark on becoming themselves.

23 John C. Robinson, *Death of a Hero, Birth of the Soul: Answering the Call of Midlife* (Tulsa, OK: Council Oak Books, 1997).

When we give up the futile project to be "good," we can spend our time and energy loving people, but love can only be love when we have enough to overflow with it. That means we have to learn to love ourselves.

Questions for Brad

Okay, but how do I learn to love myself?

People ask me this every day. I'm sure there are many ways to do this, but the one I have found to be most effective is to find somebody—a friend, a therapist—who shows up for you in a way that reveals your lovability. Jeff is not quite there yet in the story. He still has some time to go before his hero death will occur.

Jeff expresses a lot of shame about his relationship with Christopher. I really relate, but you've said that there's no such thing as healthy shame. How do you "unshame" situations like this one?

Think about how common it is. We all experience this temporary loss of our senses. Life moves differently when you're falling in love. You can lose your appetite. You can be inclined to let everything else in your life fall to a distant second, third, or fourth place in the list of priorities. The prospect of someone filling our emptiness is so exhilarating that our minds become distorted. Some call it a love-induced psychosis.

Every story of mishap, every story of falling into the deep hole, though, is an opportunity for us to learn what is missing instead of hiding under the cover of anger and shame. From the vantage point of shame, we can only peek out long enough to blame the other person for betraying us, for deceiving us about who they really are. Of course, both parties are guilty of the bait and switch. Nobody goes on a first date without carefully considering their outfit, wearing their best makeup, and putting on their brightest, most charming face. And this is supposed to be a recipe for getting to know someone?

The real work, of course, comes when the blindness subsides and we decide if we're willing to do the work of healing our wound ourselves. If we've found a partner who is willing to wake up to that same project, then that relationship can become a lifelong union.

Reflection Questions

1. Have you ever lost yourself in an impossible relationship? Have you done this repeatedly?
2. What role have proving and protecting had in your life? Have you seen your parents or your children prioritizing prove and protect?

49

Jeff

In the aftermath of Christopher, I used people to validate me, and I used alcohol and drugs like ecstasy, LSD, and coke to shrink the Unlovable Monster and quiet its voice. That's not to say I was living a life of reckless abandon in Drugland. Not yet. I was using more and more, but not all day, every day. I was a functional person who used drugs recreationally. Sure, this form of recreation was becoming quite frequent, but I liked to brag that I could always get myself home.

But then I started to get closer to the danger zone. I would use and drink to cope with any feelings, people, or situations I couldn't handle. And then I started to create conditions that I had to cope with so I would have good reasons to use. For example, I would pick a fight with one of my friends so that I could prove I was unlovable. Voila! The perfect excuse to use.

I hung out with a lot of people who were worse off than I was. In fact, I started taking in people who had nowhere else to stay. It may sound like generosity, but it was actually a sign that my downward spiral was beginning. If I kept people around who were a little more out of control than I was, it made me look good. One guy I took in was a drug dealer and user. I shot up meth with him once to see what it was like. It was awful. It kept me awake forever.

Oh, hold up, you might be saying. *Did Jeff just say he shot up meth?* For some of you, that means something, but others may be like I was: totally naïve to the magnitude of shooting up such a powerful drug (as opposed to snorting, smoking, or swallowing it). Basically, shooting up meth gives you an immediate, very intense high and is more likely to lead to hardcore addiction. It also puts you at higher risk of overdosing. I was clueless to all of this. I'd grown up with the mindset that all sins—smoking cigarettes, drinking coffee, theft, adultery, murder—were just plain bad and to be avoided. Consequently, I didn't have any sense of nuance when I took up some of those taboo vices myself.

Soon after I shot up meth for the second time (yes, I tried it again even though I hated it), I got some news that proved to be my tipping point. Remember that college job? The one I'd gone back to school for? The one I needed in order to afford my life? It was taken right out from under me and given to someone else.

Devastated, I felt like I'd run out of options. Sure, I could have become a bank teller or a grocery clerk during my nonteaching hours, but these jobs would do nothing to prove what a big deal I was.

With my hopes snatched away and financial ruin at the door, I decided it was time to die, but I couldn't go through with suicide outright. What would surely kill me yet keep me numb in the process? I knew just the thing: Meth. I'd seen it destroy the lives of so many gay men, and I believed I had a life ripe for destruction.[24]

Meth had another benefit, I thought. If I chose to take such a self-destructive path, God would have no choice but to abandon me. And I was more than ready to sever all ties with God or Spirit or Source. I didn't deserve any of their attention or love, and they stopped getting mine. Prayer and meditation and all of that other woo-woo nonsense would now be things of the past.

At first, I would shoot up every other week or so, just enough to escape into my thoughts. When I was high, my shame evaporated, and I felt like a million goddamn dollars—until I didn't. Then I wanted to die more than ever. I actually felt most connected to this comedown phase: ten days of feeling depressed, drained of life, repeating to myself phrases along the lines of *I can't have any of what I need to be happy. I deserve my fate.* I also had an excuse to do nothing. When you spend your life getting over your latest high, you don't have to make decisions or move forward. You just wait to feel better so you can get high again.

My meth suicide march had begun in mid-autumn. By Thanksgiving, I was using in isolation, shooting up and staying up all night. I spent most of the winter high, making discoveries and saying things I couldn't say when I was sober. Tapping into a spiritual plane, I learned things about God I'd never been taught. I was dumbfounded because I'd thought for sure I'd given God the slip, but there God still was, revealing to me the patterns of my partnership obsession. Could these insights be real? Or were they the fruits of a crazed brain?

---

24 The prevalence of meth usage among gay men has been widely acknowledged and studied. See Michael Kaliszewski, "Crystal Meth Abuse in the Gay Community," https://americanaddictioncenters.org/lgbtqiapk-addiction/crystal-meth-addiction-gay-community.

That spring, I learned from a fellow user that I'd been doing meth wrong. I'd been doing it mostly in isolation to open my mind, and then I'd stop when I started feeling awful. My friend set me straight: "You know how if you feel gross on other drugs, you stop doing them? Well, with meth, you just take more."

So I started doing meth the "right" way, and that's when everything started to nose-dive.

Gone were the days of my using and proudly getting myself home. I started blacking out, and I became hypersexual.

I did meth nonstop all summer. Occasionally someone I was using with would look at me and say, "You don't belong here." Other meth addicts I knew even refused to use with me. I remember being furious with them at the time, but now I feel nothing but gratitude. I can see that these people were spiritual messengers trying to nudge me away from destruction.

One Tuesday afternoon, as was my ritual, I left my studio (yes, I managed to teach through all of this) to pick up drugs. As I drove to meet my dealer, I said to myself, "This is a problem." It was clear to me that I was an addict, and I knew I couldn't stop. The good news was that I cared. Some part of me wanted to live—but I still went to my dealer.

Then I hit rock bottom, which I guess had been my intention all along. I'd been on a bender for a few days and was getting ready to stop. As soon as I decided to come down, though, someone I'd been wanting to use with called up to see if I wanted to keep it going. Of course I said yes. We plunged into some real *Fear and Loathing in Las Vegas* shit, roaming around in the middle of the night and ending up at a seedy hotel. I woke up before dawn with needles coming out of my arms. I was deeply dehydrated and malnourished, my heart racing a million miles a minute. Though I was seriously strung out, my self-preservation instinct kicked in, and I called Alex, a trusted friend who is a nurse. I'd met him through Kelly, and I'd become a regular confidante for all of his girl problems. He'd also had to stay on my couch during a few rough patches. In return, he offered me a safe emotional space—he was completely nonjudgmental and impeccably trustworthy.

And on this night of madness, he figured out where I was and brought me IV fluids. He saved me. (The friends who bring IV fluids to your fleabag motel at four in the morning are the friends you keep forever.)

After that experience, I was ready to be done. I knew for sure I didn't want to die. I could finally see that I had friends, family, and a job I loved. I'd seen people lose all of those things to meth, but something in my mind, some touch of the divine, told me that I would not be one of those people.

Miraculously, some recovery thinking started to emerge: I reasoned that I had identified my unhealthy relationship patterns, so maybe I could also identify other unhealthy patterns in my life—like regularly shooting up meth, for example. Maybe I could even change these patterns. I knew I'd need help, so I determined to tell my parents that I was an addict. They were in St. George, and I immediately jumped into the car and drove the four hours to tell them in person.

When I arrived, I said, "Mom and Dad, I'm a drug addict, and I can't stop." I'm sure they'd sensed it because I'd been so erratic. "I don't know what this means. All I know is that I can't help myself, and I don't know what to do."

They recommended a return to Ken, the trusty therapist who'd held my hand while I came out and who'd walked my parents and me through reconciliation. I quickly agreed. Ken would surely help me figure out my drug problem too.

When I met with Ken, he said, "Do you still want to kill yourself?"

I paused, taken aback, and said, "No."

"That's what I thought," he responded. "You drove four hours to let your parents know the moment you knew you were in trouble. You are here in my office. You're fighting to stay alive and work this out."

His words made me feel proud of myself. But one thing I wanted to discuss with him was the validity of my meth-fueled insights. Reverting to Mormon thinking, I had doubts that anything I'd learned while high could have any value. God's spirit can dwell only in pure spaces, right?

When I voiced these concerns to Ken, he said, "Do you think that God would be happy only if your insights—including your decision to stay alive—had come about through some other, 'purer,' means? You're here, Jeff, and you don't want to die. I'd say you made some amazing and important discoveries."

I felt better at once. It felt strange—and very un-Mormon—to say that even though I wanted to stop using, I didn't want to discredit everything about my drug experiences. Positive things had come from places I knew the Jesus of my upbringing could never go.

About three weeks into therapy, I used again. I don't even remember making a decision—I just used. I was mortified! I knew I had to tell Ken, but I didn't tell anyone else. My parents would be furious, and I knew I had let everyone down.

My relapse gave Ken and me an opportunity to start identifying my patterns. We discovered that I had a three-week cycle of sobriety plus relapse. I felt out of control. Ken's kindness and acceptance amazed me. Failure to execute life perfectly had been punishable by extreme measures when I was a child, but Ken made me feel safe in admitting that I had failed when the stakes were so high.

A few minutes into our first post-relapse session, Ken said, "I think it's time for some parts work."

He had me close my eyes and envision two different versions—or parts—of myself. I placed a Jeff in the palm of each of my hands and described them to Ken. In my left palm was Rebel Jeff: four inches tall, super goth, hunched in the corner smoking a cigarette, mascara smudged, and hair in his face. In my right palm was Priesthood Jeff: also four inches tall but with perfect hair, wearing a suit and tie, righteous and worthy.

Ken asked them questions, and I'd respond for them as an impartial mouthpiece.

Ken asked each Jeff what he wanted. Both of them, in their own ways, said they wanted to kill the other version: "He has to go. We can't both live in here together."

Ken told me to ask them, "How long do we have before you kill him?"

Without any emotion or hesitation, my voice said, "Ninety days. We have ninety days before the other dies." I was stunned. If one part of me were killed, would all of me die?

Ken said kindly, "Can you give me six months?"

"I'll give you four," I blurted back, a mere translator for these two clearly unhappy parties.

"I'll take it," said Ken. "I would like to call a truce, then. Can each of you give us four months before you kill the other? And could you both please give Jeff a break? He is trying to figure out how to manage everything you've both shared with him."

The Jeffs said, "Okay. Truce."

In the weeks that followed, Ken and I dedicated our sessions to talking and listening to Rebel Jeff and Priesthood Jeff to find out what they actually needed and if we could do anything to help them. I learned from the Jeffs that I had started to splinter when I was somewhere between eight and ten years old, and this had created the two of them.

Each Jeff had been trying his best to give me what he thought I needed, but both of their good intentions were skewed by another trait they shared: neither of them trusted me to pay attention to them. Like many neglected children, they used negative behaviors to attract my notice. For example, Priesthood Jeff wanted me to get married and have children. To get my attention, he made sure that being single was always a terrible experience for me. He would conjure up dissatisfaction and guilt, so I would hunt for a relationship and give him what he wanted.

Rebel Jeff wanted me to be free and single, so whenever I was in a relationship, he made sure I was dissatisfied and felt unworthy of my partner. That way, I would get out of the relationship and give him what he wanted.

With these diametrically opposed factions at war within me, no wonder I hadn't had any peace. My happiness and well-being were casualties on a battlefield between my two unintegrated parts. They hated each other, and each resented me for not picking him. And now at the age of thirty-eight, I'd called a truce.

I thought the truce between Rebel Jeff and Priesthood Jeff would be enough to keep me clean, but my body and mind were still very dependent on meth. When the three-week anniversary of my last relapse rolled around, I fell off the wagon again. Some relapses come out of nowhere, and others have a clear trigger. This one was of the second variety.

It was October, around the time contracts for *The Forgotten Carols* are sent out. I had done the show the previous year, smoking cigarettes behind dumpsters all over Idaho, but I hadn't used any illicit drugs. This year, though, everyone was on edge.

I was lying in bed at around 8:30 in the morning, in that slow getting-up phase. Meggan came downstairs and jumped into bed with me. She lay there for a second and then said, "You know I would go through hell with you and pull you out if you couldn't do it yourself." I appreciated the sentiment, but I knew this already. She was trying to say something else.

"What's up, Meggan?" I asked.

She cut to the chase. "Dad and Mom and the tour manager know you are working out your addiction thing. You have to assure us right now that you won't use during tour. Because if you relapse on tour"—dramatic pause—"the tour will be ruined, we'll lose the house, and everything Dad has worked for will be lost. It all rests on you. Let me know by the end of the day if you think you can do it." And she hopped out of bed and left.

She wasn't out of the driveway before I texted, "Go ahead and hire someone else."

It may come as no surprise that I promptly relapsed under the weight of this anticipated responsibility—which, of course, proved my family was right to look elsewhere for a reliable soldier.

✢

Clearly, working with just Ken wasn't enough. My next step toward sobriety was midwifed by yet another divine woman who entered my life at exactly the right time.

Like Kelly, Amy was my voice student before she became my friend. Right away, I knew I was encountering a brilliant, complicated woman who had no time for nonsense. So it surprised me to discover that she struggled to accept that her voice was worthy of being heard. She believed she couldn't express herself when she sang, so I helped her find out how her voice felt in her body.

As fate would have it, Amy is a recovering addict and was starting her own practice to help people understand addiction. (I would soon learn that the only people who truly understand recovery are those who have gone through it.)

When I sobered up after my *Forgotten Carols* relapse, I said to her, "Amy, I've got to be locked up somewhere."

"What makes you think you have lost your power?" she asked.

"I can't stop the cycle. I'm a mess."

"Are you a mess, Jeff? You sound more like a baby to me. Why did you let your family dictate whether you could be in *The Forgotten Carols*? Why did you give your power up? Your family doesn't know about drug use—you do."

"Okay. Well, I should go to a facility."

"I don't know about that. Can you handle this?" she asked.

I thought for a moment. "I can handle this."

Rather than checking myself into a residential facility, I started in outpatient treatment with Amy as my guide. She held my hand and reminded me that I was powerful. I felt totally weak, and she'd say, "Don't you dare give up your power. Don't let other people tell you what to do."

She met with my parents, explaining my situation and how my parents had—and had not—enabled it. And then she said, "Here is the deal: We have Plan A and Plan B. In Plan A, Jeff recovers and turns out great. This is very possible. Your son is powerful. In Plan B, Jeff dies of an overdose or stays alive but never recovers. What can you do to prepare yourselves for Plan B?" Heavy stuff.

Amy helped me understand my addicted brain. "You're always going to want to use," she told me. She explained that the brain loves to be active. It just wants to go go go, so of course it loves extreme uppers like meth that allow it to keep the lights on all night long. My own brain became very sly when it came to getting me to use. Meth is an ego-enhancing drug, so you feel untouchable and brilliant at the top of your high. When I was sober, my brain would cut me down and make me feel small so that I would want the swift ego boost that comes with meth—and then it could get the fuel it wanted to work overtime. Sneaky brain!

Another three weeks passed, and I relapsed, true to form. "Ah fuck," I thought. "I have a therapist and a phenomenal addiction specialist, and I still can't make it."

My dad had once recommended that I go to AA. I had done a bit of reading about the program, so I was aware of some of their lingo. I rolled my eyes when my dad suggested it, and I said, "Fantastic! Then I can admit that I am powerless and can't do it on my own." Amy had taught me to hold on to my power. But after my latest relapse, the powerlessness AA talks about was starting to feel accurate.

I remember the day of my first AA meeting. I was broke, but I'd found a forgotten gift card for a local Mexican chain in my room. It had been in my Christmas stocking. I got myself a burrito, ate it slowly, and dragged my ass to the meeting I had found online. I wanted to be late so I wouldn't have to talk to anyone.

I found myself in an old historical home that had been converted into a reception venue. I slunk down the stairs and passed into a yellow basement room—bright, happy, and full of people. I will never forget this room or how I came to feel in it.

People were reading passages from AA literature aloud, and they discussed official meeting business in the collegial, informal manner of people who go way back. I started to think I might belong here.

When the time came for everyone to share, I listened to the old-timers talk about their horrific lives before AA—and I knew right then that I couldn't bullshit these people. They knew all of my tricks and lies because they'd used them too. Then they described their recovery, and they all seemed happy.

Yes, I wanted to belong.

Here was a community of people who talked openly about the reality of imperfection. This was nothing like the vague allusion to struggle I'd heard for almost three decades at church. In this room, I heard honesty. In this room, I felt the Spirit. I kept going back, both to that meeting and others. Early on, I went to a morning meeting at a halfway house in Salt Lake City. It was a tiny group since it was during the workday, and most of the people were retirees—and old-timers in AA. I noticed a man who had a similar feel to Grandpa Egg—masculine, military—but with a gentler touch. This was Bruce, and I wanted him to be my sponsor. I got up the courage to ask him, and he said I should ask this other man instead—let's call him Ed. Bruce thought Ed needed sponsor experience.

I can say it in no other way: Ed was the worst. I confided in him, including about tingle fingers, and he took it upon himself to completely break anonymity and share this information with his sponsor, whose son happened to be dating my cousin Ellie. This chain of blab resulted in rumors circulating about my dad being a creepazoid. On top of that, Ed relapsed and somehow finagled money out of me to leave town. This was maybe enough to make someone leave AA, but I was determined to find what I saw in the lives of so many of the men I met there. So I asked Bruce to sponsor me again, and this time he took me under his wing. He became one of my favorite humans. He understands what AA is all about: getting honest and developing a relationship with your higher power.

In AA, they refer to God as a Higher Power. What's cool is that your higher power can be whatever you want. I'd grown up with a God who was a platinum-haired white dude, but Bruce said, "Yeah, the doorknob can be God."

"Um, excuse me. The doorknob?" questioned Priesthood Jeff.

"Yeah. Why not?" said Bruce. "What characteristics do you want God to have?"

At this stage, Priesthood Jeff didn't know what to do with this question. He sanctimoniously reminded me that Grandpa McLean had drilled it into us that "God doesn't change!" and anyone who attempts to see God in their own way is trying to justify sin. God cannot be imagined. He is what He is, and He has demands!

Rebel Jeff piped up and reminded me of my shamanic experiences with Kelly and of my Joseph Smith experience. God is not that mean guy in the sky.

I responded to Bruce. "Maybe God is kind. Maybe he is loving."

"That's a start," said Bruce.

After this conversation, I started praying again—praying authentically. But I couldn't say *God*. I certainly couldn't say typical Mormon things like, "Heavenly Father, please bless that, nourish and strengthen this . . . " The whole Father thing was out the window. I couldn't wrap my head around the idea of God being a man.

My prayers evolved into wordless exchanges. You can lie and manipulate with words. Instead of speaking, I started to pray to God with a certain energy. Eventually, I learned that, even in the depths of despair, I am never disconnected from God. Or, if you don't like the word God, say Source. Or Tomato Juice. Or fill in the blank.

50

BRAD

Connection

If drugs are Jeff's solution rather than his problem, then what problem is his drug use solving? The answer could be any number of things, but in his sublime TED Talk on the subject, Johann Hari offers this summation: "The opposite of addiction is not sobriety. The opposite of addiction is connection."[25] It is very possible that lack of connection is the problem that Jeff's drug use is solving. And if this lack of connection is common among addicts, as Hari suggests, it's essential that we develop compassion for ourselves and for others as they struggle with self-defeating behaviors.

Questions for Brad

25 Johann Hari, "Everything You Think You Know about Addiction Is Wrong," June 2015, TEDGlobalLondon, video, 14:33, https://www.ted.com/talks/johann_hari_everything_you_think_you_know_about_addiction_is_wrong?language=en

Jeff talks about lacking nuance in his conception of sin. What do you think could help people with similar upbringing differentiate between drinking coffee and shooting up meth?

Actually, I think we must cast off the idea of *sin* when talking about mental health and addiction if we are to help individuals heal. The concept of *sin* obviously came out of an effort to control people. The idea is this: if we stigmatize certain behaviors, folks will stay away from those things. The issue is that with stigma comes alienation. We often think that offering compassion to those who are "sinning" makes us somehow complicit in their behavior. Some people may even think that showing compassion to sinners will release their own inner demons.

But Kahlil Gibran reminds us,

Of the good in you I can speak, but not of the evil.

For what is evil but good tortured by its own hunger and thirst?

Verily when good is hungry it seeks food even in dark caves, and when it thirsts it drinks even of dead waters.[26]

If nothing else, I hope this book offers a glimpse just bright enough to encourage readers to embrace the compassion and nonjudgment that our current understanding of human behavior, addiction, and mental illness lacks. We just need to learn to love those who feel unlovable. This is the antidote to mental illness and addiction.

Jeff talks about hitting rock bottom, but then he relapses several more times. What does rock bottom mean?

Rock bottom is not an objective place. Rock bottom is when you

---

26 Kahlil Gibran, *The Prophet* (New York: Alfred A. Knopf, 1923).

decide to stop digging. It's a private surrender. It's a personal moment when the pain of going on in the same way is worse than the pain of trying something new. I heard someone explain a long time ago that people stop using drugs for the same reason they start using drugs: to feel better. Though Jeff does relapse, it is after his rock-bottom moment that he changes his ways. He is no longer in his addiction alone. He starts reaching out for help.

People recovering from addiction need so much love and support. They need community. They need to be able to walk into a room full of other addicts and alcoholics and tell their despicable stories. And then they need some old-timer in the front row to motion to them and say, "You're in the right place. You are among friends." Isn't this variety of love the essence of what Jesus taught? Didn't he come for the sinners and the downtrodden? *God* is a wonderful idea for expressing this powerful love, the love that transforms. It is the kind of love the recipient realizes that they don't deserve, but it is the most healing power on the face of the earth. That's why we call this kind of love *heaven*. That's why we talk about heaven being in the sky or in the clouds—because it's above and beyond anything we can imagine. It's above and beyond anything we've experienced. Most of us have little to no experience of it on earth.

I want to have compassion for those who relapse, but I have seen it too many times. How can I be hopeful instead of angry and frustrated?

From the outside, the process of addiction can seem completely baffling. From my experience, I know how deep and powerful addiction is and how difficult recovery can be. No two versions of recovery are the same, but most everybody in the recovery world knows that relapse is part of the process.

When Jeff relapses, he knows that his parents can't handle it. All parents have limits. That is why it is so critical for addicts to draw upon resources that have much more capacity than their parents. A higher power can fill in gaps where parents and loved ones fall short. A capable therapist can give addicts a glimpse of this love. A mentor or sponsor can show them this kind of patience.

Parents and families of those struggling with addiction also need love and patience. They have been struggling, sometimes for years, to love people who can feel very difficult to love. But families don't have to do it alone. Families can also find sources of support: therapists, sponsors, and support groups like Al-Anon.[27] And just because someone hasn't found a source of support yet doesn't mean assistance isn't out there.

Jeff refers to Rebel Jeff and Priesthood Jeff as "unintegrated parts." What does that mean?

Integration is a process of discovering and reclaiming our entire selves. All the parts. We all have different parts, some of which we had to sacrifice to survive or fit in. We were told some parts of ourselves were ugly or out of place or dangerous. In integration, we learn to listen to the "unacceptable" parts of ourselves that have been quiet and closed. These disowned parts have miraculous wisdom and energy. We have to bring them back into the fold of our whole selves.

Jeff had been medicating Rebel Jeff and Priesthood Jeff. He had been keeping them at bay all along. But Ken had the wisdom to draw them out so Jeff could hear the wisdom they had to offer.

---

27 Al-Anon is for those whose lives have been affected by a loved one's alcohol or drug use. Another program, Co-Dependents Anonymous, or CoDA, can be helpful in similar ways.

Jeff says that he relapses because of family pressure. Doesn't relapse just come from physical craving for a drug?

Physical craving is part of it, but many addicts will attest to the fact that stressful situations make them vulnerable to relapse. It comes as no surprise to me that it proves to be a crushing weight when Jeff feels he is responsible for his family's lives, happiness, and well-being. So often a person struggling with addiction carries others on their shoulders. By *carry*, I mean they feel responsible for the feelings (and, in this case, the livelihoods) of those they love. It is like their empathic antenna is too open. This overdeveloped sense is often seen in those who grow up in families where everyone is taught that they are responsible for others' feelings. The message is rarely overt, although it can be in cases like Jeff's.

Codependency is the pop psychology term describing this sense of responsibility for others' happiness, which can be viewed as a lack of individuation. Contrary to what many think, codependency not only characterizes the family members of individuals suffering with addiction but is also the driving force of the addiction itself. The medications (drugs and alcohol) serve to anesthetize the identified patient from the heavy feelings of shame and guilt related to their failure to live up to the ideals and obligations cultivated in such families.

Codependency is nearly invisible and can often be observed only with the help of a professional or mentor who is trained to see such dynamics. Because codependency is subtle and difficult to discern, many parents resist the concept. They don't consciously experience themselves as asking others to carry or be responsible for them. Furthermore, parents cite a child's betrayal (that is, the child's failure to meet family expectations) as evidence that the child doesn't seem to be adhering to any family messages, conscious or unconscious. Yet it is the child's complete rejection of the family's values that reveals evidence of the codependent pattern.

Jeff seems to like AA, but my loved one can't get past the God aspect of Twelve-Step programs. Is there another way?

Many who conclude that the path out of addiction must include abstinence are drawn to Twelve-Step groups. But the AA way is indeed difficult for those who feel significant reluctance when it comes to accepting a higher power. While the Twelve-Step concept of a higher power is expansive and undogmatic, it can still remind those who belonged to conservative religious communities of an angry and shaming God. There are endless responses to this resistance toward a higher power, but I think the most important way to overcome the aversion is to wait to define a higher power until later in the recovery process. And that definition will likely change as time goes on. (Secular recovery programs also exist, like Secular AA, SMART Recovery, and Secular Organizations for Sobriety.)

Reflection Questions

1. Think about what parts of yourself may be unintegrated. What can you do to welcome them back into your full self? (Working on this with a therapist is recommended.)
2. If you struggle to have compassion for addicts in your life, can you think of any part of yourself or a repeating pattern of your own that you feel powerless over?
3. Do you feel responsible for anyone's happiness? Do you expect anyone else to be responsible for yours?

51

MICHAEL

A Parent Like Me

Jeff's meth abuse—and the life that was crumbling around it—came as a bigger surprise to me than his being gay. And I was not naïve about addiction. I'd become familiar with the Twelve-Step recovery model through the dependency struggles of close friends, business partners, and extended family members. I'd even performed at recovery conferences all over the country, drawing on songs from an album my close friend John Batdorf and I had put together.

But when it came to my own son, I was blind. And I realized that I'd had a hand in his ability to live a double life. How many years had he had to hide his gay identity as the son of a prominent Mormon? To survive, he'd had to learn how to fool most of the people almost all of the time.

So, I had been blind. And now I was broken. In my pain, I turned to the Twelve Steps, pondering especially the first two:

We admitted we were powerless over alcohol—that our lives had become unmanageable.

Came to believe that a Power greater than ourselves could restore us to sanity.

As I intently read these words, I knew I needed to apply them to myself. I was powerless over my son's addiction, and I wanted to believe that God could restore my own sanity along with my son's.

So I knelt with Lynne at the side of our bed and prayed. *I can't do this, God. I'm clearly the worst possible father for this kid. I have prayed for him since he was born, but it doesn't seem to help. I don't want to quit on him, but I can't function. I have to surrender all of this to you, but I'm not sure I can.*

That was Monday night's prayer. The next morning, Lynne woke me with a reminder that it was Temple Tuesday.

What followed is central to my change of heart, and it needs some explanation because it happened during a Mormon temple rite called *sealing*. This ceremony is how we link families together. For example, couples are sealed when they get married, and we perform sealings for dead ancestors so we can add them to our great intergenerational chain.

On this Tuesday, we walked into the sealing room and were unexpectedly greeted by Jeff's former mission leaders, a married couple. They expressed how much they loved and missed Jeff. They knew he'd left the church, but that didn't change how they felt.

This surprise encounter felt like a little wink from God—a divine coincidence telling me that Jeff was on His mind. And then as the officiant spoke the names of our ancestors, I heard or felt something—not quite words, but almost: "Michael, we've been waiting 160 years for this. You and Lynne are doing something for me and my family that is a big deal to us. We want to help you with something. We've got Jeff's back. We will follow up in ways you can't, and we will rally others who love him."

Over the next forty-eight hours, everything fell into place for Jeff's recovery process. We organized a support structure without the prohibitive expense of a treatment facility.

Soon after, Jeff told me, "I felt Grandpa Egg next to me in the AA meeting today. He said that our family can do hard things and that they would help me."

It was remarkable to experience all of this after my own version of the addict's prayer. But here's what was most significant to me: if our ancestors were rallying to help Jeff without judgment, maybe I could suspend judgment too.

Without judgment is key. Yes, watching Jeff's recovery journey was terrifying for me, but it opened my mind. I learned that God is in all parts of our lives—not just those deemed "worthy." God is with us in the parts of our lives that parents like me don't want to hear or think about. And what is a "parent like me"? Well, I had a sincere desire for each of my children to have a real relationship with God, to know that they are not, nor would ever be, alone. To that end, I taught them to approach God with respect and reverence. I emphasized worthiness and repentance so that my children would avoid the sins and mistakes that might take them off the righteous path. I wanted my children's truth to mirror my own. I wanted to protect them from all immorality.

But then Jeff ended up finding God through his addiction and even through his lying, cheating, and manipulating. God was present for every part, and Jeff says that if he had to go through every single awful thing he's experienced to arrive where he is now, he'd do it again. So would I.

52

BRAD

Looking at Ourselves

Many religions talk about the omnipresence of God in the world. Yet at the same time, these religions (including Mormonism) suggest that God does not visit the dark corners of the world.

Jeff's story suggests something quite different. It is often in our deepest despair, under our beds or in our closets, where God is closest to us. I have found God just about everywhere I have looked. I find God in therapy all the time. I find God in Twelve-Step groups that support individuals struggling with sexual addictions, substance addictions, and all manner of struggles.

If you think that God has abandoned you or that, because of your sin, God can't be anywhere near you, you have accepted a very limited view of the creator of the universe. You have most likely adopted a God from someone who saw very little of God at work.

In the foreword of *Mere Christianity*, C. S. Lewis posits that if we look close enough, turning coins over to see the other side, we will see God and virtue in every person: "I have a reluctance to say much about temptations to which I myself am not exposed. No man, I suppose, is tempted to every sin. It so happens that the impulse which makes men gamble has been left out of my make-up; and, no doubt, I pay for this by lacking some good impulse of which [gambling] is the excess or perversion."[28] Where there are demons and sin, virtue and heavenly beings sit close by.

If you have come to believe in a God who punishes struggling people rather than loves them when they are in pain, I am here to tell you that God loves you no matter what. Jeff's story shows us this. Michael's story shows us this. Every story of any fallible human that I know of proves the same thing.

Questions for Brad

Michael wonders if he had a hand in Jeff being able to live a double life. What do you think about parents' roles in children developing addiction?

Sometimes we wonder why our children develop the way they do. We wonder why they lie, why they are susceptible to peer pressure, and why they display a whole host of other issues. An honest and courageous look at ourselves as parents will give us answers. If our children learn to hide as they're growing up in our families, they will have that same instinct when they go out into the world.

If we want to be part of the healing process when our children struggle with addiction or mental health issues, we must be willing to look at ourselves. There is no other way, but we can enlist help from someone who can show us the connections between our actions and our children's reactions. Heroic parents look

28 C. S. Lewis, *Mere Christianity* (New York: HarperCollins, 1952), xii.

inward and are willing to accept the most difficult truth—that they themselves are a primary source of their children's mental health issues.

For example, one of the most common problems I hear about from parents is the issue of peer pressure and the related issue of kids being overly vulnerable to what other people think. Simultaneously, almost every parent I have met has one thing in common: a propensity to tell their children how they, as parents, feel about them. We tell our children when we're upset with them, when we're happy with them, when we're worried about them, and when we're proud of them. The result is clear: Our children learn that what other people think about them is the truth and may even be more important than what our children think about themselves. In short, children's susceptibility to peer pressure is created by their parents.

I love the story of Jeff's mission leaders expressing love for him in the temple, but my queer child thinks they are being phony. Can we both be right?

This is tricky. The sort of love expressed here is often experienced by those in the LGBTQ+ community as condescension and pity. I don't know Jeff's mission leaders, and I certainly don't know their hearts. I can only tell those who are in a religion that marginalizes queer people to follow Michael's injunction to stay in the room and to listen and learn. Ask those who feel marginalized to share their experiences and feelings, and then *believe them*. Don't defend yourself or cling to your choice of words. This is the kind of love that Christ, Buddha, and Yoda taught.

Reflection Questions

1. Have you felt cut off from deity in dark times, or have you felt bolstered?
2. How can you practice and express unconditional love to the people in your life?
3. If you have addiction in your family, can you see a parental role in how it developed?

53

JEFF

Making It Through the Night

In December, my latest three-week stint in sobriety was drawing to a close. My sweet friend Shireen came to me and said, "Hey, if you have a twenty-one-day cycle, let's change it! Come with me to run a 5K in Moab." I said yes. (Shireen is sweet, but she's also a politician. She's got serious persuasive game.)

Two days before the trip—day twenty-one of my cycle—I was lying in bed late at night. My body knew I was supposed to be looking for meth. That's the power of a pattern. I checked in with every part of myself, the time ticking by. I prayed my new kind of prayer—wordless and energy-based. I thought about Bruce and other people in AA. I knew I could call them, but I felt weird since it was so late. At three o'clock in the morning, I realized that this was the moment three weeks before when I'd last used. I did not move. I simply lay there and checked in with myself and God.

And you know what? I made it through the night. I broke the cycle.

Making it through that night changed me, but with the dawning of a new day, the real work began. I was seeing Amy and Ken every week as well as going to my AA meetings, so I was doing about ten hours a week of intensive reflection and therapy. Three months passed one day at a time. If you aren't holding on for dear life, one day at a time seems trivial. But when you're in the thick of it, sometimes all you can do is make it through the next five minutes.

When I was hanging on minute by minute and hour by hour, I found myself continually praying for strength—like all day! Praying so frequently challenged one of my core beliefs, which was that God had to conserve his time and energy for people who really needed Him (and I wasn't one of those people). I should ask for God's help only after exhausting all other resources. But it turns out that the God of my childhood is not a good God for recovery, because if addicts don't ask God for help—a LOT—they relapse.

One day after I'd gone to my ninetieth meeting in as many days (widely called a 90-in-90 in Twelve-Step circles), I was hanging out with a friend I used to do meth with, and I said I'd had a rough day.

"Hey, do you want to use?" my friend asked.

And I said, "Sure!"

Just like that.

My high was intense because I hadn't used for so long. I was high in the canyon just west of Heber all day because I couldn't go back home. I was spinning out of control, feeling like I was not in my body. I was supposed to meet with Amy, but I didn't want her to know I was high doing who knows what.

I couldn't bring myself to tell my parents, but I eventually told Amy. She knew before I told her—of course she knew. She said,

"Yeah, relapse is a part of recovery. Sometimes relapse is the only thing that can teach you what you need to know."

I'm sure someone (or many someones) mentioned this in the meetings I'd attended daily, but I hadn't been able to hear it. The popular recovery phrase *progress, not perfection* was for lesser people. I couldn't accept my latest relapse as anything less than a calamity.

"But I used!"

"Yep. But you know what? You're not still using, are you?"

"No."

"Well, let's get back on it."

✢

I went to my mom's birthday party in mid-March, and on the way home, I got a little glimmer of post-relapse hope. A stranger reached out on Facebook Messenger to tell me how much my music had meant to him. He'd listened to my album *Something's Changed*, which includes a cover of Michael Jackson's "Man in the Mirror." The stranger's name was Mitch. He said he was gay and Mormon but hadn't gone on a mission.

I looked at his profile and saw that he was gorgeous, with long, flowing hair. Like Jesus.

I decided to respond to him: "Hey, let's hang out." And we did. We couldn't stop talking, couldn't stop making out.

I was instantly in love with him. He was the most beautiful man I had ever met in my life, both inside and out—he had been sober for seven or eight years, and he'd felt the call to help homeless youth. I mean.

A couple of weeks into this lovefest, the same buddy from my last relapse reached out: "Things kind of suck. Do you want to use?"

And I answered, “Yeah, sure.” I was heading back to my twenty-one-day cycle.

I reported my relapse to everyone who needed to know, including Mitch. I was surprised when he said, “Oh, I can’t be in a relationship with someone who isn’t sober.” Remember how partnership is the most important thing in the world to me? I wasn’t about to lose Mitch, so that relapse was the last one.

March 22, 2017, is my sobriety date. I stopped using that day. And for the next two years, even if I wasn’t totally aware of the fact, I had a new name for my higher power. It wasn’t God, Doorknob, or Tomato Juice. It was Mitch.

PART 5

Loved

54

JEFF

Toning It Down

As I've told you before, this book is a love story. No, I don't end up with Josh or Christopher or even this new guy, Mitch. Remember, this is a self-love story. Here in the final part of my story, the culmination of my recovery and therapeutic work is near, but first, I have a few more things to learn. I need to figure out how to manage my feelings and reactions. And I need to come to terms with the idea that God has the audacity to love me.

Of course, any relationship with Mitch was ultimately doomed. I was sure my devotion to him would keep me sober—and it did. But putting this kind of pressure on a partner had not exactly worked out well in the past.

For the time being—and for the first time—I used my strong need for partnership as a catalyst for good. My time with Mitch was just a little healthier than the time I'd spent dating any other man. He and I never used drugs together—a first for me. And we didn't rush into sex. In fact, we never slept together.

It was a step in the right direction, but my old patterns

certainly still cropped up. Mitch had a lot of hang-ups around dating me when I was so newly sober. He refused to be my official boyfriend, which activated my drive to prove that I was the best possible choice for him. His reticence, coupled with my casting him in the higher-power role, made for a dramatic and traumatic quasi-relationship.

But I had tools in the mix that had been absent in my other relationships. Not only was I in therapy consistently and regularly, but my connection to God was burgeoning. I had found a new spirituality and connection with Source in AA, but I felt a yearning for even more. I decided to try Transcendental Meditation.

I found a meditation teacher in my neighborhood, and he looked and behaved like the quintessential Mormon Church leader—tall, mid-sixties, a little balding, a little full in the belly, clearly of Scandinavian ancestry, and soft spoken. In fact, he was indeed deeply committed to the Mormon faith, but had been doing Transcendental Meditation since before I was born. Entering his home was like entering a Mormon temple or at least the home of a patriarch—a deeply spiritual Mormon man who administers patriarchal blessings. I found deep comfort in the pristine, quiet Mormon familiarity twinged with Hindu-based language and activity.

The guru-bishop-patriarch took me through a ceremony to get my own mantra. I was supposed to make an offering to God during the ceremony, so I'd brought six peonies and six strawberries.

As I was leaving, the teacher said, "Wait, these are for you," and handed me one strawberry and one peony.

"What do you mean?" I asked.

"You gave an offering, and now you get some back."

"I do?"

My impulse was to say, "God only takes." The Mormon God, still lurking in my brain, requires everything and more. I could never give enough, never do enough.

I went to my car and sat with my offerings. The tears came, and I knew I needed to tattoo this strawberry and peony onto my body so I could have a constant reminder of my relationship with God. Soon after, I went to a tattoo parlor and came away with the peony, the strawberry, and a crown on my arm.

Why the crown? The simple answer is that crowns symbolize power, and I was reclaiming mine. But there's a longer story behind the specifics of my crown, which features eleven spires and six little balls.

Very early in sobriety, my tongue started to seize up, and swallowing became difficult. My voice had been wrecked from the drugs, smoking, voice lessons—and, most recently, from all of the talking in AA. So Jeff the voice teacher headed to vocal therapy.

The voice therapist gave me two disturbing pieces of news: my larynx had started to crush itself, and I had a cyst on my cords. I was a straight-up vocal mess.

I had always believed that my voice would just be there when I opened my mouth. It was humbling to learn that something so tied to my identity had limitations and needs.

The therapist said, "Jeff, you are at an eleven, and you have to be at a six." I'd always thought I had to be at an eleven to be enough. If I stopped screaming, no one would listen. But now it was time to speak softly and to speak less. Hence my tattoo crown of eleven spires and six balls—my eternal reminders to tone it down.

Slowly but surely as I continued vocal therapy, my tongue began to relax, and its mobility returned. A certain fear was gone from my life, replaced by empowerment: the worst had happened to my voice, and I'd rebounded.

I'd spent so much of my singing life trying to protect my voice instead of trusting it. Now to find my voice again, I had to acknowledge its needs. This experience made me more understanding as a teacher. I started teaching kids to trust themselves and listen to their bodies and their voices, to not be afraid of hurting themselves.

When I'd put together several weeks of sobriety, I started to work the steps with Bruce. This process clarified a lot for me. The Fourth Step, for example, is taking a full inventory of everyone and everything you resent or fear. When I did Step Four on my dad, Bruce helped me find my accountability even in situations where Dad had wronged me more than I'd wronged him. Coming to that kind of self-awareness is difficult, but Bruce showed me how it's done after I told him this story:

My dad always wanted to be a tennis player. He was brilliant at it, but my grandparents made it clear they didn't have the money for him to seriously pursue the sport. Dad's unfulfilled dream meant that we played a lot of tennis growing up.

Dad's skills extended to table tennis, and we got a Ping-Pong table for Christmas when I was ten. In a mildly manic phase, Dad told me, "If you can ever beat me, I will give you $1,000." I got dollar signs in my eyes.

After that, Scott and I played Ping-Pong together for hours every day after school. I honed both my Ping-Pong skills and my manipulation skills, learning that if I could throw Scott emotionally, I would always win.

One Saturday when I was twelve, I took Dad on. I could tell he was a little flustered, that his mind was somewhere else. It would be easy to get under his skin, just like with Scott. So with my two years of practice in both Ping-Pong and mind games, I won. I shouted in jubilation. Dad started to run off, but then he came back, grabbed me, and threw me into my bedroom. He said, "I don't have to give you $1,000" and itemized the reasons why not: shelter, food, everything else it cost him for me to be alive. I couldn't believe he was weaseling out of the deal. It was official: my dad was a jackass.

Bruce listened and then asked how I'd been able to beat my dad.

"I just said," I began. "I practiced and worked hard! He was in the wrong."

Bruce kept pressing. "Yes, he was. But this isn't about him. Tell me how you won again."

"Hard work," I said.

"How did you win?"

I finally saw what he was getting at. "I got under his skin," I said.

"Was that fair?" Bruce asked.

"What do you mean, 'Was that fair?' He was the unfair one!"

"What's your part in this, Jeff?"

I relented. "Oh, I tried to show Dad that he was an idiot. I paralyzed him."

Bruce elaborated. "You showed him the person he didn't want to be: a failed tennis star. You triggered your dad's personal trauma on purpose. That's your part."

Now I had a brand-new perspective on one of my foundational childhood tragedies. Seeing my part gave me space to forgive Dad—and myself.

"Isn't it cool to own your part in things?"

I paused and took a moment to ingest this new way of thinking. "Yeah, it is, in fact, really cool."

(Sidenote: Years after the Ping-Pong incident, I got a note of apology and a check for $1,000 in the mail.)

As I continued working Step Four, I was challenged to see my part in many other situations. When I examined my relationship with Josh, I realized that I'd never believed he could truly see me. What could my part possibly be in this?

The answer to this question came to me one day while meditating: I hadn't let him go. I'd caged him in my mind, freezing him in time as the guy who had always let me down. The season for this thinking was over. Whoever I thought Josh was, I gave him to God.

Three weeks later, Josh called me. This wasn't a completely uncommon event. We chat every so often.

That day, he said, "Jeff, I've been thinking about what I want to say to you for the past month. I want to get it right." And then he paused for thirty full seconds before he spoke again: "Jeff, I see you. I've always seen you. I just couldn't tell you before, and I'm sorry." He went on to tell me what he'd seen in me, what he'd loved.

I hadn't told anyone about my decision to give Josh to God. I hadn't even spoken aloud when I'd done it. But somehow, I'd energetically made space for Josh. And when you make space, change and healing are possible.

From my experience in AA, I came to believe that everyone should declare themselves an addict of something just so they can go through recovery. Imagine dedicating at least three months to sitting with your choices, owning them, and working through them. Imagine you have a community that agrees to support you during this healing process. That's recovery.

In AA, I learned how to sit with the emotions—and Unlovable Monsters—I had long hidden from. I took it even further than just sitting with my monster. For the space of three months, I voiced aloud the Unlovable Monster's words. And not just when I was alone. People would ask me how I was, and regardless of who it was, I would say, "I'm unlovable." You can imagine that it made everyone wildly uncomfortable. I actually got a lot of guff, like *How do you think that makes your mother feel?* I allowed these people to feel their feelings, but I wasn't ashamed. If a person got past the initial shock, some vital, deep conversation often ensued. As other people got honest with me, I learned that I was not the only one with a monster twin.

Eventually, what was once true for me—*I am unlovable*—became less true, and I stopped saying these particular words aloud. But I continued to voice what I believed and felt. If I had disarmed the formerly terrifying monster by being honest, what else could honesty do?

This line of questioning led me to finally admit to myself that my house was too expensive. It was crippling me, in fact. I knew I always had a place in Heber, so I sold my house and moved back in with Mom and Dad.

✢

There's an ongoing joke about recovery newcomers: they either become addicted to fitness or they get chickens. Being an overachiever, I did both. I started with the fitness, and it segued into chickens.

Here's how it happened: I was obsessively going to the gym and eating a lot of protein like a good newbie AA. One day, I gazed down at my meat-heavy meal and thought, *Where did this meat come from? Who raised it? And*—most importantly—*did anyone sing to this animal?* I determined then and there to make farm animals a part of my life. How could I consume meat when I was so alienated from its source?

Heber has a rich 4-H and Future Farmers of America tradition, so I called my oldest local friend, Tom Hansen, and asked him if his boys were raising steers for the fair that year. When I say Tom is my oldest friend, I mean it. Our mothers were pregnant with us at the same time, and they accompanied each other to satisfy their joint cravings for McDonald's Diet Coke and French fries. Tom was born a few months before I was, and Mom liked his name so much, she gave me Thomas as a middle name. This was back in the Salt Lake days, but as luck would have it, both the McLeans and the Hansens ended up near each other again in Heber.

A feminine boy in Heber couldn't have asked for better luck than to have Tom Hansen as a friend. He was popular, definitely one of the cool kids, but also incredibly loving and kind. If I was the last one picked for a team, he'd make a point of consistently passing me the ball. If he had a birthday, I was always on the invitation list. Tom was my only confidante when I threw myself down the stairs to get out of football.

When I came back to Heber, Tom was one of the first people I reconnected with. And when I asked about whether his boys were raising steers, he said that each of his two boys had one. I asked if I could help with them. He and his boys agreed, and thus began my daily hangouts with Chancie and Tall Tale, two Black Angus steers who won my heart.

Once the steers were in my life, it was time for chickens. I took a piece of land that was not being used for alfalfa, and I made a chicken yard and coop—well, it's more like a chicken fortress.

Every omnivore and carnivore on Earth enjoys eating chickens. I couldn't leave my ladies vulnerable! With hard work, heavy machinery, and much braving of the elements, I established Von Chirp Manor (I named all of my chickens after characters from *The Sound of Music*).

And, yes, I sing to my chickens. Of course.

I created an Instagram persona, Farmer Jeff, to chronicle my life with the steers and chickens. And then more animals began to arrive. Two months after I finished setting up the coop, my niece won a pig at her church raffle and asked if I would take care of it. Hello, Oliver. Our neighbors moved, and we adopted two of their horses. Hello, Sally and Little Lady, and thank you for showing me how effective equine therapy can be. I acquired a pair of alpaca. Hello, Gentlemen.

I spent hours hanging out with these amazing creatures, earning their trust. We didn't need words, just love and energy exchange. If my addiction stemmed from a deep belief that I am unlovable, then nothing was more valuable than surrounding myself with creatures that were so easy to love and that loved so easily in return. When I was surrounded by so much pure affection, it became simpler to shrug off the Unlovable Monster (who occasionally took on a little of its old power).

55

BRAD

Mythologies

Sometimes you hear somebody explain a principle and you think to yourself, "This is not true. That is not the way things are." But if that person uses symbols and metaphors to illustrate the concept, you can more readily understand the wisdom behind the idea. The role of myths, symbols, and metaphors in our lives can serve to offer us depth.

The term *myth* does not suggest that a story is true or untrue. The concept refers to formative and vital stories that offer perspective and provide us with insights into the deeper layers of the meaning of life. Religion is a shared myth, an organized set of symbols and metaphors that invite us into a higher plane of consciousness. The symbolic nature of religion is illustrated in the frequent description of heaven and God as being above and beyond the Earth, which conveys the idea of their being outside our daily experience.

We can have personal mythologies as well. The peony, strawberry, and crown are symbols of Jeff's personal mythology. Jeff literally imprinted himself with these symbols to point himself to his higher consciousness.

Questions for Brad

I am interested in the idea that we play a part in many of our negative experiences. Can you explain this further?

I spend a lot of time teaching parents about accountability. I explain how important it is for them to recognize and accept that they have dented their children. But that's just part of the story. The parents, of course, have been dented themselves. J.D. Gill explains, "Of course no one has come from a perfect context—whatever that might be. Therefore, each person will have dents and bruises left over from earlier experiences. It is wise to consider all dents and bruises important and worthy of compassionate understanding."[29]

As we grow, we must take responsibility for healing our dents and bruises. Part of that work can be talking to a therapist—an empathic other—and telling the story of our childhood. No matter what, we must learn to move through our wounds, not for our parents' sake but for our own. Every new and not-so-new adult has to go through this process so they can be free. We have to be willing to look into the hurt and anger in order to move through them and let them go. If we refuse to look at and feel the pain, we will carry it around for the rest of our lives, thinking that our parents should somehow change or make it better. If we do this, we are still expecting our parents to come through for us. We expect them to be something they aren't, and we abdicate the responsibility to grow up and take the lead role in our own happiness.

29 J. D. Gill, *Seeing in Intimacy and Psychotherapy* (CreateSpace, 2016), 47.

A caveat: Though we can take responsibility for our healing, when we go looking for "our part" where we have been victims of abuse or assault, this can be more damaging. Process abuse and assault with trained mental health professionals.

Do you agree with Jeff that "everyone should declare themselves an addict of something just so they can go through recovery"?

I love Jeff's enthusiasm about his experience in AA, and I do agree that the systematic way of approaching life that the Twelve Steps offer is valuable for many people. The groups that form around this system are not just about sobriety or abstinence. They are about recovery from a way of thinking (*It's not the drinking, it's the thinking* is a common phrase in AA). Undoing shame while cultivating humility, the Twelve Steps encourage thorough but compassionate self-evaluation. Anything can come under scrutiny, even something as temporal as the amount Jeff was budgeting for his house.

Twelve-Step programs exist for not just alcohol and drugs. You can find programs for issues as varied as hoarding and gambling. Many of these programs have ancillary programs for loved ones. Just like Al-Anon supports families of alcoholics, groups like Codependents of Sex Addicts support those affected by another person's sex addiction.

Because Twelve-Step groups are made up only of recovering addicts, they rarely succumb to the condescension that can arise when saints make it their mission to save sinners. Everyone in a Twelve-Step group is a "sinner"—an imperfect person learning to support and lean on other imperfect people.

So often, those who have waded through mental illness or addiction have the most to offer other wounded people. When they were hurting in the darkness, they learned what they themselves needed, so now they know the needs of those who still suffer.

The Twelve-Step model is so valuable that the Mormon Church even started its own program based on the Twelve Steps. The participants I've spoken to have told me they like it better than church. They describe how it addresses, in a very practical way, the dilemmas they face. My own son told me that while he was a Mormon missionary in New York City, he found the program to be a sensible guide to help people understand spirituality.

Spirituality isn't necessarily about religion or God. Spirituality is about transcendence. If you can find transcendence in God or religion, fantastic. For some, though, anything that sounds or smells like God and religion is unsafe because they have historical trauma surrounding those entities. These people may have to find spirituality in situations that bear little resemblance to the religions in which they grew up. That can be Twelve Step or therapy or meditation or any number of options.

I wish my addict loved one could have an experience like Jeff with the farm animals. Since we are city dwellers with allergies, what else could we do?

Jeff's experience with the farm animals is simply an exercise in mindfulness. In lieu of alpaca and steers, you and your loved one can find another way to incorporate mindfulness into the healing process. In a very fundamental sense, using drugs and alcohol is an attempt to not be present in our lives. Therefore, mindfulness—which centers being present—is the antidote to substance use and other self-medicating behaviors. If we can learn to be present in our world, we won't need drugs or alcohol to take us out of it.

The Buddhist teacher Thich Nhat Hanh explains a connection between mindfulness and recovery:

When you drink whiskey, learn to drink it with mindfulness. "Drinking whiskey, I know that it is whiskey I am drinking." This is the approach that I would recommend. I am not telling you to absolutely stop drinking. I propose that you drink your whiskey mindfully, and I am sure that if you drink this way for a few weeks, you will stop drinking alcohol. Drinking your whiskey mindfully, you will recognize what is taking place in you—in your body.[30]

Those who suffer with worry or anxiety for themselves or their family members can follow a similar practice: "I am anxious and worried. I know this is fear. I am mindful that I am feeling fear. I will allow it and notice what it is doing to my body."

Reflection Questions

1. What are some of your personal mythologies? How do you manifest them in your life? If you're a parent, how could you support your children in their own mythologies?
2. Think about some of your formative negative experiences. Can you see your part in these? (And remember to be very careful when considering "your part" in cases of abuse and assault.)
3. How can you bring more mindfulness into your life?
4. Have you considered pursuing Twelve-Step work either as an addict or as a loved one of an addict?

---

30 Thich Nhat Hanh, *You Are Here: Discovering the Magic of the Present Moment*, ed. Melvin McLeod, trans. Sherab Chödzin Kohn (Boston: Shambhala, 2009), 68.

56

MICHAEL

Proud Dad

Watching my son in his Farmer Jeff role and seeing how tender he was to the animals was beautiful. But it was not surprising. Can I brag about Jeff for a moment? Remember, I'm a storyteller, so my boasts come in the form of a few stories that encapsulate how kindhearted and thoughtful Jeff is.

The first story involves our dear family friends, Keith and Suzanne Ross. They are known to my kids as Uncle Keith and Aunt Suzanne, and their two kids call us Uncle Mike and Aunt Lynne. When we get together, it's like a family reunion, and the family keeps growing. Keith and Suzanne's firstborn grandchild is the lovely and very animated Grace. The child is so precocious that it is impossible not to love her instantly.

When Grace turned five, our families joined in a princess-themed birthday celebration. A few minutes after the party started, I noticed that Jeff wasn't there. It seemed strange to me because Jeff adores Grace. Twenty minutes later, however, Prince Charming and his steed (a pony borrowed from nearby friends) made their way down the gravel road toward Grace's log castle. Prince Charming was attired as only a noble prince would be, and as he approached, he called out for Princess Grace!

I will never, if I live to be a thousand years old, forget the expression on Princess Grace's face when she saw Jeff.

"He's here! He's here! My prince came to my party, and he brought a PONY!"

I felt like I was in a credit card commercial. Princess costume: $50. Cake and ice cream: $40. Prince Charming and a pony: priceless.

What is it in Jeff, that child of mine, that not only thought of something perfect for Grace but also pulled it all together—the tights, the crown, the *pony*? Whatever it is, I cherish and celebrate it.

The next story illustrates Jeff's ability to accept his mom and me for who we are. One Sunday afternoon I was headed out the door for a meeting with one of my church leaders. Jeff asked where I was going, and I told him I was going to get my temple recommend renewed. (Every two years, Mormons who want to go to the temple answer a series of questions to show they are faithful and worthy). Jeff had been to the temple and was aware of the questions I would be answering.

"Dad, I have a tip." He motioned me closer. He smiled and said, "The answers are: yes, yes, yes, nooooo, yes, nooooo, yes, no." His smile broke into a chuckle. I asked him what his point was.

"Dad, you and Mom are excellent Mormons, and you need to be in that temple. That's just who you are. So when they ask you questions that may open the door to talking about what the church teaches about homosexuality, don't elaborate. Don't express concerns. Just say yes, yes, no, yes, no. I don't want you to feel like you have to stop being faithful Mormons to show your love for me. Loving someone should never require us to abandon our authentic, true selves."

This last story takes us back in time a little, but I saved it for this point because it is so sacred to me.

In the final days of my father's life, he was scared and in tremendous pain. He grew confused about what was happening to him, where he was, and who was around him. Hospice did all they could to keep him comfortable, but every time Dad's morphine wore off, he was trembling and terrified.

As my father lay dying, Jeff was in his final performances with the Legally Blonde tour. He had a vacation planned for when the show closed, but when I told him about Grandpa McLean's situation, he canceled his plans. He came right home to be with us and his grandfather, who no longer knew who Jeff was.

My sister and I were in the room with Dad those final agonizing hours, and Jeff joined us. When Dad's morphine wore off, Jeff saw his frightened grandfather unable to calm himself, so Jeff started to sing. He sang my father's favorite hymns a cappella with that sublime voice of his.

I can bear witness that in my father's final hours, I heard and saw an angel. The son I'd labeled gay, prodigal, and lost was an angel on earth, comforting and blessing the grandfather who had hurt and shamed him. Jeff showed up. He taught me that day what it means to stay in the room.

57

BRAD

Face to Face

Jeff says that this book is a love story—specifically a self-love story. But there's another love story here: the reconciliation story between Jeff and Michael. They reconciled not just with each other but also with God and with themselves. At its core, this love story is about two people who connected to their authentic selves. Some people describe this connection as finding themselves or discovering themselves, and others think of it as creating who they are. Sometimes people talk about it in terms of finding and healing their inner child. For some, it's about learning to tell the truth about themselves to others.

Regardless of how we choose to describe the relationship we have with ourselves, it becomes a template for all our other relationships. As most therapists will tell you, the dilemmas and difficulties we have with life, the conflicts we have with others, are merely reflections of the relationship we have with ourselves. Self-acceptance inevitably begets loving others, but if we don't make peace with ourselves and learn to love and honor ourselves, we are that much less capable of loving and relating to other people.

As author, minister, and psychologist Connie Zweig writes, "I began to believe that the way I led my life was the source of my pain."[31] In the end, we have to learn that we are responsible for our happiness, and self-love is a significant part of that happiness.

Questions for Brad

I feel like could not write a chapter like this about my child yet, but I would love to get there. How did Michael get to the point that he sees so much good in his son?

Michael had to be willing to confront and integrate ideas and parts of himself that he had been told to reject. He waded into the dark waters—or his rejected unconscious—to find the gift.

In his First Epistle to the Corinthians, Paul says: "For now we see through a glass, darkly; but then face to face: now I know in part; but then shall I know even as also I am known."[32]

As Michael tells the story of Grace's party, it is clear that he now sees Jeff face to face. He loves Jeff, and his gifts, just as he is. It is vital to see children as individuals separate from us as parents. To be able to do this, we must do the difficult work of embracing all of the parts of *ourselves*. This work allows us to see and love other people more easily. In other words, we shall know (and see and love) others even as we are known (and seen and loved) by ourselves.

---

31 Connie Zweig, *Meeting in the Shadow of Spirituality: The hidden power of darkness on the path.* [E-book]. iUniverse, 2017, Chapter 1.

32 1 Cor. 13:12 (King James Version).

Jeff says earlier that he has no good memories of Grandpa McLean, but I find it moving that he sang for him in his final hours. Do you have any thoughts about serving people who have been abusive to us?

It's beautiful how Jeff comforted his grandfather as he lay dying. But this is a very delicate situation. We must be careful about praising children when they forgive their parents and grandparents. In therapy, forgiveness is not a virtue. Forgiveness is just something we may do when we have done the work.

Many children are better at taking care of their parents and grandparents than taking care of themselves. Therefore, we must be careful about praising caretaking behavior. This praise may suggest to children that they are "good" when they deny their own needs. I'm not talking about guiding children to be selfish or self-centered. I'm talking about allowing them to be human.

I'm happy Jeff could work through what he needed to so that he could be there for his dad and grandfather. But if he had still been stuck in the hurt and the anger toward his grandfather and had chosen not to go, I wouldn't be disappointed or upset with him. I would just know that he still had some healing to do.

Reflection Questions

1. If you are estranged from or struggling with a parent or child, do you want to reconcile with them? What will it take for you to do this?
2. What is your relationship with self-love?

58

JEFF

Finding Me at Finding You

Mitch and I had been drifting in and out of each other's lives while I'd been counting sober days, raising farm animals, working with my sponsor, and healing in Heber. We were a pair of flakes with a half-decent friendship. Only I wanted more, which he knew because I'd asked him to be my boyfriend twice. I didn't go down without a fight. I turned on my charm. I wrote him songs. His response was always the same. *No.* And then he'd disappear for months.

With each rejection, I had to sit in my feelings. I didn't escape them with drugs. I didn't ignore them. I would lie in bed and let waves of emotion sweep over me.

One beautiful morning in early November, I made another move. I ordered breakfast for the two of us from the local greasy spoon, Chick's Café, and set the food up at Whiskey Springs, a picturesque spot a few miles up the canyon from home.

As I poured syrup over my buckwheat pancake, I asked Mitch—for the third time—if he wanted to date me. Both times

I'd asked before, I'd made grand, romantic gestures, and both times he'd said no (and started dating someone new). This morning was no different. He still didn't want to be my boyfriend. Heartbroken and convinced I couldn't do healthy relationships, I revenge-downloaded Tinder that afternoon. My very first match was Joe, a downright pretty man. We started texting, but we wouldn't actually go on a date for six months.

I decided to drown my Mitch-related sorrows in work. A coffee shop was opening in town, and I heard they had good insurance for part-time employees. I got a job as a morning barista so the hours wouldn't interfere with my teaching. Of course, I had to work a full week at the café to make what I did in two hours of teaching, but this job wasn't about the money. It was about the insurance and about staying busy so I wouldn't keep pouting over a boy.

Short story shorter: I got fired two days before I qualified for insurance.

Short story a little longer: The atmosphere at the café pinged my shame and rage.

Behold the mindfuck that ensued when I overcooked a pastry one day:

Annoyed Supervisor (*we'll call her Joan.*). What's wrong with this picture?

Me. What picture?

Joan. What's wrong with this pastry?

Me. "I don't know."

Joan. It's been overcooked. Why did you overcook it?

Me. Sorry, I didn't realize I had.

Joan. If you don't take it out immediately, it will overcook.

Me, *aggressively, and thus terrifying the sweet yet shame-wielding nineteen-year-old Joan, who, if you haven't noticed yet, was Grandpa McLean incarnate.* Just tell me that, then! I didn't do it wrong ON PURPOSE!

It was shit like this all the time. Pushing all of those Grandpa shame buttons over and over.

The flashbacks to missing remote-control batteries and shoes in the wrong place became too much, and I eventually snapped at a traveling manager who also had a little bit of Grandpa in her. She saw on the wall a little cheat sheet that our manager had put up so we'd know how many pumps of syrup each drink size got. She ripped it off the wall and said, "YOU SHOULD KNOW THIS ALREADY!"

That was it. "Don't SHAME me!" I yelled. She began to cry, and I got the axe.

I knew before this incident that I had shame, of course, but I hadn't put it together that rage was my reaction to shame. With my new self-awareness from therapy and recovery, I knew I couldn't ignore my rage-management issues. I needed a solution, and a possible solution presented itself.

One of my students was the child of Brad and his wife, Michelle. I hadn't met Brad before, but I heard that he and Michelle run a week-long therapy intensive called Finding You.[33] I decided to sign up because I couldn't address my shame and rage on my own, especially because I was particularly fragile: in the course of three months, beautiful Simone died of cancer, the man I'd dreamed of marrying rejected me yet again and started dating someone new, and I got fired from a job I was completely overqualified for. I was sad and alone and grieving, my temper was on a hair trigger, and I had to own that several of the trials in my life were on me.

---

33 Check out the program's website to learn more about their therapeutic intensives at *FindingYouPrograms.com*

I needed help paying for Finding You, and I pitched it to my parents as one-tenth the cost of inpatient treatment. They agreed to sponsor me. I had no idea what I was getting myself into.

I drove the fifteen miles from Heber to Park City on a Wednesday afternoon in February 2019. The air felt enchanted. Sundance Film Festival had just finished, and a special quiet descends after such a massive event. I was nervous but hopeful as I pulled up to the snow-covered cabin that would be my home for the next five days.

Claire, a therapist, greeted me, and six other human beings arrived one by one. Over the next five days, we would become family as we embarked on intensive psychodramatic therapy, where we'd attempt to heal our trauma by reenacting it with guidance from a therapist. We all ate together, slept under the same roof, and shared our deepest pain. It was one of the most beautiful experiences of my life—being held and honored by people who learned things about me that I thought nobody could hear and still go on liking me.

The first couple of days we spent reconnecting to our inner children and exploring our childhood wounds. It was hard, beautiful work. Emma, one of the therapists, taught us about boundaries using a metaphor called relationship circles. The gist is that any relationship has three circles: your circle (where you learn what is true for you), the other person's circle (where they learn what is true for them), and the relationship circle (where you negotiate and work out how to stay connected without abandoning your truths). The rules are that you can't leave your circle and you can't hang out in anyone else's circle. You can put one foot into the relationship circle, but that's all.

The importance of our inner-child work became clear: you need to make peace with yourself in order to truly exist in your circle. I'd believed for too long that to love someone meant abandoning myself (leaving my circle empty) and trying to fix them (taking over their circle).[34]

The second half of the week was devoted to our current traumas. We would each take turns processing them over the course of two days. I decided to go last because I wanted to see the process in action—and because I was afraid of what I needed to work through. I spent the first day supporting my fellow participants' healing processes. As the day ended and the next day's session came closer, my mind became plagued with panic, fear, and every imaginable emotion. As I had been learning to do in recovery and therapy, though, I sat with these emotions. I looked at them and honored them. I didn't sleep a wink.

When my turn came the next day, I created a huge circle with ropes and stood inside it. Claire followed me into the circle after a few moments, took my hand, and kindly asked, "How do you see this going?"

"I need to invite everything and everyone to leave my circle so I have room to exist," I announced. "I'm terrified, and I need to ask God to help me."

Claire asked, "Who do you want to play God?" I laughed and chose a lovely woman named Joy. Joy put on a scarf that set her apart as God, and I asked her to stand just behind me and hold my shoulder. I then asked someone to represent my parents and someone to stand in for all of my friends. Someone was drugs. Another was gay. Another was Mormonism. I kept adding to my circle: My grandparents, my Vegas days, my New York life. Josh. Christopher. Mitch. And then with Joy-God at my shoulder and Claire helping me when I couldn't find the words, I spoke to each

---

34 Brad discusses the circles concept extensively in his book *The Audacity to Be You: Learning to Love Your Horrible, Rotten Self* (self-pub., 2020).

entity one by one. When I said what I needed to say, I invited them to leave my circle.

Some people were hard to let go of. Others were easier. Sometimes I had to reverse roles or play both parts until I was ready to move on. I owned my voice, screaming and yelling when I needed to and whispering when that was enough.

I thanked drugs for helping me cope, and, assuring them that I could make it without their help, I invited them to leave.

I apologized to Casey Nicholaw for being a brat. I thanked the whole theater world for helping me grow and giving me a safe place to land when I came out as gay. But now I needed to trust myself over their opinions about me, so they were excused.

I told Grandma and Grandpa McLean that I hadn't deserved their abuse. I invited them to leave.

I spoke to my parents and was surprisingly gentle with both of them. I told them I understood why they'd done what they did. I told them we were going to be okay and that I loved them. And I asked them to step out of my circle.

I apologized to Christopher for hurting him and for claiming to love him when I didn't know what loving someone meant.

I did the same for Josh.

Finally, one last person remained: Mitch. I held his hands and said, "I'm terrified that if I let you go, I won't be able to stay sober. The dream of having a family with you has been so powerful and motivating for me that it kept me clean for two years. But it's time for me to learn sobriety for myself, by myself." Weeping, I hugged him, told him I loved him, and asked him to leave my circle.

In the end, I stood in my near-empty circle, just me and God remaining. The entire process had taken a couple of hours. I was shaking, but I kept breathing until the tremors slowed and then stopped. I was connected to myself, and I stood with a loving, supportive, constant God. I thought I'd learned connection in that chakra class with Kelly, but now I saw that I hadn't been ready back then. I hadn't fully understood. Now, though, I was ready to return to my life, knowing that trauma healing is possible.

When I went home, I went to my tattoo artist to have my sleeve finished. On my left bicep, close to my heart, a representation of my inner child joined the peony, the strawberry, and the crown. I would never abandon him again.

59

BRAD

An Exquisite Lesson

In many religions, including Mormon, Jewish, Islamic, and Christian sects, faith is seen as the great gift to carry us across turbulent waters. In Buddhism and other Eastern religions, this idea is replaced with something called *radical acceptance*. Radical acceptance says that the universe operates in a certain way, and this holds an exquisite lesson that leads to many treasures. When we spend time focusing on the way things should be or the way that we wish things were going, we miss these treasures. Radical acceptance invites us to find the meaning in our trials and our pain. The sister characteristic to radical acceptance is mindfulness, or the act of being present with our feelings. Perhaps Rilke, the renowned Austrian poet, says it best: "Let everything happen to you: beauty and terror. Just keep going. No feeling is final."[35]

---

35 "Go to the Limits of Your Longing," in *Rilke's Book of Hours: Love Poems to God*, trans. Anita Barrows and Joanna Macy (New York: Riverhead Books, 2005).

Questions for Brad

Jeff says that his boss at the coffee shop pushed all of his "Grandpa shame buttons." How do you deal with encountering people who are your abusers (without getting fired)?

Our childhood contexts and relationships shape us in certain ways. It's like we're cut into a certain kind of puzzle piece, fitting with people who resemble the characters from our childhoods. For example, children (or grandchildren) of narcissists often end up in relationships with narcissists. The similarities between spouse and father may appear scant on the surface, but the commonalities will eventually reveal themselves. These patterns also frequently surface in our professional relationships, as they did with Jeff at the coffee shop.

We go back and work through our early childhood experiences not to assign blame or identify villains, but to heal. And until we do this work, we are prone to relationships that look like the ones we had in childhood. If we are reluctant to look back at childhood for understanding, we are most likely still carrying around dysfunctional defenses.

The circle exercise that Jeff does at Finding You feels impossible to me. How do you let go of everything and stand alone in your circle?

The circle exercise is a beautiful illustration of Campbell's idea that "We must be willing to get rid of the life we've planned, so as to have the life that is waiting for us."[36] Sometimes the life we'd

36 Robert Walter and Diane K. Osbon, eds., *Reflections on the Art of Living: A Joseph Campbell Companion* (New York: HarperCollins, 1991), 5.

planned is taken from us. Sometimes we let it go. But it is the same either way. We must be willing to keep moving after failure and heartbreak and disappointment to find what is waiting for us around the next turn. It is not an easy process. It is oftentimes so painful and powerful that, in myth, death is often—and aptly—used to symbolize the process. We must be willing to die over and over again to make room for the life that is waiting for us. The snake that does not shed its skin will perish.

At Finding You Therapy Programs, we use these intensive therapeutic group processes as a tool to help people discover who they really are. We look back on our lives to find out how our earliest contexts shaped us. We look back to find out why we are struggling today. The process is nearly impossible to describe, but it's so beautiful that virtually everybody who has participated in these workshops has described them as life-changing.

Reflection Questions

1. Had you heard of radical acceptance before encountering it in this book? How can you start to practice it in your life?
2. Do you find yourself in relationship with, or working with, the same types of people over and over?
3. Can you envision a life where you remain in your own circle and step just one foot into a "relationship circle" with others?

60

MICHAEL

Following in My Son's Footsteps

It must be clear by now that I was raised in a traditional household, and I had to unlearn a lot of my parents' ways of doing things. The beginning of a song I wrote, "Listen to Me," illustrates their approach:

> Listen to me
> The first words I remember hearing from my dad
> Listen to me
> He started every conversation that we had
> Listen to me
> My youngest son, there are some jobs that must be done
> Listen to me, listen to me

I knew that this parenting method had been damaging for Jeff and me. Going forward, I knew I needed to listen to Jeff. I went even further. I wanted to listen to what he listened to. I wanted to do the things he was doing.

I took Transcendental Meditation classes because he had, and I began a twice-daily meditation habit. I attended the Finding

You therapy intensive after Jeff did. It had profoundly affected him, and I wanted to learn the language he'd learned at the retreat.

I watched several videos about the addictive brain and learned from some of Jeff's mentors, sponsors, and teachers about how difficult Jeff's challenges were. I learned about the inevitable relapses that are part of the recovery process. And I learned that I had to accept the fact that my son might, in fact, end his life—that oftentimes my attempts to try to prevent his suicide were in fact the very triggers that made his burden worse.

61

BRAD

Common Ground

Michael's decision to explore recovery for Jeff's sake is not uncommon. Parents go to Al-Anon meetings or therapy or workshops to support their children and find some common ground. But in the end, the parents often walk away with their own personal treasures.

Reflection Questions

1. Did/do your parents take time to listen to you, or were/are you expected to listen to them with no reciprocation?
2. As a parent, what can you learn from your own child's journey, even if—or especially if—it differs from your own?

62

JEFF

Partnered with God

I left the Finding You therapy retreat with just me and God in my circle, and with the help of a therapist the program recommended, I kept it that way. I changed my perspective on partnership. I'd been told coupling up was the only way to grow, but now I saw that I could be partnered with God or myself. No spouse required. It was disorienting at first not to live for another person, but I began to get used to it. And then I began to love it.

As I'd told Mitch-in-the-Circle, I really did start choosing sobriety for myself. No longer was I staying sober so that I could be in a relationship with someone else.

The more I partnered with God, the more I saw that my value had nothing to do with my job, who I knew, or how much I would bend over backward for others. That insight allowed me to value others for who they were—not for what they could do for me or what I could do for them.

I found that I loved myself for who I am and without condition—I told you this was a love story.

My reentry into life after Finding You yielded some unexpected side effects as well. I soon found myself collecting new interests—cross-stitch, yoga, baking—not because other people would think they were cool but because they genuinely appealed to me. I said yes to everything my heart wanted to say yes to.

I started thinking about getting my master's degree in psychology and combining it with my voice teaching. I could be the Brené Brown of vocal teachers. I also built an app and website where Dad can house all of his past work as well as create new content and share stories like only he can.[37]

The Finding You therapy team put me in touch with a brilliant therapist after the Finding You retreat. Each therapist I've had in my life has built upon the ones who came before, and I believe Dr. Jami Gill is the greatest one to date.[38]

She and I began working with the voice in my head. This voice is related to the much-diminished Unlovable Monster, but it is a little more articulate. It may bear a resemblance to a certain Grandpa McLean. Jami had me write down everything the voice said. I recorded such gems as, *All of your friends hate you, and you don't deserve anyone's love* and *You don't deserve to be alive* and—my favorite—*If only you would die and end it all, everyone would be so much happier. In fact, they would dance on your grave.*

Obviously, none of this was true. But why did it feel true? Jami suggested I read the statements the next day. And sure enough, the next day, they'd lost their power. They were laughable.

Following this writing practice, I began to detach from the voice, which I began to realize was on my addict brain's payroll. With continued meditation practice, I've learned to acknowledge

37 Check out allthingsmichaelmclean.com to experience the joy that is my father.

38 For a list of Jami's books, search for the author J. D. Gill.

and release these thoughts. Don't get me wrong, though. I still think the most outlandish things at times. A delightful example: *Not only do your friends hate you, but right now they are sitting around discussing all the ways that you disgust them.*

When my addict brain tries to bait me with a statement like this, I can make one of three choices:

1. Agree with the voice, spiraling into a wormhole of nasty thoughts.
2. Berate and punish myself for such stupid thoughts.
3. Say to my brain, "Interesting thought. I think you might be feeling rejected."

In the first two choices, I'm allowing my addict brain to win. In the third choice, I'm healthy and aware, not shaming my addict brain, but not giving in either. I'm grateful to say this is where I live most of the time. I let my dark feelings exist and then shower them with love. Of course, I still go with choice one or two sometimes. I'm human, after all. But the difference now is that I don't take up residence in these choices. If I do, I will use. Simple as that.

✢

From this place of clarity and love and really living, I decided to go on a brunch date with Joe, the guy I'd matched with on Tinder six months earlier. It was the first Sunday in April 2019.

Joe was really, really pretty. To be honest, I thought he seemed a little fake. He used photo filters and knew how to pose a little too well (he is a social media marketing expert with quite a following on Instagram). But I decided to just go with it and see him for who he was—no expectations. I wasn't trying to impress him.

I didn't need him to like me so I could like myself.

We brunched. And talked. And walked. And kept talking. And made out. The kissing was epic, so we kept kissing.

After that first day, it made sense to keep seeing each other. It was effortless. It was the first non-codependent relationship either of us had experienced, so we didn't even recognize what was happening: we were slowly coming to love each other in a mature, beautiful way.

Joe is driven and sexy and nerdy. He needs an invitation to speak, but when he gets one, the most amazing things come out of his mouth. Our chemistry is remarkable, and we can say brave, honest things to each other that I never would have imagined with a past partner—like, "When we break up, let's be better off than when we met."

All of these things are terrific, but the most beautiful thing about Joe is that he is *kind*. After all the relationships and all the drama, I simply wanted someone kind who would inspire me to be kind.

When Joe and I were in the initial exploration stages, I traveled to Tulum, Mexico, and started working on this book. Telling my story brought me panic and fear. I knew I wanted to write to heal myself and to try to help LGBTQ+ children, but what if what I really wanted was attention, to be the most interesting man in the room? What if I found out that my story wasn't worth writing after all? I felt those feelings, thought those thoughts, and then let them pass. I just wrote and proved to myself that I truly had experienced healing.

A little while later—when Joe and I had been dating for a couple of months—I went to visit some friends in LA I felt a little stirring. What was it? Oh. I missed Joe. I'd always been used to bombast, but this was subtle. I was experiencing something new.

When I got back, Joe and I were lying in bed, and I asked him if he wanted to be my boyfriend. I was terrified. My heart had been ripped to shreds. How could I have made myself so vulnerable?

But Joe smiled and said *yes yes yes*. It felt glorious.

For a day.

Doubt and skepticism set in. Had I made the wrong decision? Wasn't failure inevitable?

Joe was sweet. He just let me be in my drama but didn't get involved. He had never been through the circles exercise, so I didn't understand how he knew to stay put in his own circle. I was impressed. Here was a man who could be true to himself.

The very next week, Joe lost his job. His ex had left him to tend a failing business, and it went belly-up. Joe would have to live off his Instagram ad revenue. I wanted to help, so I made some choices that I felt a little apprehensive about: When Joe's computer broke, I bought him another one. I paid for his gas since he had to drive from Salt Lake to Heber to see me. I helped him furnish and organize his room. In short, I overextended in true McLean fashion, showing up for him more than anyone ever had.

My apprehensions kicked in because I saw myself following an old pattern—giving and giving with little in return. But this time around, something was different. Fresh out of Finding You, I had enough perception to figure out what the difference was: I didn't feel an ounce of desperation. I wasn't buying things for Joe in an effort to keep him around. I'd learned how to be okay if he decided to walk away. No, I was simply trying to show up for my partner, trusting that the returns would come later and that my choice to help would be worth it. And I'm happy to report that it was. Life with Joe was just plain good. We spent most nights together. When we got agitated, we talked it out. We held each other without trying to carry each other.

And then the world stopped. We were in LA meeting with some casting directors who had worked on *Project Runway* and *Making the Cut*. They wanted to discuss making Farmer Jeff into a reality TV show. The next day, the vague news I'd heard about some virus became front-page material. COVID-19 shut everything down.

We had to quarantine, but Joe and I wanted to be together. So my mother invited Joe to move in with us. Yes, you read that right. Lynne McLean of *seeing as how you are living in disgusting sin* fame invited her gay son's boyfriend to shack up with the whole family. (Oh, and, Grandma and Grandpa McLean, if you're reading this in the great beyond, we share your old room.)

Scott moved home, too, and we all got closer, working on our projects and growing. Joe began pursuing his dream of writing and producing music, and he put out a few EPs.

I kept writing my book and building the app and website for Dad. I also created a video series featuring the basics of my vocal approach. It's called *Find Your Voice: Anyone Can Sing*. I'm another step closer to becoming the Brené Brown of voice.

63

BRAD

Walking Together

Without space, a couple becomes one person. But since no two people can truly become one, what really happens is that one partner, at least, is left out of the equation. It's like what I heard an older gentleman advise a new couple at their wedding many years ago: "If you're not fighting with each other, one of you is an idiot." Kahlil Gibran says it a little more gently:

> But let there be spaces in your togetherness,
>
> And let the winds of the heavens dance between you.
>
> Love one another but make not a bond of love:
>
> Let it rather be a moving sea between the shores of your souls.
>
> Fill each other's cup but drink not from one cup.
>
> Give one another of your bread but eat not from the same loaf.
>
> Sing and dance together and be joyous, but let each one of you be alone,

> Even as the strings of a lute are alone though they quiver with the same music.
>
> For the pillars of the temple stand apart,
>
> And the oak tree and the cypress grow not in each other's shadow.[39]

I think this is a very different idea from what most people think about when they think about intimacy and love. Loving somebody means helping them get to where they need to go. Love and intimacy are not about the fusing together of two people into one. Intimacy is about two distinct people deciding to walk together on their journey home.

Questions for Brad

I like Jeff's insight that he and Joe hold each other but don't carry each other. What happens if you need to be carried?

Our wives, our husbands, and the people we love can't always carry us. They have their own pain to deal with. I find that it's essential to find somebody whose job it is to hold us—a support group or a therapist who helps us carry the heavy load of guilt, shame, and fear that comes with changing family patterns. Is the Apostle Paul anticipating the wonders of therapy when he encourages the early Christians to "bear ye one another's burdens"?[40]

When I was younger, I thought therapy would solve my

---

39 Gibran, *The Prophet*.

40 Gal. 6:2 (KJV).

problems. Now I know that therapy is a place I go to get support to help *me* solve my problems. I go there to be found, to be seen. I go there so the load is not too heavy.

Jeff says that Joe is kind. That is appealing in a partner, but I feel like I need someone who isn't too soft on me. Is it okay to prioritize finding someone who challenges me?

A great partner is not somebody who kicks you in the butt and calls you on your crap. That quickly gets old. A great partner is somebody who loves and sees you. And in being loved and seen, we are inspired. *Should* and *thou shalt not* fall away as our walls come down and we learn to contact the light and love that was lost and buried so many years ago.

Reflection Questions

1. If you are partnered, do you feel like you and your partner are two distinct people?
2. Think about your parents' partnership. Did they exhibit the kind of intimacy that Gibran rhapsodizes about in his poem?
3. How do you offer kindness to your loved ones?
4. Do you receive enough kindness from those in your life?

64

MICHAEL

Honoring Separate Paths

For many years, I saw Jeff's failed relationships as evidence that gay relationships are doomed because they are wrong. Then Jeff met Joe. From the time they started dating, I noticed that Joe brought out the best, most authentic parts of Jeff, and vice versa. They worked together well, and they complemented each other professionally and personally.

Seeing this functional and deeply good relationship, I began to wonder if the Biblical statement *It is not good for man to be alone* pertains not just to an Adam and Eve and a Michael and Lynne but also to a Jeff and Joe?

I'm sure I'm not the only conservative, churchgoing, God-fearing father to wrestle with these issues, but my experience in transitioning from *tolerating* to genuinely *loving* has been facilitated by a guy named Joe. (If they ever split up, I think I might miss Joe more than Jeff would!) I also found that the more I accepted Jeff and Joe, the more they accepted and supported me.

Jeff had pitched to me a subscription-based website that

would gather all things Michael McLean—my albums, books, musicals, and sheet music. Oh, and a podcast. I started to rack my brain for a big idea that would bring people to the website. One night in December 2019, it occurred to me that in April, the church would be celebrating the 200th anniversary of Joseph Smith's First Vision. I knew that people who had bought my albums and attended *The Forgotten Carols* each year would be happy to hear something new celebrating this anniversary.

I wrote a song called "He Looked Up." It was about the First Vision, but it was from the point of view of Joseph's older brother Hyrum. I created a demo with a simple piano track and vocals by a singer I knew in Arizona.

I sent the demo out to potential orchestrators, arrangers, and well-known singers. No one was interested. They liked the song, but for whatever reason, they didn't want to get involved. The closer we got to April 2020, the more desperate I became. When COVID-19 hit, recording the song in a polished, professional way seemed officially impossible.

Because the song was so linked to the church Jeff had left, I didn't want to trigger him by asking for his help. But he knew I was having a hard time. About a week before the window to release this song would close, Jeff came into my studio and said, "Dad, I think God wants me to help you get your song out there. I have a producer friend who's young and dynamic. I think he can take the tracks you have and build something awesome. He would keep the spirit of the piece, but it may be a little bit hipper than you imagined."

I was touched by the offer and by Jeff's belief that he could pull it off, but I had my doubts. Four days later, though, he played me the song, and I wept. It was perfect.

Joe—who had also been raised in the church—created a video of the song and put it up on YouTube. He marketed it so beautifully that within a week, the song had over 70,000 views. My social media pages were filled with praise for the song. It was reaching more people than I had ever imagined. As I write this, there are now over 248,000 views.

People can honor and support and sustain each other on their separate paths. Jeff and Joe exemplified this in another experience shortly before the pandemic:

Jeff asked Joe to join him in supporting a favorite cousin, Jane, at her eight-year-old daughter's baptism and confirmation. I didn't learn until later how reticent Joe was to attend. He worried that showing up as a gay couple might be awkward. But Jeff insisted, "What better way to see if you really want to be a part of this family than to go to a baptism?"

After the confirmation, Jane embraced her daughter, May, and thanked everyone who came to support them: "I want May to know that this church isn't perfect. As a member, you'll sometimes wonder if you can find peace and connection in this community. But, May, now that you're part of this imperfect organization trying to follow a perfect God, you have a chance like all of us here to try to make it better."

Later that evening, I learned about Jeff and Joe's discussion on their drive home. Joe felt the love and acceptance of the family and told Jeff he was glad he went. Jeff replied, "That's what we do in this family. We show up. We show up and love on 'em when they're baptized, and we'll show up and love on 'em if they leave."

65

BRAD

Willing to Work

It wasn't just Michael who had made his way back to Jeff. Jeff also made his way back to Michael. It's a two-way street. Each person's ability to reach out and connect to the other is founded in their personal work. And you can't rush it, force it, or require it just because you've done your part. It's each person's personal responsibility and decision to do their work. The great Ram Dass says it this way: "I can do nothing for you but work on myself . . . you can do nothing for me but work on yourself!"[41] Reconciliation is the practical outcome of two people who are willing to do their work.

Questions for Brad

How has Michael been able to reinterpret various religious teachings to support his son?

---

41 Ram Dass, *Be Here Now* (Santa Fe, NM: Hanuman Foundation, 2010), 44.

Michael's ability to apply the phrase "It is not good for man to be alone" to his gay son is an example of spirituality. His interpretation of the concept is beyond the fundamental and dogmatic interpretation that many people have. He is in touch with the divine. He understands the spirit of God. So many people get caught up in how many angels can dance on the head of a pin. But real spiritual transformation is always about love.

How can Jeff be so supportive of his family's Mormonism?

I admit I had the same question when I embarked on this project. I didn't know if there would be enough room in this story for both the Mormon Church and Jeff's pain. I didn't know if we could walk the middle path. But as the seminal stories of our time teach, villains aren't all bad and heroes aren't all good. The middle path began as a Buddhist idea that refutes the dualistic ideas of good and evil, of right and wrong. In mental health, we understand that thinking in terms of polarities is a common ailment associated with mental illness. All of my favorite stories—the ones about our complex humanity—are about the middle path. The story of Jeff and Michael is just such a story.

Reflection Questions

1. How do you feel when you consider walking the middle path?
2. What work are you doing to know yourself better and to help you connect better with your loved ones?

66

JEFF

Let's Go Live

The second travel opened up, Joe and I jumped at a chance to visit Tulum. We were alone for the first time in a year, and we spent the trip rediscovering each other in a new way. One day, we had an intense spa experience involving passionfruit paste and roaming naked through the jungle. It ended up with a massage and energy work. The massage was terrible, but the energy work was transformative. At one point, the shaman held his hands over my heart, and all I could do was cry.

The next day, Joe was feeling sick after all the mud and passionfruit and saunas and cooling pools from spa day. As we lay in bed, I had a feeling. I realized that the shaman had energetically opened my heart, and I could feel a question starting to emerge. I rolled to face Joe and said, "Joe, will you marry me?" His eyes filled with tears, and just like before, he said *yes yes yes.*

⁘

It was weird to be engaged because I had been excited about being single. And I didn't want to change the ending of this book, which was in development at the same time as my relationship with Joe. I didn't want my story to end with anything resembling *And then Prince Jeff and Prince Joe got married and lived happily ever after.*

I admit that I also didn't want my mom to be right about a certain something. For years, if I told my mother about any discovery I'd made that would improve my life, she'd say, "Now you're ready to get married!"

Once I said to her, "Mom, can you stop with the marriage talk? I am working through a serious addiction that stems from a fervent belief that my only value in life is to get married. Please! Stop!"

Her response was classic Lynne. She looked at me and said, "Of course. You are making such good progress. Now you are ready to get married."

I couldn't help but laugh and hug her. "Okay, Mom, now I'm ready to get married. You're right."

I talked to Jami about my marriage concerns. She said something that I'd never heard before and will never forget: "Jeff, you are getting married, but not just to Joe. You are marrying yourself. That means you're learning how to stay committed and to integrate all the parts of yourself." So I would take my commitment to Joe seriously, and, even more importantly, I would take my commitment to myself seriously.

One Friday, I became very serious indeed. Joe and I strolled into Heber's town hall and got ourselves a marriage license. We had thirty days to get married. My last wedding had been such a spectacle—so much of my life had been a spectacle—we wanted to keep it simple. We just wanted to be married. We called Mayor Kelleen Potter and asked if we could get married in her office on the Thursday morning before our license's expiration. I'd met the mayor when we'd both addressed the Gay-Straight Alliance at a local middle school. She is a great LGBTQIA+ ally, galvanized by her experience as a mother to queer and transgender children. She'd been responsible for a set of beautiful banners along Heber Main Street that said, "Pride in the Wasatch Back" (the east side of the Wasatch Range is the Wasatch Back, while the west side is the Wasatch Front). The town received national attention when a group of concerned citizens tried to force the banners' removal. That dubious attention brought more attention, and the HBO show *We're Here*, which features drag performers bringing their acts to small-town America, considered shooting an episode in Heber. The casting director interviewed me for a couple of hours, and we discussed doing a drag performance with me and my dad. It didn't end up happening—*We're Here* chose St. George, Utah, instead of Heber—but it got me thinking about how comfortable I am in my masculine persona and how scary it is for me to think about giving that up to put on makeup and feminine attire.

On July 15, 2021, the last possible Thursday covered by our marriage license, Joe and I and our tiny wedding party—Mom, Dad, and Scott—went to Chick's Café for breakfast. At ten o'clock, the mayor married us in her office at the town hall. As we walked out of the historic building, I pointed out to Joe the exact place where I'd learned about Steve Smith. The earth I'd stood on when I learned that gay meant death and AIDS. Thirty years later, my husband and I posed in that spot for our wedding pictures. Profound change is possible in this life.

Nine years after God had called me home to heal, Joe asked if we could move to LA—West Hollywood, to be exact, a walkable oasis in car-clogged Los Angeles. *Yes yes yes*, I said.

After a crazy search for a place, a little gem fell into our laps. The apartment next door to a dear friend became available, and Joe drove down to look. We signed the lease before it even went on the market.

A few weeks later, we packed up and planned to drive through the night to our new home. I will always remember stepping out of the Heber house and walking down the gravel road to where our U-Haul was parked. I stopped for a moment under a sky full of stars and scanned the space that had been my home. It had taken me in. I had learned to hate myself here, but I'd also learned to heal. I uttered a little prayer of gratitude. *Thank you, Heber. Thank you, home. Thank you, God, for everything that brought me to this plot of land in the middle of Utah that will always be a refuge from the storm.*

Joe was waiting for me in the truck. "Everything okay, babe?" he called.

"Everything's great." I took my place in the driver's seat, started the truck, and pulled out of the driveway. I turned to Joe and said, "Okay. Let's go live!"

67

BRAD

Find New Lands

On occasion, my adult children have asked me advice on looking for a marriage partner. I'm reluctant to offer much in the way of advice as this part of the journey is one's own responsibility. But I do counsel them to look for a partner who is willing to grow and change. Because no matter who you are and who they are, you will both be different people in ten or twenty years. If you're the same person twenty years from now, you've wasted twenty years. So find somebody who's willing to let go of the shore to find new lands. Find somebody who's willing to accept new ideas and go into the forest where it's darkest. This is the adventure!

Reflection Questions

1. What about Jeff and Joe's marriage appeals to you?
2. Think about points of major transition in your life. Did you meet them with excitement, apprehension, terror?

EPILOGUE

Michael

I've experienced applause and standing ovations before in my five decades of performing. But nothing before felt quite the same as the applause I received after giving the keynote address at the 2021 conference for North Star, an organization for Mormons who also belong to the LGBTQ+ community.

I shared with the audience some of my experiences as a faithful Mormon with a gay son, and I debuted a new song there:

Maybe you've been judged or hurt or shamed

Those are surely wounds that need to heal

It's not for me to blame you hating those who should be blamed

But maybe we can change the way we feel

Just because your journey has been hard

Doesn't mean it has to stay that way

Just because you thought you'd never have to climb so far

Doesn't mean you won't arrive today

Trusting is what will lead to
Believing what you need to find a way to end a lifelong war
You've been fighting but don't need to anymore

Could it be we're limiting the Lord,
Setting boundaries for the work He does?
Maybe we could burn those gates down with a flaming sword
And cross those borders straight into His love
Just because you took more time to find the faith to see
Doesn't mean God wasn't there or that He'll never be
Maybe it's the hope you long for and need most somehow
It's the gift that heaven gives, so why not receive it now?

As the afternoon progressed, we laughed and cried, and at the end of my address, we joined together to sing one of my oldest hits, "I've Got to Find Out Who I Am."

And then came the final applause—the different applause. I felt something new. I don't think the group was clapping because they loved my songs or because I performed them particularly well. I believe they were thanking me for seeing them, for celebrating them in all their diversity, for embracing our shared humanity, and for acknowledging that God is with us on this journey. Jeff was the catalyst. My experiences with him made me open to these gifts: the ability to see, celebrate, embrace, and acknowledge.

✣

Now that we've become so close, I feel comfortable sharing with all of you a journal entry I wrote as Jeff, Brad, and I came to the end of collaborating on this book. I hope it can serve as a benediction.

Today, two important moments collided. I don't think it was a coincidence.

Jeff called from California to give me an update on how his life is going, how he and Joe are doing in LA, and how close we are to finishing this book. He then said that if there was anything about our telling this story that was uncomfortable for me or triggered me in any way, he was willing to shelve the last three years of work so that I wasn't put in an awkward spot. He said that he was rather amazed at how the process of writing it with me, and with Brad Reedy, was such an essential part of his healing.

This call came right after I had seen a film called Swan Song *starring Mahershala Ali. The movie explores how far we will go, and how much we're willing to sacrifice, to make a happier life for the people we love.*

Writing and revealing our family saga/secrets in Stay in the Room *is, for me, about my own exploration of how much I would sacrifice to make a happier life for the people I love. The book ultimately begs the question,* Am I willing to sacrifice how people see me now that they've read this story, seen all the flaws and mistakes and struggles I've had with my son, my faith, my church, my understanding of God?

You pay a price when you choose any form of sacrifice, but you also give yourself a gift when you make that choice. It's the gift of discovering what it means to take yourself out of the equation, to put your faith in the power of facing and sharing your truth and freeing yourself from the fear of what consequences might follow. I've spent my life as a songwriter, filmmaker, playwright, and performer trying to use art to reveal truth. And now, in the final chapters of my life, I'm trusting that my unvarnished truth, learned with my son and shared through this book, may be the only truth that matters.

EPILOGUE

Jeff

I just got off the phone with my dad. Deep in the edits for this book, we had to discuss parts of our unpleasant past. I asked if he wanted to comment and if I could help him process the events. He dodged my questions. In the past, I would have immediately shifted into super defense mode. Instead, I had this weird feeling.

Peace.

Weirder still, I heard the following come out of my mouth *completely snark-free*: "Dad, if you're this uncomfortable, why don't we just shelve the project?" It was a genuine offer that came from a place of love. I found that I didn't need to protect myself, and I didn't need to teach my dad a lesson. But where were the old Jeff and his Unlovable Monster sidekick?

I attribute my change in approach to one major skill: taking ownership. Owning your story and your feelings—writing them down, sharing them, processing them—is powerful and transformative. Owning your story allows you to change the narrative. Today, I make the choice to treat myself and others differently than I have in the past. I choose to treat us all with love. The more I love myself, the more I can give others love in an honest and authentic way.

I envision giving this love out in great quantities, showering it on you, on myself, on the little Unlovable Monster, on my dad. These love showers have proven to be the antidote to my anxieties and resentments.

Where do I find all of this love? From the ultimate source, of course: my relationship with the Divine. And I've become adept at storing up good feelings. When it's easy to feel happy, I set some of my contentment aside for a rainy day. The rainy days always come—sometimes with gale-force winds. Instead of letting the storm blow me this way and that, I draw on my stores of love and ask my feelings to come closer to the surface. I ask, *Why do you feel less than, Jeff?* Perhaps Scared Jeff responds, *I'm terrible at budgeting! I always fail. Why try again?* When I hear that kind of talk, I know it's time to shower Scared Jeff with some love. The last thing he needs in that moment is a scolding or even a budgeting lesson. He needs some compassion and patience.

Sometimes I travel through time and space to bring love to the different parts of myself. I've visited petrified eight-year-old Jeff on his baptism day. I've held him and told him that God is in everything: the good, the bad, the ugly, the joyful, the disturbed, the nasty, the pure. I've assured him that regardless of how much he ostensibly screws up his life, he can never be disconnected from God and Source and Love.

I feel so lucky that I could share my truths in this book and even luckier that my amazing therapist, my editor, and my beloved dad helped me hold these truths as we send them out to you, dear, dear reader.

EPILOGUE

Brad

As we work through any relationship, we run up against our own outmoded mindsets. One I had to unlearn is the notion that as a therapist (or husband, father, or friend), my role is to take away people's pain or to make them feel happy.

I saw the error of this belief years ago as I sat on a broken fence in the rain with Adam, a young man who was grieving the loss of his mother. I could not "make Adam happy"—nor would it have been appropriate to try. As I cried with him, I learned that my job was to sit with people in their pain. I couldn't remove their suffering, but I could keep them company so they didn't have to suffer alone. When others are suffering, the last thing we can offer them is our company. To sit with someone in their unsolvable problem is perhaps the greatest expression of love.

Since I began practicing therapy, I have often wondered if it is possible to pass on to others the deep wisdom that is forged through suffering. Can you truly teach others these hard-earned, hard-fought lessons? I had my doubts until I became more conscious of Campbell's writings on the hero's journey, especially the last stage of that journey: the return.

Before the hero's return, the hero surrenders. They have adventured through the darkest of trials—traversing the desert, facing dragons—with little reassurance. The hero's surrender is not the loss of all hope but rather the giving up of an old way of life. This surrender is the death of old dreams, of the life the hero once imagined. These must be forfeited to make way for something larger. This larger thing is a new birth, a new self, a new way of being in the world. The hero—and we—cannot put new wine into old bottles, nor can we build houses on cracked and crumbling foundations.

The hero brings back to their community an elixir acquired during the journey. The elixir was never in the plan. The hero thought they were looking for the grail (as in King Arthur tales) or the plan of immortal life (as in the ancient story of Gilgamesh). But the elixir eclipses these former ambitions. It is a healing balm.

The hero's story itself is the healing elixir. In the journey's last stage, the hero shares their story so others can find themselves in it.

Storytelling has always been a principal tool for teaching complex ideas. It is more effective than mere explanation when the goal is to convey esoteric concepts inherent to the higher levels of consciousness. Stories act as metaphors, evoking feelings and senses without getting bogged down in specifics.

Prophet's stories don't provide details like how to repair a refrigerator or whether we should pursue a career in orthopedic surgery. Instead, they provide rich with profound truths. They tell us the story of one person or one group as if to say, "This is how this person or these people awoke to find themselves. This is a story about one truth."

We must make the choice to actively make connections between these stories and our own lives. As we make this choice, we can take a story, turn it into a seed, and plant it in our souls, where it becomes a template for our lives.

The elusive deep wisdom I thought was near-impossible to impart is passed along through storytelling. We sit in circles and tell our stories to those who haven't traveled yet. We describe our initial refusal to answer life's call. We recount how magical helpers or teachers appeared when all hope seemed to be lost. We show our scars and describe epic dragon battles designed for us alone, and we explain how we defeated (or made peace with) our dragons. We reveal the treasures we discovered on the other side of what frightened us most. While we can't fully transmit our lessons to others further back on the path, we can inspire hope if we are willing to tell our stories.

The problem is that many people can't hear the full richness of our stories. These folks have rejected the mystery and uncertainty that characterize both spirituality and the great stories, swapping them for the safety and security of explanations, dogma, and rules. Roger Waters and David Gilmour posit it this way:

> Did they get you to trade . . .
>
> Hot air for a cool breeze?
>
> Cold comfort for change?
>
> Did you exchange
>
> A walk-on part in the war
>
> For a leading role in a cage?[42]

42 Pink Floyd, "Wish and You Were Here," *Wish You Were Here,* released September 12, 1975, Harvest Records and Colombia Records.

I agreed to work on this project because I could see a healing elixir in Jeff and Michael's story, a balm for the many children who suffer alone because their contexts tell them that who they are is unacceptable. The McLeans' story needed to be told in all its mystery and uncertainty. It is both a very specific true story as well as a metaphor for the expansion required to reach higher levels of love and connection. Each of us must learn to stretch while still staying grounded.

✢

As I practice therapy, clients constantly confront me with questions like "*What should I do?*" and "*How do I do it?*" It is tempting to answer these questions, but I have learned to stay silent and to listen more deeply for the real question.

The real question is the one that comes from deep within. It is a search for hope, meaning, or tranquility. It is a search for the self. Finding ourselves is a messy business—difficult and nuanced. As Michael Meade once observed, "Becoming who we truly are requires the greatest amount of change."[43] Because the process is so taxing, we often settle for a paint-by-numbers sort of life. We don't learn how to paint a masterpiece, but we do learn how to color inside the lines. The truth is, however, that each person contains a masterpiece, a magnum opus, and it is their life. Discovering who you are is nonnegotiable in creating a more authentic life.

Father Richard Rohr says it best: "Could human life's central task be a matter of consciously discovering and becoming who we already are and what we somehow unconsciously know? I think

---

43 Michael Meade, *Why the World Doesn't End: Tales of Renewal in Times of Loss* (Vashon, WA: Mosaic Multicultural Foundation, 2012).

so. Life is not a matter of creating a special name for ourselves, but of uncovering the name we have always had."[44]

In my experience, we don't become ourselves alone. We must find somebody else who can stay in the room with us. It makes sense, doesn't it? We are healed in the same way we are wounded: in relationships. We must find somebody who can see us as we are.

During a recent talk to a group of parents, my adult daughter succinctly described how essential these willing helpers are: "Breaking free from my dysfunctional family patterns brings with it a lot of guilt. I go to therapy so my therapist can help me to carry this guilt."

The people who genuinely see us may seek us out. Or we may find ourselves in their stories. We may find these companions and narratives when we enter into a church, a Twelve-Step meeting, or a quiet conversation with an empathic and trusted friend. Expert therapists also create conditions where clients can find themselves. In fact, therapy is the art of helping people to become whole—to become who they are.

All of these contexts—church, recovery, friendship, therapy—are holy. Campbell taught that "Your sacred space is where you can find yourself again and again."[45] In my opinion, this was the initial significance of churches or temples: they were places to go to find yourself, your true nature. But like many things, the message got lost along the way and gave way to others dictating the way things *should* be. And it is understandable. The people who love us don't want to see us suffer, so they offer us clear guidelines

---

44 Richard Rohr, *Immortal Diamond: The Search for Our True Self* (San Francisco: Jossey-Bass, 2013), 12.

45 *A Joseph Campbell Companion: Reflections on the Art of Living*, ed. Diane K. Osbon (New York: HarperPerennial, 1991).

for avoiding pain. But a fully lived life is marked with pain, sorrow, fear, and grief. If these are not present, or to the extent that they are not present, the individual cannot feel joy, serenity, happiness, and freedom. As Kahlil Gibran notes, "Your pain is the breaking of the shell that encloses your understanding."[46]

Because it is natural to want to prevent the pain of those we love, parents, therapists, church leaders, and others can fall into the advice trap. They tell us to practice gratitude, be vulnerable, set boundaries, and so forth. The problem is that such behaviors are usually the *result* of self-discovery, not steps to finding the self.

Prophets and poets understand that advice and explanations fall short. No explanation, no advice, is adequate for showing people how to find themselves. No one taught Picasso to paint *Guernica*, nor could they have taught Shakespeare how to write *King Lear*. If the goal is to find yourself, as I believe it is, therapists and parents and friends cannot provide you with a step-by-step to get there.

The poet Matsuo Basho counsels, "Seek not the paths of the ancients; seek that which the ancients sought." Becoming who we are, unlearning what we were taught, finding enlightenment, and transforming: these are the most difficult and painful roads we travel. As a mirror image to the claim I cited in the introduction ("evil is a consequence, not a cause"[47]), enlightenment or self-actualization isn't found by doing the right things. Enlightenment is discovered through the process of becoming a self, and doing the "right thing"—that is, the authentic and courageous thing—can come only after that discovery.

---

46 Gibran, *The Prophet*.

47 Charles Eisenstein, *The More Beautiful World Our Hearts Know Is Possible* (Berkeley, CA: North Atlantic Books, 2013), 186.

We must walk into and through our fear, resentment, and guilt to escape the prison of self-doubt, self-hatred, or self-abuse. I've seen many clients get stuck here. They want the negative emotions to disappear, but, as every traveler who knows the path will tell you, the only way to let go of anger and resentment (toward self or others) is to battle the dragon of *should and should not* (in other words, the dragon of guilt and fear).

⁂

I hope you have found yourself in the McLeans' story. I hope you can see that you are not alone. We are not suggesting that you have to adopt Jeff's or Michael's ways of thinking. "Take what you like and leave the rest" is a popular saying in Twelve-Step groups. I encourage you to embrace this principle when it comes to this book. It does not contain a dogma but rather a story for those who feel alone in the world.

Seek what [peace and freedom from suffering] the ancients sought." We tell the story in this book for one reason: so you can see that reconciliation is possible. This book shows how the McLeans did it. These are their lives, and this is what it looked like and sounded like when they found their deeper truths. Each aspect of their story contains concepts that can help guide you to your unique solutions. Determining whether Jeff's and Michael's stories offer any solutions to your own dilemmas is part of your journey.

For those of you who love someone who has come out, let Michael's story be your guide and your hope for discovering heaven right here, right now. We must break from the traditions of the past to embrace the love that is waiting for us. That is the promise of the prophets—that through love, the kingdom of heaven will reveal itself here on earth.

For those of you aware of or awakening to parts of yourself that you were told would lead to your destruction and alienation, let Jeff's story be a candle to light your way along the path. You may be able to take only small steps right now, but keep going. Something waits on the other side of the darkness, and it is much bigger than anything you've heard or read about heaven. You may not yet see the entire road ahead, but you don't need to see it all to move forward. I hope the light borrowed from Jeff's story is enough to show the next foothold, the next handhold, on your way. In time, you will find that your path has been leading you to a mountaintop where the view is more beautiful and more vast than anything you've ever been promised. And the vista will be revealed by the light that comes from within you—a light bright enough to illuminate the world. And like the McLeans, you can use this light to show others that transformation is possible if only we learn to lay down our judgments, stop fighting ourselves and each other, exchange our weapons of war for tools of peace, and surrender to the love and the life waiting for us.

An important aspect of Jeff and Michael's story is that at several stops along the way, there were—and are—no guarantees. When I talk through a client's decision with a parent or spouse, I will often remind the parent/spouse that there is no guarantee that they will get what they are looking for in terms of solutions. The only thing I can promise is that if they live their own authentic life, they can be okay. But they, and most of us, often don't believe in this promise. We look instead for solutions to surface-level problems. We look for fixes. We go looking for silver bullets. We are so humanly prone to doing everything except looking inside to discover that *we* are why we aren't happy.

Jeff and Michael's story is an invitation for you to take responsibility for your own story and to live it. Magical helpers will appear along the way. Doors will open where it looked like there were no doors. A kind of death will occur. It is the death of the old life. It is the death of the old form or the old way. This figurative death is essential to a new life, a new way. This death is the precursor to what Jesus and other teachers allude to when they talk of being born again.

I hope you, dear reader, can catch a glimpse of the larger life, the larger love, and the authenticity that is waiting for you. And when and if you do, I will see you out there on the road. We can have a laugh, a smile, a tear, and a hug. We can look at each other through our knowing eyes. I would love to hear about your death and rebirth. I would love to hear the names of your magical helpers. I would love to share in your grief for those you have lost. And I would love to meet those you have found and those who have found you. But most of all, above all else, I look forward to meeting *you*. And I look forward to finding God's spirit in the connection between us.

About the Authors

Jeff McLean is a vocal coach, performer, and coauthor of *Stay in the Room*. A professional singer since his teens, he has performed worldwide, from first national tours to Las Vegas's *Spamalot*. Since 2012, he has coached artists and actors globally, guiding them to find confidence and honesty in their voices. Drawing on his personal journey of faith, identity, and recovery, Jeff's work emphasizes self-love, healing, and connection. He is also the founder of the McLean Foundation, a nonprofit creating safe spaces for growth. Jeff lives between Heber City, Utah, and West Hollywood, California, with his husband, Joe.

Michael McLean, a household name for millions of members of The Church of Jesus Christ of Latter-day Saints, is the beloved godfather of Mormon music and entertainment. Over half a billion people have seen his films and commercials. His fifty albums and half dozen books have sold over a million copies. Michael is a musical legend, spending every minute he can with his wife, Lynne.

Brad M. Reedy, Ph.D. served for over twenty-five years as a co-owner and clinical director of Evoke Therapy Programs before founding Finding You Therapy Programs. While at Evoke, he created Finding You Intensives, an attachment-based, experiential therapeutic intensive program that helps participants to connect their past to their current questions and issues. Finding You Intensives offer participants an accelerator and complement to their therapy work. He is the author of *The Journey of the Heroic Parent* and *The Audacity to Be You*.

www.ingramcontent.com/pod-product-compliance
Lightning Source LLC
LaVergne TN
LVHW020653110826
845149LV00012B/1979

* 9 7 8 1 9 6 9 9 3 5 0 5 3 *